About the author

NIKI CHESWORTH is the author of and contributes regularly to *Telegraph Money* and other national publications. Her down-to-earth style demystifies the complex world of finance.

The Daily Telegraph

Living on a
FIXED
INCOME

How anyone on a restricted budget can enjoy a better quality of life

Niki Chesworth

ROBINSON
London

Constable & Robinson Ltd
3 The Lanchesters
162 Fulham Palace Road
London W6 9ER
www.constablerobinson.com

First published in the UK by Robinson,
an imprint of Constable & Robinson Ltd 2006

A copy of the British Library Cataloguing in Publication
Data is available from the British Library.

ISBN-13: 978-1-84529-231-7
ISBN-10: 1-84529-231-6

Printed and bound in the EU

1 3 5 7 9 10 8 6 4 2

For Katie and Jack

Contents

*An asterisk next to the name of an organization in the text means that contact details for the organization are at the end of the chapter.

Introduction

A fixed income usually means a fixed standard of living . . . but not necessarily. If you know how, it is relatively easy to increase your spending power by reducing your outgoings and boosting your income.

Whether it is shopping around for best buys on energy bills, ensuring you do not pay too much tax, claiming benefits to which you are entitled or more drastic measures such as releasing equity from your property or downsizing, there should be a way to turn what could be a subsistence existence into a more comfortable lifestyle.

So if you are living on a fixed income, which you probably will be if you have reached retirement age, have taken early retirement or are out of the workforce, for example, owing to ill health, this book should prove an indispensable guide.

While others may be able to earn more, those on fixed incomes can – at best – hope to have an income that rises in line with inflation. This presents a challenge, particularly because items such as Council Tax tend to rise by well above the rate of inflation. So, while their income remains static, those on a fixed income often find that their cost of living increases year by year, leaving them far worse off the older they get.

In fact, research done by the Halifax, based on the latest Office for National Statistics data, shows that the cost of owning and running a house rose by 5 per cent in 2003/4, more than four times the rate of consumer price index inflation, the government's preferred inflation measure.

As a result, many of those on a fixed income feel trapped. They dare not spend too much today or dip into savings, for fear that they will not have enough to live on in the future.

There is an alternative . . .

Typical readers of this book will probably be like my mother and may find some inspiration in how she tackled exactly the same problem.

Capital-rich but income-poor, she started her retirement early without the luxury of an occupational or private pension. Faced with ever-decreasing savings, which she was using to supplement her income, she has tried numerous ways to increase her income and reduce her overheads and has even taken some drastic steps, completely changing her lifestyle.

What makes her different? Unlike many of those on a fixed income, she does not have a fixed view of life.

She has rented out a spare room under the tax-free rent-a-room scheme, offered bed and breakfast, downsized to release capital, moved to a nearby town to a much smaller property to reduce the overheads of owning her home and now – after improving her smaller property – is planning to release some of the profits she has made to fund her future retirement.

In addition, she has – despite some trepidation – used the Internet to earn a higher rate of interest on her savings, to buy airline tickets and even to sell unwanted items on eBay. Ensuring that she gets the best deal on everything from her insurance to her travel costs means that she has enough money spare to live rather than merely exist.

As a result, she travels abroad regularly and has even managed to buy a new sporty little car. Yes, she still worries about the future . . . the difference is that she is doing something about it, rather than simply accepting that her income, and her lifestyle, are fixed.

The income gap

According to the Office for National Statistics, older people who rely on the state pension 'have regular expenditure exceeding income'. Indeed, research conducted by the Prudential financial services group in 2005 found that the average gap between desired income in retirement and actual income is around £4,000 a year.

Over a retirement lasting 25 years, that is an income gap of over £100,000.

Some pensioners are far worse off than others. One in ten of the UK's 11 million pensioners now lives on less than £5,000 a year, according to the Prudential's annual retirement index. Nearly a quarter survive on less than £7,500. Generally speaking, income after retirement drops to less than half the average wage.

This means that drastic steps need to be taken to bridge this income gap.

An estimated 2.1 million pensioners have been forced to cut back their spending on holidays, while the same number are eating out less and 1.8 million are spending less on entertainment and leisure activities, according to the same survey.

Some 1.6 million have been forced to return to work to meet their income shortfall and, more worryingly, large numbers of people were also being forced to cut back on essentials. An estimated 1.7 million people have reduced their spending on clothing and 1.2 million are trying to cut their heating bills.

About 740,000 retired people also said they were trying to spend less on food, while 430,000 were even cutting back on medicines and visits to their GP.

In addition to spending more than they have coming in, pensioner households are also increasingly still paying a mortgage. Nearly half of all UK homeowners now have a mortgage they will still be paying when retired – a figure which has almost doubled since 1992.

Where the money comes from

Most retired households rely heavily on state benefits – the retirement pension and other benefits such as the Pension Credit – which, according to latest Department for Work and Pensions (DWP) figures (for the financial year ending April 2003), averaged £142 a week. This is how the income of the average pension is made up, according to the DWP.

Where pensioners get their income from

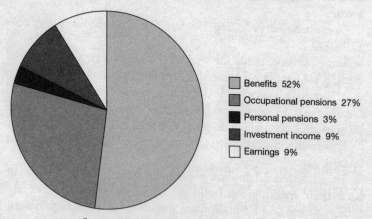

- Benefits 52%
- Occupational pensions 27%
- Personal pensions 3%
- Investment income 9%
- Earnings 9%

Source: Department for Work and Pensions.

The growth in benefit income has outstripped the growth in income from other sources. While occupational pension income has also increased rapidly, investment income has fallen, reflecting the slump in stockmarkets. The graph below shows that despite increased awareness of the need to fund one's own retirement, individuals still rely on the state to provide most of their income.

Pensioners' gross income by source

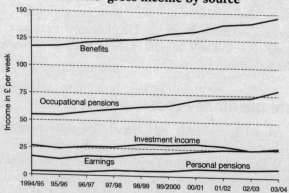

Source: Department for Work and Pensions.

A growing problem

The number of pensioners – currently 11 million people of pensionable age, including women over 60 and men over 65, and comprising 18.5 per cent of the total population – is rising and set to soar by 40 per cent by 2050.

The demand for extra cash among those in retirement has never been greater. People are living longer, and in many cases can expect their retirement to last 20 years (if not more), which is almost half their working life.

What you can do to help yourself

People living on a fixed income can take a number of steps to improve their finances, and this book examines them in detail.

Maximizing your income

Even if you cannot work to earn more money, you can get the most from the state – over 1 million pensioners do not claim their pension credit and many miss out on numerous other benefits. You can also get the most from your private pension – including shopping around for the best annuity rates, which more than half of all those retiring fail to do.

Making the most of your assets

Equity-rich, cash-poor – that is the lot of many pensioners. However, there are ways to release some of this equity or use the capital tied up in your home to boost your income, including using equity release schemes, downsizing, renting out all or part of your home/taking in a lodger, or running a business from home or using your home as a business.

Reducing your outgoings

The average family can save around £2,000 a year just by shopping around for the best deals. Easy ways to cut costs include getting the right amount of insurance at the right rate and making the most of being an older homeowner.

Minimizing your tax bill

According to IFA Promotion, an organization which promotes independent financial advice, nine in ten of us pay more tax than we need to. This book looks at the simple steps you can take to reduce your tax liability including making the most of your income tax allowances, investing in tax-free schemes, using your capital gains tax allowance and making the most of being married.

Maximizing your investment returns

Maximizing the returns on your investments can make a big difference to your standard of living. The options the book looks at include savings and how to get the best returns on them, guaranteed investments and where to get investment advice.

Thinking ahead

The book considers some of the difficult decisions you may have to make, such as going into long-term care and considering your own mortality – planning to avoid inheritance tax and making a will.

Think positive – and act now

Like you, my mother has had to consider much of what is discussed in this book – and has successfully made changes to increase her fixed income and reduce her outgoings.

As a result, she turned what could have been a subsistence retirement on a basic pension into a much more comfortable and enjoyable time of life.

If you are on a fixed income and have a fixed view of life, it will be less enjoyable. Take a leaf out of my mother's book and do not get stuck with expensive insurance and utility bills, locked into uncompetitive savings rates or saddled with a home that is too large and too expensive to run. Explore all the possibilities.

Part One
MAXIMIZING YOUR INCOME

Warning All tax and benefit rates were correct at the time of writing but will be subject to change in future years, particularly following the annual budget. Readers are advised to check rates before making financial decisions.

Introduction

When you are living on a fixed income, it is vital to make every penny work for you – and to make sure that you are receiving every penny to which you are entitled.

Just because your pension or pensions are fixed at a set amount (or in effect fixed, as pensions usually only rise in line with 0 each year), it does not mean that your income has to remain static.

Hunting around for better rates of interest on savings, making the most of tax-free and tax-efficient investments, and claiming benefits and tax credits can easily boost your income.

The other side of your balance sheet – your outgoings – can also provide you with much-needed extra income and is examined in detail in Part Three of the book.

Maximizing your income will take time and effort – and you cannot afford to be complacent. Savings rates vary and benefits and tax credit rules change, so it is important to review your finances regularly to ensure you are getting the maximum income possible. Every time a bill arrives or an insurance policy is up for renewal, it should become a habit to check that you are still getting the best deal or rate.

Sadly, many of the best buys are reserved for those prepared to shop around and to buy online. As these tend to be younger members of the population, older homeowners, who are less likely to have access to the Internet, tend to lose out. If technophobia puts you off going online, ask your children or grandchildren to help.

Don't be reluctant to claim

There is an age divide when it comes to claiming benefits. Many older people are reluctant to claim benefits to which they are entitled because they see them as a handout rather than an entitlement, and for many older claimants there is a stigma attached to receiving financial support from the state.

Many also resent the intrusion (means-tested benefits require individuals to reveal a large amount of personal and financial information), and the lengthy forms are offputting in themselves.

However, even those entitled to only a small amount of help should consider the following:

- you are not a drain on society – you and your family have paid taxes and National Insurance to the state and have probably paid in far more than you will ever get back
- even a small amount of benefit – for example, £5 a week – is valuable. Over a 20-year retirement it adds up to £5,200 (and that does not take into account annual increases)
- some 20 per cent of the poorest pensioners are failing to claim the main benefit – Pension Credit – so even those who most need help are missing out
- the 12-month backdating provision for Pension Credit means you could get a lump sum by claiming now – the amount averages £1,000.

Chapter 1

Claiming what's yours

Thousands of pensioners fail to claim benefits to which they are entitled – sometimes through apathy, sometimes through ignorance because they feel the amount they receive will not be worth the effort, and often through a dislike of complicated forms.

The state retirement pension

The state retirement pension for the 2006/7 tax year is £84.25 for single people and £134.75 for couples. This can be topped up with an additional state pension – previously known as SERPS (the State Earnings-Related Pension Scheme) and now known as S2P (the State Second Pension).

This chapter shows you how you can:

- ensure you get the maximum amount
- increase the amount you will receive
- gain a lump sum or extra from the state – even if you have already retired.

How much will I get?

Contrary to popular belief, not everyone qualifies for the full basic state pension.

Only those who have made National Insurance contributions (or had NIC credits) for at least 90 per cent of their working lives receive the full basic state pension. The years in which an entitlement to the basic state pension is built up are known as 'qualifying years'. The amount of pension depends on the number of qualifying years a person has amassed before reaching state retirement age: the more qualifying years, the higher the pension.

Men need 44 qualifying years to get the full (100 per cent) pension.

Women who will reach the age of 60 before 2010 need 39 qualifying years. However, from 2020, when the state pension age is equalized at 65, the number of qualifying years will increase to 44. During the phased increase of the state retirement age for women from 2010 the number of qualifying years will gradually increase.

To get the minimum basic state pension (25 per cent) you will normally need 10 or 11 qualifying years.

Anyone earning more than the NI primary threshold (£97 a week for the 2006/7 tax year) will be credited with NICs and as such will build up their entitlement to the basic state pension. Employees pay Class 1 NICs, which are deducted from their salary through PAYE. The self-employed build up their entitlement to the basic state retirement pension through Class 2 NICs, which they pay at a flat rate.

Those who earn less than the primary threshold (not lower earnings limit) of £97 a week do not pay NICs. However, they may still be able to build up entitlement to the basic state retirement pension if they get certain benefits or are a carer who gets home responsibilities protection (HRP). In addition, employees who earn less than the primary threshold of £97 a week but more than the lower earnings limit of £84 a week (2006/7 figures) will be treated as though they had made NICs even though none are taken out of their pay. Self-employed people who earn less than the lower earnings limit can opt to pay voluntary NICs to build up their entitlement to a pension. Those who are registered as unemployed will be credited with qualifying years.

You may be credited with earnings to help you build up your entitlement to the state pension if you do not have enough earnings in a tax year and have been:

- incapable of work through illness or disability
- receiving Carer's Allowance

- getting Working Tax Credit
- getting Statutory Maternity Pay
- getting Statutory Adoption Pay
- unemployed but available for, and actively seeking, work
- on a training course
- doing jury service
- serving a prison sentence for a conviction which was subsequently quashed.

What if I am over 60?

Women over 60 can claim their retirement pension. Men who are not working or who have no liability to pay Class 1 or Class 2 NICs may be credited with contributions automatically for the tax year in which they reach 60 and the four following years. From 6 April 2010 this arrangement will be extended to women.

The raising of the state pension age for women will affect only women born after 5 April 1950. If you are a woman born after 5 April 1950 and you want to check when you will reach state pension age, you can use a state pension age calculator on the Pension Service (part of the Department for Work and Pensions, DWP) website*.

Although men cannot get retirement pension until they are 65, once they are over 60 they can claim any other benefit that a woman over 60 can claim.

What if I am a married woman with no pension of my own?

Married women who do not have enough NICs to earn a basic state retirement pension of their own can claim a pension based on their husband's contributions provided:

- they have reached state retirement age
- their husband has reached state pension age
- their husband has claimed his pension.

They can get a pension of up to 60 per cent of the full basic state retirement pension.

From December 2005 you have also been able to rely on the contribution record of someone with whom you have a registered civil partnership.

The rules for calculating how much you receive are very complicated and work differently depending on whether you are still married and your spouse is alive, you are divorced, or you are a widow or widower.

Relying on a spouse's contributions has drawbacks. The rules mean that women who are older than their husbands can find that they are left with no income until he reaches 65. So a wife five years older than her husband will have to wait until she is 70 to get any state pension.

Warning Some married women who opted to pay reduced NICs do not qualify for the basic state pension although they will – as part of a married couple – qualify for a pension when their husband retires. Reduced NICs can no longer be made, but many older women opted to pay these and have received little in return. Some 4 million wives who contributed £8 billion between them are receiving as little as 8p a week in pension.

What if I stop work before retirement?

As you will no longer be making NICs you may have a shortfall in the number of contributions needed to qualify for the full basic state pension. If so, you may need to pay extra contributions (see below).

However, if you are a man aged 60 or over you will usually get NI credits until state pension age. These start from the tax year in which you turn 60. You may also be able to get Jobseeker's Allowance, which will give you an entitlement to a credit.

What about SERPS or the State Second Pension?

Depending on your individual circumstances, you may be entitled to additional state pension. As its name suggests, this is a payment on top of the basic state pension.

Until April 2002 the additional state pension was called SERPS. It was based on your record of NICs and your level of earnings as an employee.

On 6 April 2002 SERPS was reformed as the State Second Pension (S2P) to provide a more generous additional state pension for low and moderate earners, and to extend access to certain carers and people with long-term illness or disability. When you make your claim for a state pension any additional state pension due to you will also be calculated.

What happens to my SERPS or S2P when I die?

In the past widows and widowers received up to 100 per cent of their late spouse's SERPS. However, the widow or widower of a spouse due to reach state pension age after 6 October 2002 but before 6 October 2010 can inherit only between 60 per cent and 90 per cent of their SERPS. The exact amount will depend on when, in this period, the deceased spouse was due to reach state pension age.

If the husband or wife is due to reach state pension age on or after 6 October 2010, the surviving husband or wife will receive up to a maximum of 50 per cent of their SERPS.

Increasing your state retirement pension

If you have not yet retired, you can increase your state retirement pension by making use of the following options.

Making additional NICs

If you are more than four months away from retirement you can get a pension forecast to check how much you will receive on retirement. It will tell you in today's money how much state pension you have already earned and what you can expect to have earned by state pension age. It will also include details of any additional state pension.

Application forms (BR19) can be downloaded from the Internet or requested by calling or writing to the Retirement Pension Forecasting Team*. They are also available at your local benefits agency.

Note The forecast will be based on your current circumstances, which can of course change. Also, note that you will need to quote your National Insurance number when requesting a pension forecast.

Once you have received your forecast you can use it to calculate how much extra you need to save for your retirement.

You can make additional NICs if you are to receive less than the full basic state pension. The forms you receive will tell you how to do this.

If, even after making additional contributions, you will still have less than the minimum ten qualifying years there is no point in making additional payments – you will still not receive a state pension.

However, in most other cases additional contributions will be worthwhile. It may seem expensive at the time, but when you retire you will probably be grateful for the fact that whatever happens with all your other pensions and investments, you are guaranteed to receive enough for a basic standard of living from the state for the rest of your life.

Under the normal rules, the latest deadline for making payment for gaps in your NI account is six years after the end of the relevant financial year. However, for the financial years 1996/7 to 2000/1 HM Revenue & Customs has announced an extension of this deadline to 5 April 2008.

HM Revenue & Customs has started to contact people of working age to inform them of gaps in their NI records covering the tax years 1996/7 to 2001/2. It will tell people if they have any missing contributions in those years, and what they can do to fill the gaps in their contribution record. Everyone will be given until 5 April 2008 to pay (irrespective of the year that the gap occurs).

Note You will automatically be sent details of your state pension entitlement four months before you reach state pension age, along with an invitation to claim the state pension. However, you will receive this information only if the DWP has an up-to-date address for you.

Delaying taking the state pension

It is possible to increase the amount of pension paid by postponing taking it. You can request details of how this will increase your pension when you ask for a pension forecast.

Even a short delay in taking your pension can result in a significant increase in what you receive once you start to claim the basic state pension.

This is how it increases under new rules introduced in April 2005. Figures for 2005/6 tax year.

A person who defers a state pension entitlement (basic and second state pension) of £105 would get:

£110.90 if they defer for one year
£120.80 if they defer for two years
£154.60 if they defer for five years

These figures assume that the base rate is 4.75 per cent.

Another option you have is to delay taking your pension and then opt to take a lump sum. That way you get a one-off payment and the normal weekly state pension payment – in other words, you can convert the increase per week you would have received into one large amount and still continue to get the normal weekly amount. This makes delaying retirement far more attractive. The rule changes from 5 April 2005 also mean you can put off claiming for as long as you like (under the old rules you could delay claiming it only for up to five years). However, it may not be wise to leave claiming your pension too long, just in case you do not live long enough to enjoy the increased amount.

The state pension is increased by 1 per cent for every five weeks you put off claiming it (equivalent to about 10.5 per cent extra for every year you delay claiming compared to about 7.5 per cent extra before 6 April 2005).

The lump sum payment is based on the amount of normal weekly state pension you would have received, plus interest added each week and compounded. If you opt for the lump sum, when you start to claim your state pension it will be paid at the normal rate – not the increased rate.

Deferring the state pension

The following examples of the postponement of state pension are published by the Pension Service.

Anne decides to put off claiming her state pension for five years. When she comes to take up her pension, the weekly rate she would have been entitled to, if she had not put off claiming, would have been £105. As she put off claiming for five years and chose extra state pension, the amount of state pension she will get every week will be £159.60.

Ahmed's weekly state pension is worth £105. When he reaches state pension age he decides to put off claiming his state pension for five years. When he claims his pension, if he chooses a lump sum, he will get a lump sum of around £32,306 before tax (assuming a return of 6.75 per cent) as well as his normal weekly state pension entitlement.

The compounded rate will be broadly equivalent to an annual interest rate of 2 per centage points above the Bank of England's base rate (so if the base rate was 4.75 per cent, the annual rate of return would be 6.75 per cent).

The rules for postponement of state pension are:

- you must put off claiming your state pension for at least five weeks to get extra state pension. If you choose extra state pension you will not be paid state pension for the weeks you gave up claiming it as you will get higher pension instead
- you have to put off claiming your pension for at least 12 months to qualify for the lump sum payment. If you do not, you can either claim an increased pension or choose to have arrears of pension paid back to you in one payment (without any extra interest). This is known as 'backdating'.

Even if you have already retired, you can choose to cancel your claim and then build up an entitlement to extra state pension or a lump sum.

Note You can do this only once.

If you would like to stop claiming your state pension and

would like to earn extra or a lump sum, contact your pension centre (the telephone number will be on any letters you have received from your pension centre).

Although you will generally be required to be normally resident in the UK you may also be able to take up this option if you are living in the European Economic Area (EEA, which comprises the 25 member states of the European Union, plus Norway, Iceland and Liechtenstein), or Switzerland and are either a national of one of those countries or otherwise entitled to live there.

How will deferring my pension affect other benefits?

Deferring your pension does not mean you can then get huge amounts of additional benefits from the state because you now have no or little income. Your Pension Credit (see Means-tested benefits, below) will be calculated as if you were getting the state pension. However, your housing benefit or Council Tax Benefit will not take into account the state pension you are deferring.

Once you receive the higher extra state pension, the higher amount will be used when working out your Pension Credit, Housing Benefit and Council Tax Benefit. Normally, if you claim any of these benefits, any savings you have above certain limits will affect the amount you get. As the savings credit is set at the level of the basic state pension, getting an increased level of state pension could mean you lose out on additional savings credit.

However, lump sum payments will be disregarded in calculating the savings credit for these benefits, so that if you choose a lump sum payment you will not get less benefit because of the lump sum payment.

Note While you are deferring your pension you will not build up extra pension entitlement just because you are receiving other state benefits such as Carer's Allowance, Incapacity Benefit, or Severe Disablement Allowance.

Will I be taxed on the extra pension?

If you receive it as extra income, it will be added to all your other income when determining whether you pay income tax and the rate at which you pay it.

The lump sum will be taxed at the rate that applies to your other income. So it will not push you into a higher tax bracket.

Note Tax – if it is due – will be deducted from the lump sum before it is paid to you.

Do I have to take the lump sum at the same time as my pension?

No, you can take it in the following tax year. This may be worthwhile if you have been working past retirement age and once you claim your state pension your income drops sharply. Your income tax rate could fall and therefore your lump sum will be taxed at this lower rate. So if you change from being a higher- to a basic-rate taxpayer you will make significant tax savings.

What happens if I die after deferring my state pension?

Your widow or widower may be entitled to extra state pension or a lump sum payment for the period you had put off claiming. Only if the claim has been put off for at least 12 months will he or she be able to opt for a lump sum.

If you are already receiving extra because of your deferral, your widow or widower will get extra pension added to their own state pension (although the part relating to the earnings-related additional pension will be reduced).

Make sure you claim your pension when it is due

You should be sent forms inviting you to claim your state pension about four months before you are due to retire. You can, at this point, decide to defer taking your pension.

If you want to take a pension straight away, rather than deferring it, remember that you can only backdate a pension claim for 12 months.

If you delay making a claim for less than 12 consecutive

months you will not have the choice of an increased pension. Instead you will get pension arrears as a one-off lump sum.

If you are not sent a claim form call the state pension claim line*.

Retiring abroad

If you are thinking of retiring abroad, find out how your pension – and other benefits – will be affected.

Your pension will be paid to you even if you live in another country. However, you may not get the yearly increases in the state pension. Your pension will therefore be in effect frozen unless you live in an EEA country or in a country with which the UK has an agreement that allows for upratings.

In 2005, of the 900,000 UK pensioners living abroad, 480,000, including those living in South Africa, Australia, Canada and New Zealand, had their pensions frozen. See also Chapter 4.

Universal benefits

These are benefits that are paid regardless of need or means. Benefits for the over-60s include:

- the winter fuel payment of £200 (rising to £300 for those over 80)
- free bus travel
- free television licences (for the over-75s)
- a Christmas Bonus of £10 a year, paid to those who get certain benefits and to people aged over 80.

In winter 2005–6, extra help was available for households paying Council Tax where someone of 65 or over was not getting Pension Credit. These households received a payment of £200 at the same time as the winter fuel payment, although the payment did not have to be spent on Council Tax itself. At the time of writing it is not known whether this one-off payment – announced prior to the General Election of May 2005 – will be continued in subsequent years.

Although take-up of universal benefits is high, some households have failed to claim their entitlement and not all of those eligible for the winter fuel payment may receive it automatically. Remember, these are available regardless of your income.

Winter fuel payments

At the time of writing, this payment is:

* £200, rising to £300 for people of 80 or over. However, some people get a reduced rate of £100 (£150–£200 for people of 80 or over): this is usually paid to those who live with someone else who qualifies for a winter fuel payment or those who live in a care home, but for those who receive income support the level of payment may differ
* tax-free
* paid to people who were aged 60 or over by the end of the qualifying week of 19–25 September 2005
* paid regardless of how cold it gets
* not paid to those in hospital (if you are there during the qualifying week or have been there for over a year) or a care home if they receive income support
* made to cover fuel costs – although the money can be spent on anything
* made automatically to those receiving state retirement pension, Pension Credit, Attendance Allowance and a range of other benefits. However, if you were not receiving these in the qualifying week in September, you will need to claim.

Cold weather payments, made when the temperature falls to a certain level, are different, and are paid only to some of those on means-tested benefits.

You have to live in the UK to get the payment.

Free bus travel

Originally offered in Scotland and now extended to England, from April 2006 people aged 60 and over and disabled people have been entitled to free off-peak travel on their local bus services. This benefits around 11 million people.

At the same time Scotland has extended its free services to include Scotland-wide travel – at any time of the day, not just off-peak periods.

Means-tested benefits

This is state help targeted at those with the most need. Even if you feel that you do not qualify, it is important to know the income and capital thresholds in case your income drops or you use up your capital.

Pension Credit

Anyone over 60 whose weekly income in the 2006/7 tax year is less than:

- £114.05 (for a single person); or
- £175.05 (for a couple)

can claim Pension Credit, which will guarantee to bring their income up to at least this level.

In addition, if you are aged 65 and over (note that women pensioners aged 60–64 are excluded) and have savings or an additional private pension income, you could still be entitled to some savings credit if your weekly income is up to:

- £158 (for a single person); or
- £230 (for a couple).

This latter payment is unlike those under previous benefit systems, which penalized pensioners who had small second pensions or modest savings. In the past these pensioners often saw no benefit from saving for their retirement because their additional income amounted only to what they would have received from the state.

Now, if you or your partner are aged 65 or over (not 60, as is the rule for the basic credit) you may be rewarded for saving for your retirement.

The savings credit is extra money (paid on top of the basic guaranteed credit) and in the 2006/7 tax year is worth a maximum of:

- £17.88 if you are single
- £23.58 a week if you have a partner.

As your private pension income or savings interest increases, the savings credit decreases. The highest levels of savings credit are payable where qualifying income exceeds the state pension by a very small amount – around £20–£35 per week.

What if I have savings or a private pension? Will I still qualify?

You may do. While Pension Credit is designed to help the poorest pensioners, many of those with private pensions and savings do qualify for the credit. Yet many do not realize they could get extra financial help from the government.

Does everyone who is entitled to Pension Credit receive it?

No. Over 1.7 million pensioners fail to claim Pension Credit, so it will be worthwhile reading this section to see if you should submit a claim. The government has set a target for 78 per cent of those eligible for the Pension Credit to receive it by 2008. (This target is subject to review.) That will still mean that thousands of those entitled to Pension Credit will not claim it.

Why do so many fail to claim it?

Pension Credit is a means-tested benefit and many pensioners are unwilling to submit themselves to a means test. Some feel that the extra income is not worth all the hassle.

The DWP's own research into people's attitudes to and knowledge about Pension Credit found that eight in ten non-recipients had heard about it but only half felt they would be better off if they received it.

The most common reason for not claiming Pension Credit is perceived ineligibility; indeed, the understanding of the rules of eligibility was generally low. The highest levels of misconception and uncertainty related to the backdating of claims: 60 per cent of those questioned did not know that they can be backdated for one year. Significant numbers of older people also believed – wrongly – that home ownership (16 per cent) and financial support from family (13 per cent) bars them from receiving Pension Credit.

How much Pension Credit could I get?

How much you receive will depend on how much other income you have – as well as any savings or investments (see below.) The average weekly award is £43.54 according to December 2005 figures.

Who qualifies for Pension Credit?

Around half of all pension householders – about 5.4 million people – are benefiting or could benefit from Pension Credit.

Of these, 2.35 million pension households qualify for the Pension Credit guarantee (this is the minimum means-tested income for all pensioners) and the remainder qualify for the savings credit element of Pension Credit (this is the part of the credit that rewards those with modest private pensions and small amounts of savings).

Note You must be at least 60 to apply for the guarantee part of Pension Credit, although it does not normally matter if your partner is under 60. Partners include a spouse or person you live with as if you are married to them.

Even if your income is more than the limits mentioned above, you may be able to get some Pension Credit if you or your partner:

- are a severely disabled person
- look after a person who is severely disabled or
- have certain housing costs – for example, mortgage interest.

What income is taken into account?
Pensions including state, occupational and private pensions, certain benefits including Carer's Allowance and Bereavement Allowance and earnings from a job are taken into account. In addition a certain amount of income is assumed depending on the level of your savings (see below).

What income is not counted?
Attendance Allowance, Disability Living Allowance, Housing Benefit and Council Tax Benefit do not affect how much Pension Credit you get.

So receiving these benefits will *not* mean that you are excluded from Pension Credit.

Payments from friends, family and charities are also ignored.

How do savings affect Pension Credit?
Only savings over £6,000 affect Pension Credit. This rises to over £10,000 if you live permanently in a care home.

Any savings over this amount are assumed to produce £1 of income for every £500 of savings or part of £500.

Savings that are taken into account include:

- cash in bank, building society or post office accounts
- National Savings Certificates
- Premium Bonds
- ISAs, PEPs and TESSAs
- income, capital or granny bonds
- shares and unit trusts
- property and land (but not including the place where you normally live).

How is Pension Credit calculated?

Assumed income from savings (if you have any) is added to your income from the state retirement pension and any other pensions as well as any other income you receive.

The following example is based on one published by the DWP and uses 2005/6 figures:

Mr and Mrs Smith	weekly income
Mr Smith's state pension	£82.05
Mrs Smith's state pension	£82.05
Mr Smith's personal pension	£14.00
Savings £8,000 (assuming £1 of income for every £500)	£ 4.00
TOTAL weekly income	£182.10

The income exceeds the guarantee element of Pension Credit, which is £167.05. Instead, the Smiths receive a savings credit. To calculate the savings element of Pension Credit, savings income is reduced by 40p for every £1 over £167.05.

So it is calculated on the difference between £182.10 and £167.05 = £15.05. It is reduced by 40 per cent, or £6.02.

The amount they receive is the maximum savings credit of £21.51 less £6.02 (a reduction taking into account their assumed savings income), which is £15.49. This brings their income up to £197.59.

To sum up, this is how the savings credit is calculated.

You get 60p for every £1 of income above the minimum guarantee level (£84.25 if you are single or £134.75 if you are in a couple in 2006/7) provided:

1. your income is more than this level – which is the same as the basic state pension, and
2. your income is less than £150.55 if you are single and £230 if you are married (although if you are very disabled, or you

are a carer, you may get some savings credit even if your income is higher than these amounts).

The maximum amount of savings credit you can get is £17.88 if you are single or £23.58 between you if you are a couple.

It sounds very complicated – is it?
It is complicated, but you do not have to go through the process every year. Your income is assessed at retirement and then every five years unless you have a major change of circumstances.

It seems a lot of effort for very little extra money
Even if you are entitled to only a small amount, receiving Pension Credit may mean that you can get help with other things such as Housing Benefit and Council Tax Benefit. While an extra £15 a week – as in the example above – may not sound like a fortune, over ten years it adds up to £7,800.

What if I should have been claiming Pension Credit, but have not done so?
You may be able to get up to 12 months' back payments. Average payouts to new applicants are around £1,000, and some customers have received over £3,000. For those receiving a backdated payment, other benefits – such as Housing Benefit or Council Tax Benefit – will not be affected, however large the lump sum.

How will my Pension Credit be affected if I move abroad?
You will lose entitlement to means-tested benefits such as Pension Credit.

Council Tax Benefit

You do not have to be in receipt of any other benefits to qualify for Council Tax Benefit.

As Council Tax bills are likely to be among the biggest bills you face, it is worth exploring whether you are entitled to help.

It is:

- paid whether you rent or own your own home or live rent-free
- given as a rebate on your Council Tax bill
- paid even if you already get a discount on your Council Tax – for example, if you live alone.

Who can claim it?

Those in receipt of the guarantee credit part of Pension Credit, on low incomes or with savings of £16,000 or less are eligible to claim this benefit.

Who cannot claim it?

Anyone with savings over £16,000 (unless they receive the guarantee credit).

How much will I get?

The full amount – which means you will not pay any Council Tax – if you receive the guarantee element of Pension Credit.

Even if you do not receive this but have a low income you may be entitled to some benefit. Average rebates are over £700 but bear in mind that it will be affected by:

- any savings over £6,000 if you or your partner is over 60
- your income, including some benefits and tax
- your circumstances: age, whether you or any of your family are disabled, and so on.

The rates used to work out your Council Tax Benefit are generally the same as the allowance and premiums that make up Pension Credit, Income Support and income-based Jobseeker's Allowance.

How do I claim?

If you claim Pension Credit you will get a form to claim Council Tax Benefit with your claim pack. If you do not, contact your local council directly.

What other help can I get?

If you share your home with another adult (other than your partner) who cannot pay towards the Council Tax you may be able to get a second adult rebate. The other adult needs to be on a low income (your income and savings do not affect the rebate) – however, you receive the reduction in your bill. You may be able to get this even if you do not get Council Tax Benefit.

Note If you are entitled to Council Tax Benefit and second adult rebate, you will get the one which gives you more.

How does it affect my other benefits?

It does not – and the discount is not taxable.

What if I go into a care home?

If it is a permanent move you cannot normally get Council Tax Benefit. If it is temporary you may still receive some benefit. Contact your local council for more information.

What if I move abroad?

You will generally lose your entitlement to benefit.

Housing Benefit

The rules for this are the same as for Council Tax Benefit. This benefit too is administered by your local council.

It is paid to those on low incomes and those who pay rent.

Those over 60 in receipt of the guarantee credit of Pension Credit will generally receive Housing Benefit (even if they have savings over £16,000). Savings over £6,000 if you or your partner are aged 60 or over affect how much Housing Benefit you can get (£10,000 for some kinds of residential accommodation). If your savings are over £16,000 you will not get any benefit.

To work out your Housing Benefit, the council will look at:

* money you and your partner have coming in, including earnings, some benefits and tax credits, and other income such as occupational pensions
* your savings and your partner's savings
* your circumstances, such as your age, the ages and size of your family, whether you or any of your family are disabled, and whether anyone who lives with you could help with the rent.

The council will also look at whether the amount of rent is reasonable for your particular home, whether your home is a reasonable size for you and your family, and whether the amount of rent is reasonable for the area your home is in.

The maximum Housing Benefit you can get is the same as your eligible rent. This may not be the same as your full rent.

Cold weather payment

The cold weather payment provides additional help towards heating costs when there is a cold spell. Those already receiving Pension Credit or another income-related benefit should receive this automatically.

It is different from the winter fuel allowance.

The DWP will automatically pay you when the average temperature is recorded as, or is forecast to be, 0 degrees Centigrade or below over seven days in a row at a given weather station.

You will receive £8.50.

Central Heating

In early 2006 the government announced a £300 discount on new central heating for pensioners who do not have an existing system, with free installation for the poorest pensioners.

Benefits based on need

Attendance Allowance

This is a tax-free benefit for the over-65s with an illness or disability who need help with personal care. It is not affected by savings or another income and it is usually ignored when working out Pension Credit. Moreover, if you receive Attendance Allowance it may increase other benefits you are getting, such as Pension Credit.

When can I claim Attendance Allowance?

Normally you will have needed help for at least six months before you can claim it. However, you do not actually have to receive or pay for any help to qualify.

Special rules apply to those who are not expected to live longer than six months because of an illness.

How much help do I need to qualify?

There are two rates of benefit payable, a lower rate for day or night care, and a higher rate for day and night care.

So if you need help with washing, dressing or using the bathroom, or someone to keep an eye on you or to be with you when you are on dialysis, you should claim this benefit.

How do I claim Attendance Allowance?

Ask for form AA1 from your Disability and Carer's Service or your local society security office. If you are terminally ill and are unlikely to live longer than six months you should ask your doctor to complete form DS1500.

How much will I get?

The rates for the 2006/7 tax year are £41.65 (the lower rate for help during the day or night) and £62.25 (the higher rate for day and night care).

How is Attendance Allowance paid?

Attendance Allowance is paid four-weekly by direct debit into an account (unless you claim under special rules, in which case it is paid weekly).

What if I go into hospital or a residential care home?

Attendance Allowance will be withdrawn after 28 days or an aggregate of 28 days in hospital or certain residential care accommodation.

How do those in charge work out how much help I need?

Claims for Attendance Allowance include a section for your own assessment of how your illness or disability affects you. Some people who complete the self-assessment questionnaire will be asked to undergo a medical examination. If you do not want to fill in the self-assessment part you can ask for a medical examination instead.

How does Attendance Allowance affect other benefits?

Attendance Allowance is taken into account when fees for residential care and nursing homes are topped up. Also, it will be reduced by the amount of any constant Attendance Allowance (see Other disablement benefits, below) paid with Industrial Injuries Disablement Benefit or War Disablement Pension. If you start to get Attendance Allowance it might increase other benefits you are getting, for example Pension Credit, Income Support or Housing Benefit.

How do I find out more?

Ring the Benefits Enquiry Line* for information, and also ask for DS702 (information leaflet) and AA1 (claim form).

Incapacity Benefit

Incapacity Benefit is paid to those of working age who cannot work because they are sick or disabled. If you have already reached state pension age you cannot claim it. However, if you became sick before reaching state pension age, you may be able to get Incapacity Benefit after state pension age. It can be paid at the retirement pension rate for up to one year of sickness.

To claim it you must have paid NICs and have been unable to work for at least four consecutive days because of sickness or disability.

Incapacity Benefit is paid at three different rates.

Short-term Incapacity Benefit at the lower rate This is paid if you do not get statutory sick pay and have been sick for at least four days in a row including weekends and public holidays. For the 2006/7 year it is £59.20 a week for those under state pension age and £75.35 a week for those over state pension age.

Short-term Incapacity Benefit at the higher rate This is paid if you have been sick for more than 28 weeks and fewer than 52 weeks. It is £70.05 a week for those under state pension age and £78.50 a week for those over state pension age.

Long-term Incapacity Benefit This is paid if you have been sick for over 52 weeks, and is £78.50 a week.

You may be able to get the Incapacity Age Addition if you get long-term Incapacity Benefit and were aged under 45 on the day you became unable to work. This includes days you got Statutory Sick Pay. The age addition is currently £8.28 a week at the lower rate and £16.50 at the higher rate.

If you get the highest care component of Disability Living Allowance or are terminally ill you will get Incapacity Benefit paid at the long-term rate after you have been sick for 28 weeks.

You may earn extra pension through State Second Pension (S2P) for every complete tax year you get long-term Incapacity Benefit, depending on your NI record.

How do I claim Incapacity Benefit?

Contact your local Jobcentre Plus or benefits agency for a claim form. Alternatively, you could ring the Benefits Enquiry Line.*

As with all benefits, you should make your claim as soon as possible as if you delay you may lose benefit.

Disability Living Allowance

A person can claim Disability Living Allowance (DLA) if he or she has needed help for three months because of severe physical or mental illness or disability, and is likely to need it for at least another six months.

It must be claimed before you reach 65. However, if you are getting it when you reach 65, it can continue as long as you still need the help. There are special rules for people with a life expectancy of fewer than six months to help them get DLA quickly and easily. Moreover, you can get DLA even if no one is actually giving you the care you need. Bear in mind, though, that you may not get DLA if you are in hospital or a care home. DLA is not affected by savings nor is it usually affected by other money you have coming in.

How much will I receive?

This will depend on how much help you need. If you need looking after (the care component), you could get between £16.50 and £62.25 a week. If, on the other hand, you need help just to get around (the mobility component), the rate is either £16.50 or £43.40 a week for the 2006/7 tax year.

How do I claim DLA?

Contact your local benefits agency.

What if I go into hospital?

Your benefit will usually stop after four weeks. However, if you benefit from the Motability scheme, the part of your DLA that allows you to get Motability may continue until your Motability agreement ends.

What if I go into a care home?

If your local social services department arranges your care, your DLA will usually stop after four weeks if:

- you go into a home run by your local council and receive help with funding

- the social services department helps with the cost of an independent home.

If your local social services department does not arrange your care in an independent home you will usually continue to receive DLA.

If the social services department stops helping with the cost of an independent home, tell the office that dealt with your benefit, as you will usually be able to start getting benefit again.

Going to live in a home will not normally affect DLA paid for helping you get around, but it may be affected if the NHS arranges the care.

Note The rules are different in Scotland.

How do I find out more?
Ring the Benefits Enquiry Line.*

Community Care Grants

These are paid to those who need money so they can avoid going into a care home or to help them when they are leaving a care home.

The grants can be paid to those in receipt of Pension Credit to help them live independently. You can claim a grant if you:

- plan to leave institutional care or a care home
- need help to stay in your own home and avoid going into institutional care or a care home
- look after someone who is ill or disabled.

Savings of more than £1,000 will usually affect how much you will get (£500 if you are under 60).

These grants are part of the Social Fund and you can find out more from either your local Jobcentre Plus or the Pensions Service.

Other disablement benefits

From April 2001 it has not been possible to claim Severe Disablement Benefit, but if you had been getting the allowance before then you can continue to receive it. It is paid to those assessed as being 80 per cent disabled.

Those who are ill or disabled because of an accident or event that happened at work or in connection with work may be able to get Industrial Injuries Disablement Benefit – accidents (IIDB).

You may be able to claim it if:

- you were employed when the accident or event happened
- the work accident or event that caused your illness or disability happened in England, Scotland or Wales.

It is worth between £25.42 and £127.10 a week depending on the level of your disability.

In addition, those with 100 per cent disablement can claim a constant Attendance Allowance and there is a retirement allowance when you reach state pension age.

War Disablement Pensions

Those who have been injured or disabled during a time of war, or as a result of their service in the armed forces, may qualify for a War Disablement Pension. Contact the War Pensions Agency Freeline.*

Moving abroad

If you are claiming Incapacity Benefit, Severe Disablement Benefit or Bereavement Benefit these may continue to be claimed if you are resident in another EEA state. It is also possible to receive a widow's pension, war pensions and Industrial Injuries Benefit while living abroad: the same applies to Attendance Allowance or Disability Living Allowance if you have been receiving it since 1 June 1992. You may also be entitled to benefits paid by the EEA state you move to. Leaflet SA29, from your local benefits agency, has more information.

A few non-EEA countries have agreements with the UK, which mean you may be able to continue receiving certain UK benefits in that country – details are in leaflet GL29 from your local benefits agency.

Other benefits and financial help

Carer's Allowance

If you are looking after a severely disabled person for at least 35 hours a week, you could get Carer's Allowance. The disabled person must be entitled to Attendance Allowance, Disability Living Allowance (middle or higher rate) for personal care, or a Constant Attendance Allowance if the person is receiving a War Disablement Pension. For more information call the Benefits Enquiry Line.*

There is an earnings limit so recipients can only work part-time. If the carer already gets another benefit which is worth as much as, or more than, Carer's Allowance (for example, the retirement pension), then the Carer's Allowance will not be paid, even though the person remains entitled to it. Someone entitled to Carer's Allowance will receive an extra amount in the calculation of their Pension Credit and other means-tested benefits.

Warm Front/Deal

Anyone aged 60 or over who gets a disability or income-related benefit such as Pension Credit may qualify for home insulation measures worth up to £500. Those aged over 60 but not getting benefits can get a grant of £125.

In addition to helping you to keep warm, home insulation will lead to lower fuel bills.

To find out more, call Eaga.* See also Chapter 7.

Help with central heating costs

Homeowners and private tenants aged 60 or over may also qualify for a central heating system and a range of home insulation measures. Contact Eaga for more details. Public-sector landlords should be contacted directly. The government has also announced a £300 payment to all those over 60 installing central heating for the first time. See page 25.

Bereavement Allowance

Formerly known as Widow's Allowance, this new system of bereavement benefits for men and women was introduced in April 2001. It is based on your late husband or wife's NICs and paid for 52 weeks from the date of bereavement. It is paid to:

- widows and widowers who were aged 45 or over when their husband or wife died
- who are under state pension age and
- not bringing up children (if this is the case you may be able to claim widowed parent's allowance).

If you were over state pension age when you were widowed you may get extra state retirement pension based on your husband or wife's NICs.

If your husband or wife died as a result of his or her job, you may be able to get bereavement benefits even if he or she did not pay enough NI.

Note You cannot get bereavement benefits if you were divorced from your husband or wife or if you remarry or if you live with a partner as if you are married to them.

The standard rate for bereavement benefits is £84.25 for the 2006/7 tax year. However, this is reduced depending on your age at the time of your spouse's death (or when widowed parent's allowance stops). A woman aged 50, for example, will receive £54.76 and one aged 45 just £25.28.

How do I claim?

Claim straight away – if you delay you may lose benefit. Contact your local benefits agency for a claim form. You may also be able to claim a Bereavement Payment – a tax-free lump sum of up to £2,000 – if you are under 60 when your spouse dies.

Discount driving licence

The Driver and Vehicle Licensing Agency (DVLA) has cut the fee for a three-year driving licence to £6 for those aged 70 or over. The DVLA will send a renewal form when the old licence is about to expire. For further information call the DVLA.*

Free prescriptions and eye tests

These are available for those aged 60 or over. If you are also getting Pension Credit, you may get free NHS dental treatment and vouchers towards the cost of glasses or contact lenses. You may also get help with these costs even if you do not receive Pension Credit but are on a low income. Pick up the leaflet HC11, *Are you entitled to help with health costs?*, at your local post office.

Other health-care costs

While you may be entitled to free health care in the UK, this may not continue to be the case if you move overseas.

What health care am I entitled to if I live abroad?

Entitlement to state health treatment varies from country to country and you may have to pay a certain amount or take out private medical cover, which can be very expensive. UK nationals living in another EEA country are entitled to the same health-care benefits as a pensioner who is a national of that country. To qualify you must be either in receipt of state pension, Bereavement Allowance or long-term Incapacity Benefit in the UK. For advice on obtaining an E121 form, call the International Pensions Centre.*

Can I return to the UK for health care?

If you become resident in another European Union (EU) country you will technically not be entitled to free health care in the UK and could be charged for it should you return to the UK for medical treatment.

Free nursing care

In England and Wales you are entitled to help with nursing care costs (but not the personal care costs associated with long-term care). The nursing payments (2005/6 figures) fall into three bands:

- £129 a week – for those who need frequent medical interventions by a registered nurse throughout a 24-hour period
- £80 a week – for those who have multiple care needs and require intervention by a registered nurse on at least a daily basis
- £40 a week – for those who needed minimum registered nurse input.

If you live in Scotland the benefits are greater. In addition to free nursing care, those aged 65 or over also qualify for free personal care. Those who fully fund their own care will be entitled to a contribution of £145 a week towards the costs of personal care and a further £65 a week if they require nursing care.

The NHS helpline* can give further information about free personal and nursing care.

Ways of funding long-term care and the help available (including from insurance policies) is covered in greater depth in Part Four of this book.

Further information

The Pension Service (0845 606 0265; www.thepensionservice. gov.uk), part of the Department for Work and Pensions (www.dwp.gov.uk), has several useful guides:

Your State Pension Choice – Pension Now or Extra Pension Later: A Guide to State Pension Deferral

Pension Now or Extra Pension Later: An Introduction to State Pension Deferral
State Pensions – Your Guide (PM2).
You can also obtain these guides by calling (0845) 731 3233.

For advice on getting your pension paid abroad, and the rules applying to your country of choice, call the International Pensions Centre (0191-218 7777 or 0191-218 2828) and ask for Customer Liaison.

The Pension Credit line (8am–8pm Monday–Friday) is on (0800) 99 1234. Staff can fill in your form over the phone and post it out to you for you to sign. Alternatively, visit www.dwp.gov.uk. On the Pension Service website is a Pension Credit calculator (www.thepensionservice.gov.uk/pensioncredit/calculator/home.asp) where you can get an estimate of a possible award.

The state pension claim line is on (0845) 300 1084.

Retirement pension forecasting is on (0845) 3000 168. Staff can fill in the form over the phone. You can also write to the Retirement Pension Forecasting Team, Room TB001, Tyneview Park, Whitley Road, Newcastle upon Tyne, NE98 1BA – ask for a forecast application and a return envelope to be sent to you.

Age Concern Information Line (0800) 009 966
Benefits Enquiry Line (for people with disabilities and their carers) (0800) 882 200
Enquiry lines for:
Attendance Allowance (0800) 220 674
Attendance Allowance and Disability Living Allowance Helpline (0845) 712 3456
Carer's Allowance (01253) 856 123
DVLA (0870) 240 0009
Eaga England (0800) 316 6011; Northern Ireland (0800) 181 667; Warm Front Scotland (0800) 072 0150; Wales (0800) 316 2815; www.eaga.co.uk
Help the Aged SeniorLine (0808) 800 6565
NHS helpline (0800) 22 44 88
War Pensions Agency Freeline (0800) 169 2277
Winter Fuel Payment helpline (08459) 15 15 15

Chapter 2

Making the most of your private pension

The average pensioner household receives almost a third of its income from private pensions. But private pensions – either from occupational schemes or personal pensions – could provide even more income as:

- many pensioners fail to shop around to get the best rates from annuities (these are purchased to give an income for life from private pension funds and money-purchase occupational schemes). This could cost a person a total of £18,500 over his or her retirement
- many smokers and those with a history of poor health – some 40 per cent of annuitants – are failing to opt for what are known as enhanced annuities (which reflect their shorter life expectancy) and as a result are losing out on up to 30 per cent more income each year
- some £6 billion of occupational pensions are unclaimed
- pensions are often taken even though income is not yet required (for example, if the individual continues to work). Deferring the pension will increase it
- taking a larger lump sum could lead to a smaller pension but that, in turn, could mean more Pension Credit (see Chapter 1)
- retirees may get a better return by investing the maximum tax-free lump sum they are allowed to take on retirement rather than using the money to buy an annuity
- those retiring may be better off deferring the purchase of an annuity until age 75 (there is a campaign to increase this to 85) rather than buying one on retirement.

Annuities

What is an annuity?

An annuity is income provided to you for life from the proceeds of your pension fund (but not a final-salary occupational pension). Annuities are provided by life insurance and other specialist companies and can be sold by a range of advisers.

An annuity purchased with the proceeds of a pension fund is known as a 'compulsory purchase' annuity.

When you retire, you have the right to shop around for the best rate, known as the 'open-market option', rather than simply buying the annuity offered by your pension provider.

Despite this, the Association of British Insurers' latest figures for 2004 show that two-thirds of people still buy their annuity from their pension provider without shopping around.

According to the Bank of Scotland Annuity Service, this could mean a loss of almost £18,500 over their retirement for a 65-year-old man and his 62-year-old wife with a pension fund value of £100,000. The research found that many people fail to shop around for the best annuity deal because of loyalty to the company their pension fund is with and the expectation that there will be only a very limited gain for considerable effort.

Warning An annuity is a one-off purchase. Get the decision wrong and you will be stuck with a lower income for life.

Who must purchase an annuity?

Members of money-purchase employer pension schemes, those with stakeholder pensions, investors with personal pensions, some with additional voluntary contributions (AVCs), people with free-standing AVCs and those with S32 buy-out plans all have to purchase annuities.

However, not all of them are allowed to shop around. For those who have AVCs and those who belong to money-purchase schemes, it depends on the scheme rules.

Note New rules allow those with pension funds of less than £15,000 to take this as a lump sum – they no longer need to purchase an annuity. This limit includes the capital value of any pensions in payments.

How much income will the annuity provide?

The larger your pension fund, the larger your pension.

The annuity rate (what income you will get from this fund) depends on a number of factors:

- annuity rates at the time of retirement or purchasing the annuity if this is later
- your age and gender
- your health and past health
- whether or not you smoke
- whether you want to protect your pension against the ravages of inflation
- if you want a guarantee that you don't lose out because you die shortly after purchasing the annuity (you can buy a five-year guarantee)
- if you want a spouse's pension
- if you want to take some investment risk and buy a newer type of annuity.

Basically, the higher the risk you will die shortly after retirement, the higher the income you will get. Older men who smoke and have had a past history of heart problems can expect a much higher income than a 60-year-old non-smoking woman. This is because the company will have to pay her – in all probability – a pension for much longer than it will for the man.

The more protection you want – against losing out if you die, inflation, or your spouse missing out on your pension – the higher the annuity costs and therefore the lower the income.

Those with a poor health history and smokers should ask for what is known as an impaired life annuity.

If you smoke ten or more cigarettes per day and have done for the last ten years, are suffering from ill health or have had any previous illness or major surgery which is likely to reduce your life expectancy, including diabetes, liver impairment, hypertension which cannot be controlled by medication, a heart condition or cancer, you can expect an enhanced annuity rate – hence a higher income.

Do not forget to include your spouse's or partner's health history when applying for an annuity as this too could increase the income you receive.

Another type of impaired life annuity is socio-geo-economic annuity. If you are or were in a manual occupation or if physical labour accounted for a large part of your work, and you live in certain areas of the UK, you may qualify for this annuity, which tends to offer a higher annuity rate than the top standard annuity rate available.

How can I boost this income?

Shop around – you can get 30 per cent more by simply checking out the alternatives.

Everyone should now be informed that they have a choice (an open-market option).

The difference in rates can vary widely. It also depends on what extras you buy (see *Choosing an annuity*, below).

According to Financial Services Authority's (FSA's) comparative tables, as at mid-2005 there was a 14 per cent disparity between the top and bottom annuity rates for standard lives. The difference between the worst standard rate and the best enhanced rate (for smokers, for example) is 30 per cent – equivalent to nine years of lost income.

Does it always pay to shop around?

Not always. The annuity offered to you by your existing pension provider may be the best deal, particularly if you bought a personal pension with a guaranteed annuity rate (GAR). Such an annuity is hard to beat and if you opt for the open-market option you will give up this guarantee. Also, your ability to shop around may depend on your scheme rules if you are a member of a money-purchase employer's scheme or contribute to an employer's AVC scheme.

Warning Check before shopping around if you have a GAR. If you have one, retire on the stipulated date to take advantage of the guaranteed rate, which will usually be far higher than rates in the open market. If you chose to waive your right to a GAR you may be offered an additional income to make up for the reduced annuity.

What if I change my mind?

To put it bluntly – tough. Once you have purchased an annuity, that is it – you are stuck with it for life. You cannot decide after a year or so to switch to a different or better deal. You will, however, be given details of your rights to cancel should you change your mind upon purchase.

What if I need to buy more than one annuity?

You may be able to combine the proceeds of various pensions into one annuity. However, this will depend on the types of pension. Also, as the annuity rate is not affected by the size of your investment, there is no incentive (as there is with a savings account, for example) to pool your money. In fact, you will probably be better off keeping them separate. You then have the maximum flexibility as to when to purchase the annuities and what benefits they offer.

You can also phase your income so that you receive different amounts at different times (quarterly, six-monthly or annual annuities paid in arrears offer far better rates than annuities which pay income monthly in advance).

Why do annuity rates vary?

The annuity rate you are given depends on your expected life expectancy (which in turn is based on your age, gender and health) and the benefits you want to buy – a spouse's pension, inflation-proofing etc.

However, the economic environment is also significant. Annuities are investments. The income they pay reflects the income they can afford to pay.

When gilt yields (the return from government bonds) are low, annuity rates also fall. This can dramatically hit the value of your annuity. For example, a man aged 65 with a pension pot of £100,000 would have been able to achieve an annual annuity income of around £15,000 ten years ago. Today, the same man would be able to secure an annual annuity income of only about £8,000 a year.

Different types of annuity

Standard annuities

Standard annuities are the most popular type of annuity. With them, your income is guaranteed at least for the rest of your life. Once you know the benefits you want to take, the annuity is selected purely on price (that is, the annuity provider paying you the highest pension income).

You will be paid an annuity rate – for example, 6 per cent. This means that if you have a £100,000 pension fund your annual income will be 6 per cent of this, or £6,000.

Standard annuities carry no risks other than the annuity company going bust (see *How safe is your annuity?* below).

Value protected annuities

These are new (they are expected to be introduced in April 2006) and pay back the residual fund – the value of the annuity less any money paid out – on death if the member dies before their 75th birthday. The lump sum is subject to 35 per cent tax.

Investment annuities

Investment annuities include with-profits, conventional with-profits, guaranteed with-profits and unit-linked annuities.

With-profits annuities carry some risk. Relatively new, they were launched when interest rates were low and stockmarket returns high. They aim to provide income growth through steady investment performance. However, bear in mind that the income from some with-profit annuities can go down as well as up, so you could get poorer, not richer, as you age.

Some have a guaranteed minimum income level, below which the annuity income can never fall.

Conventional with-profits annuities have no guarantees but you can select a level of first-year income at the lower end of what you expect the bonus to be. Each year the provider will declare the bonus level it has achieved in the preceding year. If the total bonus is less than your anticipated bonus level, your income will be reduced for the next 12 months to reflect this fall. Obviously, if your provider achieves better results and the total bonus is greater than your anticipated bonus level your income will be increased for the following year.

The annuity is linked to the investment performance of the insurance company although with-profits funds are designed to smooth out investment returns in a volatile market. Some with-profits funds are harder hit by stockmarket falls than others, so you need to check the financial strength and stability of the insurance company and its fund and its ability to give good future growth.

So with a conventional with-profits annuity you have no certainty, and your income will vary on an annual basis – and may fall as well as rise.

Note Any protected rights benefits (the benefits that replace the State Earnings-Related Pension Scheme, SERPS, or the State Second Pension, S2P) cannot be taken from with-profits, or investment linked, annuities. They must be taken from a guaranteed conventional annuity. In other words, you will need to buy a conventional annuity for your so-called protected rights contributions and this annuity must rise by a set amount each year (either by 3 per cent for contributions made before 6 April 1997 or by inflation for the proportion built up after this date).

Guaranteed with-profits annuities are similar to the conventional with-profit annuities, but have minimum income guarantees, which in some instances will never be less than the starting income. Some providers have also scrapped the requirement to select an anticipated bonus level and have modified the bonus structure in order to simplify the product. However, the annuity is still linked to investment performance.

Warning As with-profits annuities are complex investments and carry a degree of risk, you should seek independent financial advice before making any decision.

Although, once it is purchased, you cannot change your mind about your annuity – it is a once-only decision – some with-profits annuity providers do allow you to switch to their standard annuity under certain circumstances. You cannot, however, move to another provider or switch back into a with-profits, or unit-linked, annuity.

Unit-linked annuities are the riskiest of all. Your income may fluctuate and your investment is completely linked to the stock-market – there is no ironing out of fluctuations as there is with a with-profits annuity.

Unit-linked annuities are suitable only for younger retirees who are prepared to gamble that stockmarkets will recover faster than the rates they can expect to get from a conventional annuity, and only a few providers offer this type of annuity. Generally, if you want to opt for this type of annuity, you need to have other sources of retirement income and not rely on it as your main source of income in retirement.

You should seek specialist independent financial advice and ensure that this is ongoing so that you can change your invest-ment strategy to maximize returns and minimize losses.

The annuity provider works out an income it will pay based on age and the size of your pension fund. This then buys units of the pension fund or funds and the value of these units fluctuates in line with market conditions.

You can choose an anticipated growth level and take a gamble that investment performance will be higher than this. If it is not, your income will be cut.

Some unit-linked annuities allow you to choose your invest-ments (these are known as self-invested annuities). However, they are riskier as they are invested directly in shares, gilts and unit and investment trusts. Once you reach 75 you can no longer self-invest.

Choosing an annuity

In addition to choosing the type of annuity (most will be standard annuities), you have other decisions to make:
- when to buy it – the older you are, the higher the income (see *Income drawdown*, later in this chapter)

- whether you want inflation-linking or other pension increases, or a flat-rate annuity
- whether you want a pension for a spouse.

Your choices will affect the income you receive, as the tables below illustrate.

The tables show the best rates on offer at the end of June 2005 and how your age, gender, whether or not you want a spouse's pension and the type of annuity you purchase affect your pension income.

Bear in mind that these are the best rates: you may get up to £1,000 less each year by failing to shop around.

The figures below assume an annuity purchase price of £100,000 and are shown as gross annual income. All the figures are based on payments being made monthly in arrears, with a guarantee period of 5 years, and with a spouse's benefit of 50 per cent. All the annuity rates shown for smokers are based on someone who smokes an average of ten or more cigarettes each day.

Not inflation-linked, single life

Provider	Income	Provider	Income
Male 60		Female 60	
Scottish Equitable	£6,414	Scottish Equitable	£6,091
Male 65		Female 65	
Scottish Equitable	£7,171	Scottish Equitable	£6,689

Not inflation-linked, joint life

Provider	Income	Provider	Income
Male 60, Female 57		Male 65, Female 62	
Scottish Equitable	£5,919	Scottish Equitable	£6,469

Inflation-linked, single life

Provider	Income	Provider	Income
Male 60		Female 60	
Standard Life	£4,188	Prudential	£3,866
Male 65		Female 65	
Standard Life	£5,100	Scottish Widows	£4,584

Inflation-linked, joint life

Provider	Income	Provider	Income
Male 60, Female 57		Male 65, Female 62	
Standard Life	£3,692	Prudential	£4,266

Not inflation-linked, smoker

Provider	Income	Provider	Income
Male 60		Female 60	
Reliance Mutual	£7,002	Reliance Mutual	£6,525
Male 65		Female 65	
Reliance Mutual	£8,191	Reliance Mutual	£7,441

Not inflation-linked, smoker, joint life

Provider	Income	Provider	Income
Male 60, Female 57		Male 65, Female 62	
Reliance Mutual	£6,234	Reliance Mutual	£7,105

Source: The Annuity Bureau

Although a pension for a spouse dramatically hits the amount you receive, it does at least guarantee that your pension does not die with you.

In addition, the following can affect what you receive as an income.

- **Frequency of income** An annuity is normally paid monthly but it can be paid less frequently – quarterly, half-yearly or even annually. Income paid monthly in arrears is around 4 per cent less than annual in arrears, according to the Annuity Bureau. For a man aged 65 with £100,000 to purchase an annuity that can be the difference between £9,250 and £8,859 a year.
- **Whether income is paid in advance or in arrears** If you take out an annuity and receive your payment the same day, you are being paid in advance. If you are paid a month later, it is in arrears. The difference in income is around 1 per cent. For a male aged 65 with £100,000 to purchase an annuity that can be the difference between £8,859 and £8,792 a year. You can opt for this to be 'with proportion' if you receive

your payments quarterly, six-monthly or annually. This means that when you die, your estate receives the annuity income to which you were entitled. So if you die three months after receiving your last six-monthly payment, your estate will get three months' of annuity income.

- **Whether you opt for a guarantee** You could choose to have a guarantee that will make payments for a certain period even if you die within that period. It protects your pension if you die shortly after retirement and is suitable for those with dependants other than a spouse who do not want their annuity to die when they do. While a spouse's pension will provide the spouse with an income for life, the guarantee provides income only for a limited amount of time – usually five or ten years after retirement. So a spouse's pension will usually be a better option. If you do not die within the guarantee period, your spouse receives nothing. The guarantee is expensive and for a man aged 60 could result in 1 per cent less income, aged 65, 2 per cent less, and aged 70, as much as 3 per cent. The rates are lower than for women. The guarantee can either be for income to continue to the end of the guarantee period – five or ten years after retirement – or for an equivalent lump sum to be paid. New value protected annuities – which pay a lump sum (less 35 per cent tax) of the annuity price less any payments made – also offer protection. See page 42.
- **Whether you opt for an escalating or level pension** If you inflation-proof your annuity your starting pension will be lower. A 65-year-old man would receive 36 per cent less – a high price to pay. However, bear in mind that a man aged 65 is likely to live for a further 19 years and a woman aged 65 for another 22 years. According to the Annuity Bureau, a 65 year-old man would be in his 80s before the total payments from an escalating annuity match those from a level annuity. So it is a gamble you must take. With inflation-proofing you will preserve your spending power. Even low inflation has an impact. After 15 years of inflation averaging 2.5 per cent, the buying power of £1,000 is just £684. On the flip side, if inflation is negative, however unlikely, your pension will decrease.

You can also opt for limited price indexation – 5 per cent or inflation (retail prices index, RPI) whichever is lower – or a fixed percentage of up to 8.5 per cent a year. If you cannot afford full inflation-proofing, opt for a lower percentage.

- **Spouse's pension** Instead of your pension dying with you, an income – usually half your pension – is paid to your surviving partner for the rest of his or her life. You can choose anyone as your partner – unlike, in the past, with most occupational schemes you do not have to be married, nor does your partner have to be of the other sex. All that is required is that the person is financially dependent upon you. The age of your spouse is the biggest factor affecting costs – particularly if your partner/spouse is significantly younger. According to the Annuity Bureau, for a man aged 65 with a wife aged 62, the starting income would be around 14 per cent less than a single life annuity, if he chose a 50 per cent benefit for his wife. This income would fall to around 24 per cent less with a 100 per cent spouse's pension. Most couples, however, opt for an income between 33 per cent and 66 per cent.

- **Overlap** This is usually available only to retirees from company pension schemes in which a five-year guarantee period and a spouse's pension are required. When the person receiving the annuity dies, the spouse's pension starts immediately and – if death is within the guarantee period – the remaining guaranteed pension is also paid. Without overlap, annuities start paying the spouse's pension once the guaranteed period of pension finishes.

- **Dependant's pension** If you are not married, widowed, or living with your partner but still have a dependent child (for example, one with special needs), you can provide a pension for this person. However, you will need to show that he or she is financially dependent on you. This type of pension is expensive and not all annuity providers offer them.

Finding the best deal

Most independent financial advisers should be able to help you shop around for the best annuity rate. However, you may prefer to use a specialist company if you want to opt for a less conventional annuity or income drawdown (see below).

For standard annuities you can surf the Internet for 'best buy' tables. Contact IFA Promotion,* the organization that promotes independent financial advice, for details of advisers in your area who can advise on annuities.

If you have access to the Internet, go to the FSA website* and do a search of the 'best buy' annuity to meet your needs.

How safe is your annuity?

No one who has had an annuity has been left out of pocket so far. However, annuities are not ring-fenced in a separate fund and, as such, if their pension provider goes bust they could lose money. However, if that happens, up to 90 per cent of the money would be made up by the Financial Services Compensation Fund.

Income drawdown

You are required to purchase an annuity by the age of 75 but in the meantime can invest your pension fund in the hope that you will be better off as a result.

This will be the case if:

- your fund is invested well, giving a better return after charges than what you have given up by not purchasing an annuity
- annuity rates when you finally buy your annuity have not fallen from the levels at retirement.

However, few retirees can afford to leave their pension pot invested until they reach 75.

So the rules allow you to draw an income from the pension fund which is roughly equivalent to the income you would have received if you had purchased an annuity on retirement.

There are big risks with this option: you are swapping the certainty of a guaranteed income for one subject to the volatility of the investment markets; annuity rates may not improve in future and could deteriorate; and you will have to pay charges for investing your money, which will eat into your returns.

Also, this option is open to only those who can afford it, who:

- have at least £40,000 to invest
- have other forms of income (so do not have to rely on their income drawdown scheme)
- can delay purchasing their annuity for a long time – long enough for investment markets to improve and interest rates to rise
- do not need the income today or may want to vary the income they receive.

Even if you do not need the income today, you are required to withdraw a certain minimum amount (set by the Inland Revenue) from your pension fund annually. What remains when you reach 75 must be used to purchase an annuity. New rules to be introduced in April 2006 offer another option. The Alternative Secured Pension enables income drawdown past the age of 75.

Those who have very short life expectancy and fear they may die shortly after retirement or before age 75 may also consider the investment option – if they do not need to rely on this for their income – as the death benefits are more generous.

Anyone who has not yet purchased an annuity can leave their entire fund to their relatives and are not restricted to simply providing a pension for their spouse. However, note that this lump will be subject to a 35 per cent tax charge – although it will not form part of your estate for inheritance tax purposes.

This is still less than the 40 per cent tax you would normally pay if you have exceeded the inheritance tax threshold (£300,000 from April 2007).

These schemes also put the investor in control, so you can choose where your money is invested. However, in general these schemes are not a safe bet in the current environment.

Even if you delay purchasing your annuity for two years and this results in an extra £500 of income a year, you will have lost two years of income – for example, £10,000 – so will be far worse off. It could take you years to 'earn' this back from the extra £500 you get each year.

How do I know if income drawdown is a good idea for me?

Income drawdown schemes became popular when the stock-markets were booming but some of those who took them out are now nursing losses. A specialist adviser will look at the costs, expenses and risks before producing a critical yield comparison, which looks at what your investment will need to produce in order to match a conventional annuity. If you want to see how this works visit the Actuarial Profession's website.*

However, for many it will not come down to economics but how they feel. Generally if you:

- have less than £100,000 in your pension fund
- want certainty in retirement
- are dependent on your fund for income
- are concerned about returns from equities
- do not even bother to consider an income drawdown option.

Income drawdown may be more attractive following the introduction of short-term (a maximum of five years) annuities in April 2006.

Phased retirement

The other alternative to buying an annuity with your pension fund is to purchase an annuity gradually over a number of years. This option, also known as phased retirement, may be suitable for you if you:

- want to contribute to one of your pension plans to boost your long-term retirement income
- don't want to cash in all of your pensions at a time when stock-markets have still not recovered
- need to take some of your pension but not all of it
- don't need to have all of your tax-free lump right away.

Phased retirement involves investing in a personal pension fund which in turn is divided into different segments. You cash these in as and when you need income. Each time you do so, you can take up to 25 per cent of that segment as a tax-free lump sum. You can, for example, cash in very few in the early years when – perhaps – you are working part-time.

As with all personal pensions, you must use the remaining fund to purchase an annuity by the time you reach 75.

The benefits, while similar to income drawdown plans (except that you do not have control over your investments), can be more tax-efficient.

- Death benefits are more generous than with an annuity. The entire remaining fund can be left to your dependants. Moreover, unlike what happens in an income-drawdown scheme, the entire fund can be left to your estate with no tax imposed.
- You can continue making pension contributions – and therefore receive tax relief – provided you are still earning a living.

However, there are still risks. Your fund remains invested and could still suffer from stockmarket falls (although you can switch to much safer funds near or shortly after retirement).

Note You can take your tax-free cash entitlement only each time you buy an annuity.

Taking a lump sum *vs* income

Those with occupational and personal pension schemes need to decide whether to take a lump sum or opt for a higher regular pension income.

Although taking a lump sum from your pension when you retire will reduce the amount of pension income you receive, it is not always an unwise decision.

Those in money-purchase employer schemes and with personal or stakeholder pensions can take a maximum lump sum of 25 per cent of the fund. Those in final salary schemes can generally take a maximum of one-and-a-half times final salary as a tax-free lump sum.

Investments *vs* pensions

One advantage of taking a lump sum is that you could make better use of the money if you invested it instead of using it to buy an annuity or taking the maximum pension from your occupational scheme.

While annuity rates tend to be higher than savings rates, they have still been beaten, historically, by the stockmarket. Use £50,000 to buy an annuity and you may get an income of £3,000 a year (depending on the type of annuity and your age). Invest the same amount in the stockmarket and if your portfolio rises by 10 per cent you would have a return of £5,000 (this is before tax but is below the capital gains tax threshold). You could either take your profits to boost your income or watch your money grow and buy an annuity with a larger lump sum later on.

However, if the market grows by only 2 per cent, you will only receive £1,000 a year. Worse, still, given the steep falls in share prices in the early part of the 21st century, you could end up far worse off – losing money and facing a poorer retirement as a result. In such a market, investing is a high-risk option. Also, if annuity rates fall further you could find that you are hit twice – once by the value of your investments falling and second by receiving a lower annuity rate.

Why a lump sum may be better

You do not have to invest your lump sum in risky stockmarket investments. Put it in a high-interest savings account and you could still be better off than with an annuity. There are other reasons why taking the maximum lump sum may be worthwhile.

Pensions restrict your choice One reason for taking the maximum lump sum is to spread your risks of investing and to get a wider choice of investments. You could, for example, use the money to invest in a balanced portfolio of shares and bonds or to pay off borrowings so you can reduce the amount of income you need. If you forgo taking a tax-free lump sum these options will not be open to you.

Your pension may die with you If you die after buying an annuity all the money you invested in it (less any income you already received) is lost unless you pay extra for a guarantee or a spouse's/partner's/dependant's pension or one of the new value-protected annuities. However, even then your widow or widower may only get half of your pension. You can buy a guarantee that the annuity will pay out for at least five years – but it will still be far less than the 15 or 20 years you could have expected. The same applies to company schemes. Your spouse gets half your pension. However, if you are not married or widowed and have no dependants your pension will usually die with you. So you may have worked hard all your life to build up a decent pension which, because you die shortly after retirement, turns out to be very poor value.

You can leave a lump sum to whomever you want There are restrictions on what you can do with your pension from a company scheme or income from an annuity. These pensions can be used only to provide a widow or widower's or dependant's pension and with some annuities a partner's pension. You cannot, for example, pass on some wealth to your children in the form of a lump sum.

With a lump sum you are not locked into low interest rates If you choose to take a lump sum, you are not locked into the prevailing low interest rates and therefore annuity rates (although this is not a problem if you are in a final-salary scheme).

You could keep back a lump sum and use this to buy an annuity at a later date if rates improve. However, a word of caution – rates could move down.

Pensions are taxed – lump sums may not be Pensions paid from an annuity or employer pension scheme are subject to tax (unless your total income falls below the tax threshold). However, your investments may not be. You can invest up to £7,000 in a tax-free ISA each year (£14,000 for a married couple) as well as money in National Savings products.

But a pension means certainty However, there are many advantages to using all or most of your fund to buy an annuity or boost your occupational pension (rather than taking the maximum lump sum):

- you are guaranteed an income for life. Your money is not at the mercy of the stockmarkets and is not affected by future changes in interest rates (although you can reduce risks by purchasing one of the new short-term annuities)
- you will not be tempted to spend the money – leaving you with less to live on when you get older
- any money you have saved or invested may be subject to inheritance tax, whereas your pension will not be.

So should I take the maximum lump sum?
On balance, yes. According to the financial organization Legal & General, annuities are good value for money only if you live to be at least 82. The company says that given an average pension fund of £23,000, pensioners would need to live to 82 before an annuity would prove to be better than investing the money in a building society – and even that is at the low interest rate of 4 per cent.

However, if you live a long time, you may be grateful for your annuity. Research done by Legal & General claims out of every 1,000 men retiring at 65 and buying an annuity, 304 will be alive to celebrate their 90th birthday. There is even more food for thought in the fact that for every 1,000 women buying an annuity at 60, a staggering 499 will live beyond 90.

An annuity today *vs* an annuity tomorrow

This section does not apply to most people in final-salary schemes unless they transfer to a personal pension before retirement to alter the way they receive benefits. If they do this they will, however, be giving up a guaranteed pension for an uncertain future so it is not usually recommended.

Most people in employer money-purchase schemes can exercise their right to shop around for the best annuity rate.

However, there are usually conditions – you must buy a five-year guarantee and a spouse's pension, which will eat into your pension income. It is possible to switch to a personal pension or income drawdown plan to restructure the way you receive your benefits on retirement as well as to give you the flexibility to retire earlier or later than your employer's scheme allows.

What is the best option for me?

If you want more flexibility and are prepared to take an element of risk, then take the maximum tax-free lump allowed.

If, however:

- you do not need the lump sum (to repay a mortgage, for example)
- you have other savings, investments and sources of income
- and have used up your tax-free ISA allowances

you will generally be better off opting for a lower lump sum and taking the certainty of a larger pension.

Remember, this is the rest of your life you are gambling with.

Rules for contracted-out pensions

If you are contracted out of SERPS and S2P, that part of your pension fund must be used to purchase an annuity at the age of 60 for women (due to increase to 65) and 65 for a man.

If you contracted out through a money-purchase occupational scheme, this pension is known as the guaranteed minimum pension or protected rights.

Boosting your pension on retirement

Immediate vesting

Immediate vesting means investing a lump sum into a pension, getting tax relief and withdrawing your 25 per cent tax-free lump sum at the same time.

It is an option available to those over 50 who are self-employed and have net relevant earnings.

Basically, you can invest a gross premium of £10,000 of which £4,000 is tax relief (if you are a higher-rate taxpayer) so it costs you only £6,000. You can then take £2,500 out as a tax-free lump sum, leaving you with £7,500 invested – still more than your pension has cost (although this is a simplistic calculation that does not take into account charges, it illustrates how financially advantageous this option can be).

Most stakeholder providers allow immediate vesting without any conditions. Some impose qualifying periods ranging from one day to one month or even one year.

By investing a large lump sum just before you retire you can therefore boost your pension pot and benefit from tax relief.

Continuing to invest

If you have sufficient capital or income you can continue to invest in a pension after you retire. The stakeholder rules allow you to invest up to £3,600 a year and receive tax relief even if you are no longer working. If you are planning to work part-time after retirement you may be able to contribute more than this.

After age 60 you can contribute up to 40 per cent of earnings tax-free to a pension although these limits are due to be scrapped and replaced with an annual limit of £215,000 subject to an overall pension fund limit of £1.5 million. This rule change could be implemented as early as April 2006.

Making the most of the tax breaks

1. If you are not working you can nominate to base your contributions on your earnings in any of the past five tax years – so this could be when you were a higher earner. You will therefore be able to contribute more than the £3,600 limit.

2. You can get tax relief on pension contributions at the basic rate (22 per cent) even if you are a non-taxpayer and no longer working. However, you do not receive this tax relief. All contributions are made net of tax relief. So if you want to invest £3,600

you need to pay in only £2,808 – the remainder will be paid in by HM Revenue as tax relief.

Early retirement

Pension tax rules currently allow you to retire from 50 (55 from 2010) and it is a pipedream of many to do so at this age. However, bear in mind that if you plan to retire early, you will need far, far more in your pension fund to pay for what is likely to be 30 years of retirement after only 30 years of employment.

Even if you have built up a £100,000 pension fund (over four in ten people retiring today have just £10,000 with which to buy an annuity pension), you will get just £4,000 a year income (assuming it is inflation-linked) at 55 compared to £6,000 at age 65.

So the chances are that you may not be able to afford to retire at 50 unless you start planning this when you are in your 20s. A man retiring at age 50 wanting a more decent income – say, of £20,000 a year and rising by 3 per cent per annum – would need a pension fund of almost £500,000. To fund a more indulgent £30,000 a year would require a pension fund of over £700,000.

So for most people a wealthy and long retirement is unachievable unless they have other sources of capital and income – for example, a large cheque from the sale of a business or a second home.

Enforced early retirement

Early retirement is not always a choice. Fewer than half of the people a year short of the current retirement age do any paid work. Among women only 44 per cent are still working at age 59.

If you are not working, you are not paying into your pension and therefore you will get less when you retire. Also, as you will probably be dipping into your savings and investments, you will be further reducing what you will have to live on when you retire.

So your plans should take into account the fact that you have a less than 50 per cent chance of working right up to retirement. Further, do not assume you can make up for years of under-investment in your pension in your 50s and 60s when your mortgage has been paid off and your children have grown up.

If you are forced out of the job market at an earlier age than planned you will have no scope to meet your pension shortfall and will have to make your reduced pension fund last longer than you planned.

Your rights

Legislation to prevent age discrimination is due to be implemented by the end of 2006. It should mean that older members of the workforce are not discriminated against.

Meanwhile, if your employer tries to replace you with younger staff, you have no legal protection. However, the new law means employers will no longer be able to recruit, train, promote or retire people on the basis of age, unless this can be objectively justified.

Employers in both the public and the private sector will be barred from forcing people into retirement before the age of 65. For older workers this should open up new opportunities in competing for jobs, and in staying in work longer, if they want to.

Problems in recruiting trained staff, or any staff at all, have already led to more employers introducing flexible retirement. Either they raise or abolish their mandatory retirement date, or they introduce a flexible window, during which employees can choose when to retire. This is the most popular option. A few offer greater flexibility by allowing employees to work part-time to gradually reduce their workload and/or responsibilities ahead of retirement, or after the normal retirement age.

You need to know what your employer currently offers and plans to offer, as this could affect your financial planning for retirement.

Income problems in early retirement

Fewer than seven in ten of people aged between 50 and state retirement age are in employment even though the employment rate among older workers has risen faster than for the population as a whole.

Some people can rely on taking early retirement from their occupational scheme to provide some income (although this will reduce the amount of weekly or monthly pension they receive as it will need to be paid for longer). However, for others there is a significant income gap before the state pension is payable at 60 for women and 65 for men. They therefore need to ensure they are in receipt of all the state benefits to which they are entitled (say, Jobseeker's Allowance, Income Support or Incapacity Benefit) and consider ways of rejoining the workforce.

Returning to work

New Deal 50-plus is a programme for people aged 50 or over who have been out of work and claiming benefits for at least six months.
It can provide:

- personal advice and support to find a job
- up to £1,500 in-work training grant
- access to financial support when you are in work, paid as part of the Working Tax Credit. The amount depends on your income and circumstances
- help whether you move into full-time work or part-time work and can also help you start up your own business.

Working past retirement

Working past retirement (if you still have the energy) can be an easy way to boost your retirement income because by deferring taking the state pension you will increase what you get when you do retire, you can continue contributing to private pensions thereby increasing your fund on retirement, and you can avoid dipping into savings or other capital and may be able to continue to save.

The UK has the highest number of employees working past retirement age than most of continental Europe – with 8 per cent of women and 9 per cent of men still earning in their 60s.

Pension rights

If you work past retirement you can still take your personal pension at any time from age 50 (rising to age 55 in 2010) to 75 and defer taking your state retirement pension. The government has also proposed more flexibility for occupational schemes so that employees can, for example, continue to work part-time while drawing part of their pension.

Changing your planned retirement age

You need to inform your personal pension plan provider of when you plan to retire.

If you are deciding to retire at 60, for example, but when you bought your personal pension you selected a retirement age of 65, you will need to notify your pension provider (and there may be penalties to pay).

Tracing lost pensions

There is an estimated £6 billion 'lost' in former employers' schemes and more in personal pensions. Track down your pensions well before your chosen retirement date to ensure the providers know your current address. The Pension Service* provides a Pension Tracing Service* to help you find the contact details of an old pension scheme that you may have lost touch with because you have moved jobs a number of times or the company you worked for previously has moved, been taken over or is no longer trading.

The Service has access to a database of over 200,000 occupational and personal pension schemes and can provide current contact details for the pension scheme. Searching the database is free.

Tip The more information you can give the Pension Tracing

Service, the more likely you will be able to get an up-to-date contact address for the pension scheme you are tracing. For instance, was the pension scheme an occupational pension scheme or a personal pension scheme?

The Pensions Tracing Service says that if you are trying to trace an occupational pension scheme, start by working out:

- whether the employer traded under a different name
- the type of business the employer ran
- whether the employer changed address at any time.

If you are trying to trace a personal pension scheme, start by working out:

- the name of the personal pension scheme
- the address where the personal pension scheme was run from
- the name of the insurance company involved with the personal pension scheme .

Further information

The Actuarial Profession www.actuaries.org.uk
Annuity Bureau (0845) 602 6263; www.annuity-bureau.co.uk
Financial Services Authority (0845) 606 1234; www.fsa.gov.uk
IFA Promotion (0800) 085 3250; www.unbiased.co.uk
The Pension Service (0845) 606 0265; www.thepensionservice.
  gov.uk
Pension Tracing Service (0845) 600 2537

Part Two
MAKING THE MOST OF YOUR PROPERTY

Introduction

For most people, their main asset is their home. So the most obvious way of raising an additional income is to use the family property. However, this is not necessarily a straightforward decision to make, partly because so many options are available.

Do you downsize, release capital using a specialist equity release scheme, or rent out the property? If you decide to move, how much capital do you need to release? Should you opt for housing – such as sheltered accommodation – that will see you through to your old age? Or should you indulge your dreams and head for the South of France or Spain? How will releasing so much equity affect your tax and benefits?

There are numerous questions to answer. So, before deciding, homeowners should go through a very thorough decision-making process. Do not forget – once capital has been released, it must be invested wisely to provide the maximum income possible. And if it is spent, remember that you may not have any more capital to rely on should you need money for urgent home repairs, private medical treatment or to replace the car.

This chapter explores the options in detail to help you make an informed choice. Although the aim of releasing capital and making the most of your assets is to provide more income, you will find that the decision is not a purely financial one. The family home usually has emotional attachments – it may be where you brought up your family, you may love the garden and have close friends living nearby. So you have to consider carefully how any decision you make about your property will affect the quality of your life.

Another option is to make money from property – for example, if you own a second home or if you want to use your home to make money. For those who want to remain in their property, these options should not be overlooked. Taking in a lodger or running a business from the back bedroom may not appeal to everyone. However, thousands of homeowners use these ways to make money from their homes – properties they may otherwise be forced to sell because they can no longer afford to run them.

Your home is probably also the biggest drain on your finances. How to minimize the costs of maintaining and running your home are covered in Part Three of this book.

Chapter 3

Using your property to boost income

The so-called savings gap – the difference between what people should be investing for retirement and what they need to live on – is a staggering £28 billion.

Much of this gap is being met by property – some 70 per cent of those over the age of 60 are homeowners and by 2031 the figure is forecast to rise to 78 per cent. The over-65s now own an astonishing £1 trillion of unmortgaged property, according to actuaries.

So it is not surprising that many of those approaching – and already in – retirement view property as an alternative or a supplement to a pension. In fact, the Council of Mortgage Lenders says: 'In time, equity release [the technical term given to releasing some of the capital tied up in your property] will become a core component of retirement planning.

'Many customers' lives will be improved, and some changed beyond recognition, by products that do no more than enable them to spend their own wealth during their own lifetime.'

However, relying solely on the equity in a property to provide an income – particularly in retirement – has its pitfalls.

Despite the recent surge in property prices, a report entitled *Property or Pensions?* published by the Pensions Policy Institute (PPI) in May 2004 warned that the 'majority of people will not have housing equity to allow them to retire without savings in other assets'. It added: 'Although more wealth is held in housing than in private pensions, not all housing wealth can be converted into an income. Equity release products typically allow only 20 per cent of the house value to be realized at age 65. Housing wealth – like other forms of wealth – is not evenly spread. Most houses are worth less than £130,000. Only 10 per cent of homes are worth more than £330,000, which is how much is needed for equity release to provide an income of £100 a week.'

The PPI report concluded: 'For most people, property will be at best a complement to occupational or personal pensions, not a substitute.'

How property can help fund retirement

Property can help to fund retirement and improve your lifestyle in several ways in addition to the obvious fact that owning your own home can reduce day-to-day living costs in retirement (you do not have to pay rent):

- owners can downsize, thereby freeing up some money
- equity released by homeowners can be used to provide extra income/capital
- part or all of a house can be rented out, a business can be run from home or a property can be used as part of an investment portfolio generating retirement income.

The most suitable option for you will depend on how much additional income needs to be raised and the value of the property. More than half of those aged over 35 have property and pensions, but wealth (including housing wealth) is not evenly spread among everyone. Most people have low levels of private pension saving and relatively small amounts of housing equity. For these people, the predominant benefit of home ownership will be to reduce living costs, rather than to provide a significant amount of income throughout retirement.

Downsize

Sell up and downsize

+ This can release a sizeable amount of capital but there will be costs involved (stamp duty, estate agency fees etc.). This option allows you to move to a more manageable property that is less expensive to run – reducing your day-to-day living costs. And if you move abroad you could not only get a better property and a higher standard of living, you could also release a substantial amount of equity because property prices tend to be substantially lower than in the UK.

− If you have a property that is worth about or less than the average value of £166,000 you may not be able to realize sufficient capital to significantly improve your living standards and afford a new property. For example, £50,000 of equity will probably only provide an additional income of £50 a week. To put this into perspective – you may lose the entitlement to Council Tax Benefit, worth £1,000, and some entitlement to Pension Credit, and may be only marginally better off, if at all.

So before considering this option remember that the additional capital may affect your tax position and may also affect any entitlement to means-tested state benefits.

Downsizing also means moving, something many elderly people may not wish to do particularly as it could mean a move to a smaller property, possibly in a less desirable area. Although downsizing is generally the cheapest and most advisable option from a financial point of view, it may not be the best option for you.

There are numerous older homeowners with three-bedroom properties that are in theory too large for their needs, who would never consider moving to a smaller home because they would miss the neighbours, their garden or their friends. Also they may have a strong emotional attachment to the property. These are the types of homeowner who find equity release an attractive option.

Sell up and rent a new property

+ You will release all the equity in your home – which could provide a substantial lump sum to live off.
– You will no longer have a home of your own and will have to pay rent, and possibly service charges, which will increase your day-to-day living costs. You will probably have to pay income tax and may have to pay CGT on any profits/gains you make when you invest your lump sum. You will lose entitlement to state means-tested benefits. And, once you have subsequently spent the money you have released, you may no longer be able to afford your rent, will have to subsist on state benefits and will have little/nothing to leave as an inheritance.

As a result, you will probably dismiss this as an option.

Release equity from your home

Those wanting to release equity from their homes broadly belong to one of three categories according to the equity release company GE Life.

The pension shortfallers

Pensioners who need to make up a shortfall in their incomes make up 60 per cent of the equity release market. However, equity release should be used only in the last resort, only after other, cheaper, alternatives have been considered. So people should look at other forms of raising income including checking they are receiving all the benefits and Pension Credit to which they are entitled. If they need to release equity to improve their home, grants or loans may be an alternative to equity release. Moreover, because many pensioners may find that they can boost their incomes by only £50 or £100 a week through equity release, they may find that downsizing is a more financially advantageous alternative particularly as the additional income raised by equity release may simply replace benefits from the state.

The lifestylers

This is the fastest-growing area of the equity release market and accounts for around 25 per cent of all clients. Often early retirees, they want to maintain their lifestyle – to travel the world, change their car every three or four years, or buy a holiday home.

The main issue for these homeowners is finding the cheapest way to release equity from their homes. For example, flexible drawdown (taking capital out of the property in stages) will enable a homeowner to release equity as the need for additional income increases with age – and could save vast amounts of interest.

The inheritance tax avoiders

Accounting for around 15 per cent of the equity release market, these wealthier individuals see equity release as a solution to the issue of inheritance tax (IHT). They want to keep their lifestyle and live in their home – but they don't want to leave it to the Inland Revenue.

With so much of their wealth tied up in their property, the only way for them (other than downsizing) to ensure that their home has a reduced – or does not produce – an IHT liability is to release equity. This market is likely to grow rapidly as more homeowners realize they have an IHT problem.

The pros and cons of equity release

+ You can continue to live in your property while releasing some equity to provide capital or an income.
- There are restrictions on the type of property and age of homeowner, so these schemes may not help everyone. Typically, only 20 per cent of equity in a house can be released at age 65 and you will have less to leave as an inheritance. Also, income generated by the capital released will be subject to income tax and any profits on investments could be liable to capital gains tax (CGT). Moreover, you should consider the impact of this additional income on your means-tested benefits and Pension Credit.

Even so, equity release schemes are increasingly popular. They are now the fastest-growing area of financial services and within the next five years £2 billion of equity could be released each year by older homeowners looking to make the most of their most valuable asset.

These are covered in greater detail in Chapter 5.

Make money from your home

Rent out part of your property

+ The income can be tax-free. Under the rent-a-room scheme you can earn up to £4,250 each year tax-free.
- The income will affect your benefit or Pension Credit entitlements. Also, you will have to tolerate living with a lodger. However, many older homeowners living in large properties may find it a comfort to have another person around the house. Having a lodger also involves very little extra effort for what can amount to a sizeable additional income.

Mary, a widow in her 60s living in a mansion flat in London: 'I have let out the room at the back of the flat to a middle-aged man whose family lives in the country. He is here only three or four nights a week, I hardly see him and yet I receive an extra £400 a month in income.'

Susie, a divorcee living in Suffolk who has no private pension: 'I let out a room for a while to a young girl who was working locally. It was good fun at first to have someone young around the house. However, in the end I found it hard to have someone else in my space all the time. So eventually I opted to downsize instead.'

Rent out the whole home

+ If you can rent somewhere cheaper, have a second-home abroad or plan to move in with relatives you can earn a good income *and* continue to benefit from the capital appreciation of your property.
- The income will be taxable (although some expenses can be

offset against the rent) and if you eventually need to sell the house some of the profits on the sale may be liable to CGT. Also, receiving an income from your property will affect any entitlement to means-tested state benefits such as Pension Credit or Council Tax Benefit.

Those moving abroad could find this option particularly appealing. Many of those who have made a move overseas find that when they reach their 70s or 80s and want to return to the UK they can no longer afford to buy a property because of sharp rises in UK house prices.

High rental yields from UK homes can easily fund a much more lavish lifestyle abroad, where the cost of living tends to be much lower – without the need to sacrifice the capital in your property.

This option is also ideal for those who want to try another lifestyle but need a fallback to return to should it not work out. Not everyone who moves overseas or to the country or seaside enjoys the change. Renting out your home – even for just a year or two – will give you the chance to enjoy life in a new location without burning your bridges.

However, renting out your property is not risk-free. There is always the possibility of having a bad tenant. Fortunately, most retirees do not have a mortgage to worry about so there should be no risk of the mortgage going unpaid because the tenant has run off without paying the rent.

If you are interested in this option, read Chapter 6.

Run a business from home

+ Not ready for retirement? Many of the over-50s find it hard to find employment even though they have the experience, talent and energy to continue working for many years to come. In fact, one in five of those aged over 55 are self-employed – they have created their own employment because they may find it hard to find anyone to employ them. Using your home as a business premises has obvious advantages:

- there are no premises costs
- you do not have to commute to work
- you can offset some of the costs of running your home against tax.

In effect, your home can pay its way – and provide valuable employment.

- You have to have an idea for a business that will work. Professionals and those with years of experience can become consultants. Anyone with a particular skill – from typing to dressmaking – can usually make some money by working for themselves. However, not everyone will have a money-making idea. Also, if you work from home, you never get away from the office and your business can easily end up taking over your life as well as your home – eating into leisure time that you may want to enjoy.

There can also be tax implications. Your home, which is usually free from CGT, may become partly liable if you use all or part of it to run a business.

For more information, see Chapters 6 and 18.

Turning your home into a business

+ You can make your home pay its way by using it to generate income. This is an option for those who may not have another business idea and who need or want to work but cannot find suitable – or any – employment. Turning your home into a business – a B&B, guesthouse or holiday let (while you stay with the children) – can provide valuable income for little outlay or risk.
- Running a business is not easy or risk-free. There is a lot of red tape to tackle, the Inland Revenue and possible VAT to deal with and no guarantee that your business will make money.

See Chapter 6 for more information.

Investing in property

If you can afford it, you can supplement your income by investing in property. This can include buy-to-let investments, second homes, commercial properties bought by your pension fund or property funds that are collective investments such as investment trusts.

+ Property has – at certain times – outperformed shares as an investment. It can provide both an income and capital growth. A property investment fund can add balance to your investment portfolio and require as little as £1,000 as a lump sum.

– Direct property investment is very expensive (you have to pay stamp duty, legal fees, a large deposit, etc.) and so it is an option only for the wealthy. You will also need to invest for a long time to recover these costs, and time may not be on your side if you have already retired. Moreover, there are no guarantees – prices may not recover from their recent slump for many years.

REITS – Real Estate Investment Trusts

These are a new way to invest in commercial and residential properties announced in 2005 and they can be tax-efficient if held in a tax-free ISA. Investments start at just £50 a month.

Chapter 4

Downsizing

Equity release is probably the best-known financial product that enables homeowners to raise additional income in retirement, but selling up and moving to a smaller and more manageable home is by far the most common way of releasing money tied up in a property. In addition to examining this method of downsizing, this chapter also looks at selling off part of one's property, moving into a retirement home, and moving abroad, where property prices tend to be much cheaper.

Moving down the property ladder

Contrary to popular belief, most equity withdrawal occurs as a result of trading down or last-time sales (when people trade out of owner-occupation to move into sheltered housing or long-term care, or when their properties are sold on death), rather than as a result of people increasing their debt by tapping into their housing equity, according to the Council of Mortgage Lenders.

Nearly two-thirds of all equity withdrawn from property comes from last-time sales and trading down, according to the Council of Mortgage Lenders. With the over-65s owning over £1 trillion of unmortgaged equity in their homes, this represents a sizeable amount of capital to fund a better standard of living.

Reasons for moving down the property ladder

Among people over 65 who are considering a move, the huge majority – some 88 per cent according to the Prudential's retirement index – are doing so because of financial difficulties. In other words, they need the money.

Other reasons for moving into smaller property include:

- home too large to meet needs
- property requires too much maintenance/expensive repairs
- the costs of running the home (including Council Tax) are too high
- cannot cope with the large garden
- want to be nearer children/grandchildren
- want a property without stairs
- need to be nearer to shops, doctors, the post office etc.

Despite all these practical and financial reasons, selling up and moving into a smaller house can still be a very emotional and difficult change to make – you should not underestimate the trauma of leaving a property that has been your home for 20, 30 or even 40 years, where you have raised your children, which you have improved and decorated and made the centre of your family life. Moreover, getting rid of your clutter and possessions to move to a smaller home will take time and involve parting with things which have a strong emotional attachment. This is probably why equity release is becoming increasingly popular.

Age Concern* has produced a Moving Home Checklist aimed at people over 60.

Is it an option for me?

If your aim is to increase your income by releasing capital, the overriding consideration must be that it is financially worthwhile – £50,000 is the sort of sum that makes downsizing worth it. Bear in mind that the costs of moving (see below) will eat into the capital you plan to release.

If you are moving for other reasons, such as to reduce the maintenance costs of your home by moving to a smaller property, there may be long-term rather than short-term savings.

According to the research done by Prudential, two-thirds of homeowners will be out of pocket if they downsize because of the costs of moving, which now amount to over £6,000, rising to £13,500 in London. The survey found, for example, that someone in the South East who wanted to move to the South West and remain in a similar-sized house would gain only £20,720 in equity. Almost a third of that would be used in moving costs, leaving them with only £14,520. This capital, spread over 20 years of retirement, would give them only an extra £14 a week. So to make it worthwhile they would either have to move to a much cheaper and possibly less desirable area and/or a much smaller property.

The pros and cons of moving down the property ladder

The benefits are that you can:

- release capital to improve your standard of living
- cut the costs of maintaining your home
- reduce the burden of running a larger property – maintenance, gardening etc.

In addition to the fact that moving is expensive (see below), the drawbacks are that you may:

- not be able to release enough capital to fund the lifestyle you want
- not be able to find a suitable property for significantly less money
- have to move to a less desirable area
- have to leave friends and a community behind.

The costs of moving

As mentioned above, according to the Prudential the average cost of moving in the UK is £6,200, rising to £13,500 in London.

These costs, which include stamp duty, will eat into any capital released. Therefore, according to Prudential, 'the long-held belief that downsizing is a way to plug the pension gap is only true for a minority of people, who live in detached houses or London and the South East. Not only is it practically impossible for people in some regions to downsize to release equity, it is true that the large cost of moving home will eat into their profits. They may not end up with as much cash as they expected.'

This is how the costs add up according to the latest Woolwich cost of moving survey:

WOOLWICH COST OF MOVING SURVEY 2005

House prices	Cost of selling	£	Cost of buying	£
£80,000	Solicitor	442	Solicitor	467
	Estate agent	1,227	Land Registry	60
			Searches	186
			Stamp duty	0
	Total	**1,669**		**713**
£100,000	Solicitor	460	Solicitor	486
	Estate agent	1,472	Land Registry	100
			Searches	186
			Stamp duty	0
	Total	**1,932**		**772**
£150,000	Solicitor	498	Solicitor	527
	Estate agent	2,146	Land Registry	150
			Searches	186
			Stamp duty	1,500
	Total	**2,644**		**2,363**
£200,000	Solicitor	541	Solicitor	571
	Estate agent	2,819	Land Registry	150
			Searches	186
			Stamp duty	2,000
	Total	**3,360**		**2,907**
£300,000	Solicitor	617	Solicitor	654
	Estate agent	4,145	Land Registry	220
			Searches	186
			Stamp duty	9,000
	Total	**4,762**		**10,060**

House prices	Cost of selling	£	Cost of buying	£
£500,000	Solicitor	740	Solicitor	784
	Estate agent	6,741	Land Registry	220
			Searches	186
			Stamp duty	15,000
	Total	**7,481**		**16,190**
£750,000	Solicitor	940	Solicitor	1,000
	Estate agent	10,127	Land Registry	420
			Searches	186
			Stamp duty	30,000
	Total	**11,067**		**31,606**
£1,000,000	Solicitor	1,326	Solicitor	1,398
	Estate agent	13,374	Land Registry	420
			Searches	186
			Stamp duty	40,000
	Total	**14,700**		**42,004**
£1.5m	Solicitor	1,680	Solicitor	1,783
	Estate agent	20,098	Land Registry	700
			Searches	186
			Stamp duty	60,000
	Total	**21,778**		**62,669**
£2m	Solicitor	2,170	Solicitor	2,318
	Estate agent	26,990	Land Registry	700
			Searches	186
			Stamp duty	80,000
	Total	**29,160**		**83,204**

Compiled by University of Greenwich.

The choices

1. Remain in the same area but move to a smaller property

Moving from a semi-detached house to a terraced house will release under £40,000 of equity – no matter where you live, according to research from the Prudential.

In fact, the average person moving from a semi to a terrace will release nearer £22,000, and that does not include moving costs, which will eat into the capital significantly.

So, to make it worthwhile moving you will generally need to

make a significant change – from a detached home to, say, a small bungalow.

2. Remain in the same-sized house, but move to a cheaper area
Cheaper areas are often cheaper for very good reasons. There may be fewer facilities or, in the worst case, these areas may suffer from higher levels of deprivation.

However, bear in mind that for a retired person cheaper areas may provide better facilities. Just because there are fewer jobs and facilities for younger people it does not mean that the area is undesirable for the over-60s, who are probably not interested in finding work, commuter transport or schools.

Although swapping your average semi in the South East for a similar property in the South West will generally result in just under £21,000 of equity being released (before costs), some moves are more financially worthwhile: swapping the same home for a semi in Wales will release over £64,000 of equity on average.

Of course, much depends on where you live today. Those in the East Midlands will find that property prices are cheaper only in Scotland and Northern Ireland, whereas those living in London can expect to release at least £100,000 by swapping a semi in the capital for another anywhere else in the UK.

3. Move to a smaller property in a cheaper area
For anyone living outside London and the South East or prepared to make a significant downsize in terms of the size of property, this is going to be the only financially viable option.

Selling part of your property

If you do not wish to sell all of your property, you could sell part of your house to either your children or developers.

Selling a stake to your children

Rather than opting for equity release – which is expensive and leaves less of an inheritance for your heirs – it is worth considering whether or not you can sell part of your home to your children.

This will give you extra capital with which to provide an additional income while giving you the right to continue to live in your home.

The drawbacks

Many children (even if they are in their 40s or 50s) are still reliant on financial help from their parents – to pay for school fees for their own children, for example. As most are heavily mortgaged, they will not have sufficient capital spare to buy a share of their parents' property.

Moreover, joint ownership (when the children buy a stake they will generally want to become joint owners to protect their capital) can have drawbacks. If you fall out with your children they can force you to sell. If they run up debts, your home may have to be sold.

While you will not pay tax on the capital you receive, your children will pay capital gains tax on any rise in the value of their stake in your property.

The main advantages

Selling a stake to your children (for the market value) means that that proportion of your property is no longer classed as part of your estate for inheritance tax purposes.

If, however, you give your property to your children this will not be the case. Only if you then pay your children a market rent will the property become a potentially exempt transfer (which means that if you survive for seven years, it will no longer be part of your estate for inheritance tax purposes).

Note Recent rule changes prevent homeowners from retaining an interest in assets they sell or give away to avoid inheritance tax. Seek legal and tax advice before making a decision.

Selling off land to developers

This will be an option for very few elderly homeowners. However, it is worth considering if you live in a large house with a garden that is too big for you.

In many cases it may turn out that the land is not suitable for development or that planning permission is not granted. However, if your neighbours join you in selling part of their land and help make it a larger development site, you may have found an easy way to raise additional capital.

A local surveyor can tell you if your land is large enough and suitable for development (remember, homes can be built out of part of the back gardens of a row of houses) and your local council's planning department can tell you if development is permitted.

Moving into retirement housing

Retirement housing schemes are designed for those who are at least 55 or 60. They generally consist of 20 to 40 flats and/or bungalows, which people buy on a leasehold basis and live in.

The advantages

- There is usually an alarm system so that should you fall or fall ill, a warden can be summoned to help.
- You are part of an instant community.
- The properties are elderly-friendly – no stairs, parking outside the door, low maintenance.
- There may be a guest bedroom so family/friends can visit.

So a retirement home will be smaller, more manageable, with good security and support.

However, this is not an option for everyone, and these properties tend to come at a price.

The disadvantages

- You may have to move to a new area, away from family and friends.
- You may not be able to take your pet.
- You will probably have no or little outside space.
- Retirement homes are sold on a leasehold basis and you will have to pay ground rent.
- You can sell your property only to another older homebuyer, limiting the potential number of buyers. (You could leave it to another older person in your will, but more often than not when you die the property will be sold, subject to restrictions on who can buy or live in it.)
- As retirement housing schemes tend to be fairly newly built, they may be away from facilities such as shops and transport. So while the property may be suitable, the area may not be. For example, it may be at the top of a steep hill or a 20-minute walk from the shops.
- The properties tend to be small. You will have to get rid of treasured possessions, and you may find your flat or house claustrophobic.
- You will have to pay a service charge for the upkeep of communal areas, the warden and insurance. This could be expensive and will probably rise each year (even though your income may not).

Questions to ask

To safeguard yourself and to help you make an informed decision before you buy a retirement house, you should:

- talk to other residents to find out if there are any problems (poor noise insulation, for example)
- check that the management company is a member of the Association of Retirement Housing Managers (ARHM)
- check what the warden's duties are – and how often they are available. Do they live on site? Or is there no warden at all?

For example, if there is an alarm will it be answered 24 hours a day? Remember, retirement housing does NOT provide long-term care – you will need to arrange help with your local social services department should you need home help because of a disability

- think twice before opting for a part-exchange – whereby the retirement housing company buys your house to save you the hassle and expense of selling it yourself. You will get less than the market value – a high price to pay for an easy life
- check that the flat or home is covered by a National House-Building Council (NHBC) warranty if it is new. The NHBC Sheltered Housing Code of Practice applies to all buildings built after 1990. This Code protects residents' rights in a legally binding management code and requires developers to produce a Purchasers' Information Pack detailing important information about the scheme.

Buying a retirement home

Some retirement homes are offered on a 'shared ownership' basis, which means you buy part of the property and pay rent on the rest. The Elderly Accommodation Counsel* can provide details of schemes in your area.

Alternatively, you can buy a lifetime lease, which gives you the right to live there for the rest of your life or until you move. However, while this may be a cheaper option, for example, a couple in their mid-seventies could pay around £65,000 for a life interest in a property worth £110,000, you will probably get little back if you move, and your heirs will inherit nothing when you die.

Moving abroad

Some 900,000 British pensioners already live abroad and, according to research done by the Prudential, 45 per cent of people in the UK would like to retire abroad if their finances allow.

It is no surprise that retiring to the sun is a dream for many: no more rainy, cold winters; cheap wine and food; a more relaxed way of life; and a larger home for a lot less money.

However, this dream can turn into a nightmare if it is not planned properly. As with any major decision, you need to do your research before moving overseas. Age Concern* produces a useful information sheet on retiring abroad.

The pros and cons of moving abroad

You need to examine your reasons for moving abroad in depth before taking the plunge. Once you have sold up in the UK and made a commitment to a new country, you will be out of pocket should you change your mind and decide to return home.

It is far better to try before you buy – possibly renting out your home in the UK and renting overseas. The rent from your UK property could easily cover your rent in France, for example, and provide you with an additional income while you still retain a stake in the UK property market and benefit from house price increases.

Moving abroad may not resolve the problems you face. For example, you may want to move because of the weather. However, you could find that you find living in the heat just as uncomfortable as living with cold, damp weather. Perhaps holidaying in the winter may be a better solution than moving lock, stock and barrel to a new country.

If you wish to improve your income in retirement, you will find that moving abroad will:

- enable you to release equity from your UK home as prices overseas are often significantly lower
- reduce your living costs. It is not just the heating bill that is cheaper but also often day-to-day items such as groceries.

However, you may find that you lose entitlements to benefits when you leave the UK and that as a result you are not significantly better off.

Moreover, it is not always cheaper to live abroad. According to the Prudential's 'International Costa Living' survey, Canada, Cyprus, Jamaica, France and Australia are all more expensive places to live in than the UK.

Also, bear in mind that exchange rate and interest rate fluctuations will affect your income. If you are receiving pensions in sterling and there is a 10 per cent move in sterling against the euro, for example, you could suddenly find that you are worse – or perhaps – better off.

Think long-term

One of the biggest drawbacks to moving abroad is leaving behind family and friends, especially at a stage in your life when you may have more time to spend with them and become more reliant upon them.

Age often brings illness and using a health system in another country (where you may not, for example, speak the language well enough to discuss a major operation) can be daunting.

You also need to think about what happens when you or your partner dies. One of you could be left alone in a foreign country to deal with all the paperwork and possibly repatriating the partner's body if he or she wished to be buried in the UK.

Also, if you decide to return to the UK at a later date, think about where you will live. Many homeowners who have sold up and moved abroad to enjoy a more luxurious lifestyle find that when they want to move back to the UK they can afford only a tiny terraced house.

Remember, living in another country is very different from going there on holiday. You may choose to live in a place that you enjoyed visiting as a tourist, but the area may turn out to be miserable out of season and lacking in facilities for residents.

Will I be able to retire abroad?
While it may be easy to retire in the European Economic Area (EEA, which comprises the 25 member states of the European Union, plus Norway, Iceland and Liechtenstein), not all

countries welcome pensioners. Canada and Australia will probably not allow you in unless you have family there, and the USA does not issue visitor residence permits to retirees although you can stay for six months at a time as a visitor.

Some countries will require you to have a certain level of savings to buy a property.

UK citizens have a right to live and settle in any of the EEA countries. However, you may still have to apply for a residence permit.

Doing your maths

As mentioned above, while you may gain from a lower cost of living if you move overseas, there are things that you could miss out on – and we are not just talking about your favourite television programme or Indian takeaway. For more information, see Chapters 1 and 17.

Pensions

You will continue to receive any UK state pension to which you are entitled: it will be paid in any country in the world. However, you may not receive any increases in your pension if you move outside the EEA area. As mentioned in Chapter 1, of the 900,000 UK pensioners living abroad, 480,000, including those living in South Africa, Australia, Canada and New Zealand, are the victims of frozen pensions. For advice on getting your pension paid abroad, and the rules applying to your country of choice, call the International Pensions Centre.*

Benefits

You will lose entitlement to means-tested benefits such as Pension Credit, Housing Benefit and Council Tax Benefit. However, if you are claiming Incapacity Benefit, Severe Disablement Benefit or Bereavement Allowance, these may continue to be claimed if you are resident in another EEA state. It is also possible to receive a widow's pension, war pensions and Industrial Injuries Benefit while living abroad: the same applies to Attendance Allowance or Disability Living Allowance if you have been receiving it since 1 June 1992. You may also be entitled to benefits paid by the EEA state you move to. Leaflet SA29 from your local benefits agency has more information.

A few non-EEA countries have agreements with the UK which mean you may be able to continue receiving certain UK benefits in that country – details are in leaflet GL29 from your local benefits agency.

Health

Entitlement to state health care varies from country to country, and you may have to pay a certain amount or take out private medical cover, which can be very expensive. UK nationals living in another EEA country are entitled to the same health-care benefits as a pensioner who is a national of that country.

To qualify, you must be either in receipt of state pension, Bereavement Allowance or long-term Incapacity Benefit in the UK. For advice call the International Pensions Centre.

However, one of the biggest losses comes if you become resident in another EU country as you will technically not be entitled to free health care in the UK and could be charged for it should you return home for medical treatment.

Taxes

There will be taxes such as local taxes to pay wherever you live, and not all tax systems are as generous as in the UK. You will need professional advice before you go, to ensure that your finances are protected. Inheritance and inheritance tax laws vary from country to country. For example, you may not be able to leave your property to your spouse free of tax. Dying intestate (without a will) will also cause major problems.

Becoming a non-resident in the UK for tax purposes does change your position. If you spend fewer than 91 days a year in the UK per tax year (averaged over four years) you will not be taxed on your worldwide income in the UK. However, certain income from the UK – such as letting your UK home – may still be liable for UK tax.

Doing your research about living abroad
- Do not base your decision on a fortnight's holiday. Spend some time in the country/town of your choice – both in and out of season.
- Talk to other British people who have moved there. The local British consulate should be able to put you in touch with expatriate groups. Find out what they like and do not like about living there. For details of British Consulates abroad contact the Foreign and Commonwealth Office*.
- Try before you buy. Rent a property for a while to make sure that this really is the right decision for you.
- Learn the language. In some countries this will not be an issue. However, life will be easier if you speak the local language: while the barman or local shopkeeper may know a few words of English there are no guarantees that a plumber or doctor will.
- Find out if you need a permit to drive in the country (which will probably be the case outside the EEA).

If you are a non-resident for tax purposes you can receive interest from UK bank accounts without tax deducted (gross).

In addition, the country in which you become a resident for tax purposes may charge you tax on your worldwide income.

Double-tax treaties (signed by most countries) ensure that you do not pay taxes on the same income in both countries.

The one tax you may not be able to avoid is inheritance tax. When a British person dies abroad, UK inheritance tax is usually applied to his or her estate unless he or she changed domicile (renounced all links with the UK). Seek professional tax advice before making this decision.

Tax issues for expatriates are complex and getting them wrong can be expensive, so it is worth using an accountant or tax adviser to handle your tax affairs once you move abroad – ask other expatriates for a recommendation.

The buying process

If buying a home in the UK is one of the most stressful life events – along with divorce and bereavement – imagine how fraught it can be to buy abroad, given a different legal system and, perhaps, a different language.

If you are moving to a country which has a lot of expatriate British people, things will be easier as there will be lawyers and estate agents used to dealing with UK buyers.

Even if you speak the local language well you are advised to deal with an English-speaking lawyer who can explain the differences in legal systems to you in English.

The costs of buying abroad

You may be seduced by cheaper property prices abroad and then find that you are not that much better off because of the costs of buying. These can easily add 10 per cent to the purchase price. In France, for example, stamp duty can be as high as 13 per cent.

The difficulties in buying abroad

Buying a home overseas may be very different from buying in the UK: you may find that issues you take for granted in the UK are not so straightforward elsewhere. For example, there have been horror stories in the media of UK expatriates buying homes in Spain that have no planning permission and therefore have to be demolished.

Type of property

Anyone inspired by Peter Mayle's book *A Year in Provence* may believe that buying a dilapidated house abroad and doing it up is an easy way to release capital from an existing home in the UK and make money on the one you are renovating overseas. But as Mayle discovered, dealing with foreign tradesmen can be fraught with difficulties – and far more expensive than you realize.

At the other end of the property spectrum is to buy a home on a complex. These are newer properties which require less maintenance; an on-site manager is often part of the package so there is someone there to keep an eye on your home when you are away and to help if there is a problem with the property. These complexes tend to have many expatriate communities, which is ideal for some – but unwelcome for those wishing to integrate fully into the local community.

Further information

Age Concern (0800) 00 99 66

Elderly Accommodation Counsel: National Advice Line
    020-7820 1343; www.housingcare.org

Foreign and Commonwealth Office 020-7008 1500;
    www.fco.gov.uk

For advice on getting your pension paid abroad, and the rules
    applying to your country of choice, call the International
    Pensions Centre (0191-218 7777 or 0191-218 2828) and ask
    for Customer Liaison.

Chapter 5

Equity release schemes

Equity release schemes give older homeowners a way of releasing the equity in their homes, turning some of the value of the property into cash. This can be in the form of a lump sum, regular income or both.

They break down into two types of scheme – equity release mortgages (of which lifetime mortgages are the best-known), which account for more than 90 per cent of the market, and home reversion schemes. These financial packages enable the homeowner to live in the property for the rest of his or her life while enjoying a better standard of living.

Equity release schemes differ in terms of who and what type of property qualify, what percentage of equity can be released and the risks involved.

They are also one of the most complex areas of financial services. The city watchdog, the Financial Services Authority (FSA), has already expressed concern that vulnerable homeowners may be sold inappropriate equity release schemes. In addition, home reversion schemes have yet to come under the regulatory net of the FSA, although the government plans legislation on this front shortly.

Anyone considering taking out one of these schemes should not only seek independent financial advice, they are also advised to seek impartial legal advice and to discuss the implications fully with their family. Even equity release providers admit that their schemes should be a last resort. *The schemes are expensive and only if all the alternatives have been fully considered – and dismissed – should equity release be an option*.

For these reasons, this chapter looks mainly at making the

decision about equity release – rather than which type of product is most suitable for an individual.

Would equity release be right for me?

Yes, if you want the right to live in your home for the rest of your life and are asset-rich but cash-poor. If this is the case, releasing part of the capital tied up in your property to raise extra income or a lump sum may be the perfect solution for you. However, before you decide on equity release you should consider a number of issues, ranging from the impact of releasing capital on your income tax and benefits, to the inheritance you leave future generations.

It may be worth exploring equity release as an option if you answer 'yes' to these questions.

- I want to continue living in my property – for as long as I choose.
- Most of my capital is tied up in my property.
- My income and savings are no longer/not meeting all my financial needs or I need to raise a cash lump sum (for example, to repair the roof, adapt my home, replace my car, to help my children).

Remember, equity release is only one option. Other choices, including downsizing, renting out your property and running a business from home (see Chapters 4 and 6), may be cheaper and less risky ways of solving your financial problems. You should explore these first.

How much can I raise?

You might not be able to raise as much as you think you will. If you are prepared to sell your property to a home reversion scheme provider in exchange for the right to live in it till you die and either a lump sum or an income for life, you can release most of the equity in exchange for an income. However, you will not get the full value of your home, and the income you receive will reflect the fact that the reversion company may have to continue paying you for 20 or more years.

If you want to retain ownership of your home, a lifetime mortgage will generally release only 25 to 40 per cent of the value of your home. So someone releasing 25 per cent of a £200,000 property will get around £50,000.

To put this into perspective, £50,000 may provide you with only an extra £50 a week. However, you do not have to invest the equity released, and can use a lump sum to buy a new car, improve the property or travel the world. So the equity released can have quite a dramatic impact on your quality of life.

What can I do with the money?

Some schemes provide a lump sum, others an income and some both. You do not have to spend the money on your home or buy an annuity (a financial product that guarantees to pay out an income for life).

If you want, you can – although this will generally not be advisable – blow the lot on a once-in-a-lifetime holiday. Once you have spent the money, that's it. You may not be able to raise additional funds (release further equity) from your home in future if your income fails to meet your financial needs. Most people use the money to improve their homes and to supplement their retirement income.

Key Retirement Solutions, the UK's leading independent financial advisers specializing in equity release, found in a survey of customers that the top ten reasons for releasing cash from their homes were:

1. to carry out home improvements
2. to enjoy the cash now while they can
3. to go on more holidays
4. for lifestyle improvement
5. to pay off mortgage/debts
6. to invest for a future income
7. to treat family or friends
8. to reduce inheritance tax liability
9. because they have no children/beneficiaries
10. because their children suggested it.

Can anyone take out equity release?

No. There are restrictions, although these do vary from provider to provider.

The main restriction is age. You will generally need to be at least 60 although some require that you are 65 or even 70. You also need to own your own home and have paid off your mortgage although some schemes will enable you to raise capital to repay a small outstanding mortgage.

If you jointly own the property, you will need to take out a scheme in joint names.

What type of home do I need to have?

Again, this varies from scheme to scheme. Freehold properties are normally acceptable although some schemes will allow you to release equity on a leasehold flat or a leasehold house as long as at least 75 to 80 years of the lease is remaining.

The minimum value of the property should usually be at least £50,000. The home will need to be in a reasonable state of repair, and not all companies offer schemes in all locations, so your choice of scheme could also depend on where you live.

If your home is unusual in any way, is considered hard to sell or is part of a sheltered accommodation complex you will probably not be able to find an equity release scheme that covers you.

Is there a minimum amount I can release?

To be worthwhile – and to cover the costs – most people release near to the maximum they can. The minimum is £3,000 or a monthly payment of £50 for home reversion schemes. For lifetime mortgages the minimum is usually £25,000, but some lenders will go as low as £5,000.

What happens if I live with someone else?

Married couples usually take out a joint scheme and the same will generally apply to unmarried couples. If you have a child still living at home, he or she will need to agree to forgo any right to stay living in your home when you die before you can take out a plan.

What happens if I remarry after taking out a scheme?

If you remarry after taking out a scheme, the scheme will have to be changed to include the new partner. If anyone else moves into the property, they will have to forgo any right to live there after you have left.

What happens when one of us dies?

With both lifetime mortgages and equity release schemes, if the scheme was taken out as a joint plan the surviving spouse or partner can continue to live in the property for as long as he or she wishes.

What happens if I still have a mortgage?

If you have a small outstanding mortgage, the equity release company will probably allow you (and require you) to pay this off with the capital released. However, generally, companies require the property to be unmortgaged – that means the mortgage will need to be paid off before or at the same time as the plan starts.

How do the different types of scheme work?

As mentioned earlier, there are two main types of equity release scheme. You can either:

- mortgage your home, raising a loan against the value of your home using what are now normally referred to as lifetime mortgages. This way you continue to own your home and benefit from the future growth in its value. However, interest rolls up on the mortgage (there are no repayments) so that means your debt will increase year after year, eating into the capital, or
- sell part or all of your home in what is known as a reversion scheme. The advantage is that you know exactly where you stand. However, you will not benefit from future rises in value of that proportion of your property. To release enough for sufficient income, you may need to sell your entire home – leaving your heirs with no inheritance. These schemes pay a regular income for life, which is good if you live a long time but a financial loser if you do not.

Equity release mortgages

The most common type of equity release mortgage for older homeowners is a lifetime mortgage. Almost 30,000 homeowners now take advantage of lifetime mortgage schemes each year according to the Council of Mortgage Lenders. In 2004 some £1.2 billion of loans was arranged and to date almost 85,000 homeowners have released a total of £4 billion to help them to remain in their homes and have additional income.

The market is growing rapidly, increasing 25 times in the last decade. With an estimated £1 trillion worth of unmortgaged housing owned by people over 65 there is huge scope for this market to expand even further.

Lifetime mortgages have, since October 2004, been brought under the regulatory net of the FSA, and there are strict guidelines on how they should be sold. Even so, the FSA has expressed concern that some vulnerable homeowners could be being advised to take out unsuitable equity release products.

Lifetime mortgages

How lifetime mortgages work

With a lifetime mortgage you borrow money from a bank, building society or other lender using your home as security. This mortgage is called a lifetime loan: it lasts for your lifetime and is repaid when you die out of the proceeds of the sale of your property (or when you sell the home, if that is earlier).

There are no repayments; instead interest rolls up each year. Therefore, the amount you owe continues to rise. As you can borrow only a set percentage of the property's value and property prices generally increase, you should continue to own a considerable amount of unmortgaged capital in your home.

Even so, negative equity – when the property is worth less than the outstanding mortgage debt – is a real worry for many homeowners. Most lifetime mortgages come with a negative equity guarantee (see below).

What lifetime mortgages cost

Rolled-up interest loans will, naturally, cost you money. However, if your property continues to rise in value, the increase can more than compensate for the interest costs.

Bear in mind that interest rates vary – not significantly, but by enough to make a difference over time. Just a fraction of a percentage difference in the rate can amount to thousands of pounds of interest over the life of a lifetime mortgage. Rates have recently fallen to closer to those charged on traditional mortgages, so it will pay to shop around.

In addition you will often have to pay:

- a **valuation fee** This will cost upwards of £150 and is the same as the valuation fees that all lenders charge before advancing a mortgage.
- an **administration fee** This can cost around £250 – or more – and is charged when you apply for a lifetime mortgage. (This fee is not normally charged by home reversion plan providers.)
- an **arrangement fee** This can cost between £500 and £600. It is paid when the mortgage begins and can be added to the mortgage. (Again, there is not normally an arrangement fee for a home reversion plan.)
- **solicitors' fees** Anyone taking out an equity release plan is recommended to seek independent legal advice. Although the equity release provider will usually pay for its own solicitor's fees, the homeowner is responsible for his or her own solicitor's costs. These can be between £400 and £800.

If your property fails to meet the requirements of the lender (it must be suitable security), then you may have to fund some repairs before the mortgage is advanced. If you decide to pull out of the arrangement before the scheme is completed, you may also be charged a fee to cover administration costs.

Choosing a lifetime mortgage

Features to consider when choosing a lifetime mortgage

Different lifetime mortgages offer different benefits to different borrowers, making them hard to compare. However, when you choose a lifetime mortgage, the following features need to be considered (the order of priority will depend on your particular needs).

- **Interest rate** This will be well above the Bank of England base rate. At the time of writing, this was 4.5 per cent, while most equity release providers were charging between 6 and 8 per cent. Rates may not seem to vary that widely – at the time of writing you could pay as little as 4.89 per cent or as much as 5.79 per cent for the best buys alone – or as much as 8.75 per cent if you wanted to borrow up to 75 per cent of the property value. However, remember that over the term of a lifetime mortgage – which will probably be at least ten years – this can amount to thousands of pounds in extra interest paid. So it is worth your while to shop around.

- **Interest guarantees** For greater certainty, homeowners should opt for a fixed rate plan. That way they will know exactly how much they will owe at any given time. Remember, interest may be compounded monthly (or at least annually) – that means you will also be charged interest on interest. An alternative is to opt for a capped rate. This guarantees that the rate will not rise above a certain level, which could be 3 percentage points higher than the rate offered.

- **How interest is calculated** Again, this may not appear to make that much of a difference. However, as interest is compounded (monthly or annually), it can make a difference.

- **Amount that can be borrowed** The minimum is usually £25,000 although some lenders will allow you to borrow as little as £5,000. The maximum loan-to-value rate (mortgage as a percentage of the value of the property) varies from 13 per cent to 55 per cent, depending on the age of the borrower. The older you are, the more you can borrow. However, the more you want to borrow, the higher the interest rate. At the time of writing, one provider, Hodge Equity Release, was allowing borrowers to release far more than the usual maximum of 50 per cent. It was approaching 75 per cent of the property's value for those aged at least 67 (or with a minimum age of 69 if joint buyers) but was charging up to 8.75 per cent fixed interest as a result.

- **Lump sum or income or both?** Many, but not all, schemes will offer you the option of receiving an income or a lump sum or both. The advantage of a lump sum is that you can invest it to provide an income – or spend some or all of it – giving you maximum flexibility.
- **Negative equity guarantee** Almost all plan providers now offer this. It is a guarantee that the mortgage debt will not exceed the property's value.
- **Fees** Again, charges depend on the plan provider, but expect fees of between £250 and £600 (see above).
- **SHIP membership** An organization called Safe Home Income Plans (SHIP)* was set up after past problems with equity release schemes to reassure the public and establish minimum standards. Although the sale of lifetime mortgages is now under the regulatory umbrella of the FSA, membership of SHIP offers added protection.

Who offers lifetime mortgages?

Banks, building societies, specialist equity release companies and life companies as well as newer style lenders such as Mortgage Express offer lifetime mortgages. These include GE Life, Hodge Equity Release, the Holmesdale Building Society, Mortgage Express, National Counties Building Society, Northern Rock, Norwich Union, Portman Building Society, the Prudential, Scottish Widows Bank and Standard Life Bank. According to the Council of Mortgage Lenders, 27 of its 143 members currently offer equity release schemes. However, now that the FSA regulates these schemes and they have renewed respectability, more lenders are expected to offer lifetime loans to take advantage of the growing market.

How do I find the best deals and rates?

You will need to seek independent financial advice. However, if you subscribe to a specialist publication such as Moneyfacts (subscription £89.50 a year) you can get regular lists of best buys for equity release as well as a range of other financial products from savings accounts to credit cards. It may seem expensive, but if you use all the information included you should make your money back.

Other equity release mortgages

Lifetime loans account for the bulk of all equity release mortgage schemes. However, there are some other schemes on offer.

Home income plans

Mortgage annuity plans (more commonly known as home income plans) involve a mortgage being taken out on a property at a fixed rate of interest. The money is used to buy an annuity, which pays an income (which can be level or rising) for life. This income is used to pay the mortgage interest and provide extra income.

The advantage is that the mortgage debt does not grow as interest is not rolled up. However, this leaves less income for the homeowner. As a result, these schemes have higher loan-to-value maximums, allowing borrowers to release up to 75 per cent of the property value.

The rate of interest, while fixed, is usually far higher than the most competitive lifetime loan.

Home income plans are not widely available.

Appreciation mortgages

These work in a similar way to a roll-up scheme. However, the lender charges a lower rate or provides a higher income in return for a percentage of any growth in the property when sold.

Equity release mortgages: the essentials

How much money can I release?

This depends on the lender, your age, your gender, the property type and property value. For example, Northern Rock will allow a couple aged 60 (with a life expectancy of 30 years) a maximum loan-to-value of 15 per cent (that is, a loan of 15 per cent of the property's value) and a single male age 66 (life expectancy 17 years) the same amount.

Other lenders will advance different amounts, so it is vital to get independent financial advice to seek out the mortgage to suit you.

Are equity release mortgages risky?

As most reputable lifetime mortgage schemes have a negative equity guarantee (which prevents the mortgage debt exceeding the value of the property) and the interest rate is fixed – so that the homeowner knows by how much the debt will increase each year – these are not high-risk schemes.

However, the amount owed could mount up quite quickly. If property prices stagnate or even fall, there is a risk that when the property is sold very little capital is left in the property.

Older-style home income plans were more risky. With these, an annuity was purchased with the equity released, and the income generated paid the interest on the mortgage (instead of it being rolled up as it would be with a lifetime mortgage) with the remainder providing an income. In the 1980s these had variable interest rates, so homeowners were often left with no income when interest rates rose and a rising debt which left them with negative equity.

Things have moved on since the 1980s, when thousands of elderly homeowners were left seriously out of pocket. Since October 2004 lifetime mortgages have come under the supervision of the FSA.

Even so, many of the largest lenders still do not offer lifetime mortgages. 'Significant reputational risks and the small size of the market have deterred the largest lenders from joining so far,' says the Council of Mortgage Lenders. 'However, it is expected that most of the biggest high street names will join over the next three years.'

How long can I continue to live in my home?
As long as you like – it is still your home.

What if I want to sell my home?
When you sell, you simply repay the lifetime mortgage along with the rolled-up interest.

There may be an early repayment charge. This should be clearly spelt out when you take out the loan.

What happens when I die?
When you die the home will be sold to repay the debt. If, however, your spouse is still in the home, he or she may continue to live there.

What happens if interest rates fall?
You can take advantage of lower rates and remortgage, even on a roll-up mortgage. If you can find a cheaper rate it may be worthwhile to do so. Most existing lenders will charge a form of penalty for repaying the mortgage early in these circumstances so it will be a case of weighing up the interest savings against any penalty. In future, lenders may charge more heavy penalties (particularly to those who remortgage in the early years of the mortgage) to cover their costs.

What happens if I want to borrow more at a later date?
You can do this, provided you do not exceed the maximum percentages allowable. Remember there may be additional costs.

An alternative is to opt for flexible drawdown.

Flexible drawdown

In the past, financial advisers have recommended that borrowers release the maximum allowed for their age by lifetime mortgage lenders. This is because of the charges – taking out further advances for small amounts is costly.

However, homeowners could save tens of thousands of pounds by choosing a plan that allows flexible drawdowns.

These enable borrowers to release equity as and when they need it, and to pay interest only on the money they need to borrow.

How much can be saved?

Mr Brown is 83 and his wife is 75. Saga has calculated the following example that results in a saving of more than £10,000. The Browns' house is valued at £250,000. The maximum they can borrow if they opt for a lifetime mortgage, based on the younger borrower's age, is £82,500. However, they do not need this much all at once. They decide to borrow £30,000 straight away, and then withdraw another £5,000 every two years after that. Mr Brown dies after seven years, and Mrs Brown lives for a further three years, at which point the house is sold, ten years after the original loan.

To access £30,000 today will cost Mr and Mrs Brown £495 for the arrangement fee, plus their own solicitor's fees. However, the Browns also borrow £5,000 after two years, and again at four years, six years and eight years after the original loan. So they will release a total sum of £50,000.

When the house is sold in ten years' time, the added interest means that a final payment of £86,325.59 plus the £100 administration charge will be payable.

Had the £50,000 been withdrawn in full at the start of the plan, a total £96,949.74 would have been owed after ten years (this assumes that all advances accrue interest at the current rate of 6.64 per cent per year), so the Browns have made a saving of £10,624.15. This demonstrates the advantage of taking equity from your home gradually, when you need it, rather than all at once.

Home reversion schemes

In 1998 almost all equity release products were reversion schemes but by 2004 the situation had reversed and only £41 million of the £1.1 billion market was accounted for by these products.

The essentials

How home reversion schemes work

In home reversion schemes homeowners sell part or all of their property to a reversion company. Although they may no longer own their own property, they do have the right to live in their home rent-free for life – or until they choose to leave, or move into sheltered accommodation or a nursing home.

In return for forgoing all or part of the capital in the property, the homeowners receive a tax-free cash lump sum.

Alternatively, some plan providers may offer a regular income which can be:

- fixed
- rising in line with inflation
- rising by another pre-agreed amount
- rising to partly reflect growth in property values.

It may be possible to receive a lump sum as well (although this will reduce the amount of income).

How much home reversion schemes cost

The biggest 'cost' when you go in for a home reversion scheme is the fact that you will not receive the full market value of your property – possibly as little as 40 per cent, depending on your age – and that you will forgo any future rises in the value of your home (which could amount to tens of thousands of pounds over a number of years).

Another hidden cost comes if you die shortly after taking out a scheme. Some plan providers now offer a protection against your losing out if you die or go into a residential care home in the early years after taking out the plan. This gives an extra payment.

Norwich Union, for example, will pay out 90 per cent of the open market value of its share of the property if you die within six months of taking out the plan. This gradually drops, reducing to 55 per cent by year four.

In addition, there are arrangement fees, which can amount to £600.

How much can I release?

In theory, up to 100 per cent of the property value. However, you do not actually receive that much – the amount you will receive will be less than the market value and, as mentioned above, possibly only 40 per cent.

How little can I release?

The minimum tends to be higher than it is for lifetime mortgages – around £25,000. The maximum can be as much as £600,000.

If I don't get the full value of my property, how much will I get?

This depends on a number of factors. The older you are, the more you will be paid for your property. That is because the younger you are, the longer the company will have to pay out by way of a regular income and it is likely to have to wait to get its cut. If you are in poor health – which will affect your life expectancy – this will also be taken into account and should result in a higher lump sum.

When you sell your stake – for example, 80 per cent – you will receive as a lump sum perhaps only 40 per cent of this.

A 73-year-old couple has a home valued at £150,000. In an example from Key Retirement Solutions, independent financial advisers specializing in equity release, they want to sell 50 per cent of this to a reversion company.

They could expect to receive a cash lump sum of around £33,000. That means they would be getting only about 22 per cent of their home's value. Another way of putting it is that for every pound they are selling, they are getting 44 pence. Younger homeowners would get even less.

So why such a big shortfall?

The home reversion company will have to wait many years – possibly until both owners have died – before receiving its money back. So it is investing with no return until the property is sold.

The reversion company also takes a risk – however remote it may seem today – that the property price or property prices in general will fall.

Why can't I find out more easily how much I would get?

A complex actuarial calculation involving the age of the homeowners and their health is used to determine what percentage you will receive. As each case is different, there are no easy ways such as tables to look up to find out how much you will get.

However, your independent financial adviser (remember, you should seek impartial advice before making a decision) should be able to give you a rough idea of how much you could expect.

Will I still benefit from house price rises?

You will benefit from the increase in value of your home only if you do not sell all of it. Once the property is sold, any proceeds that are left after deduction of fees and the home reversion company has taken its share will be paid to you or your estate. So if you sold 80 per cent of the property, the home reversion company will expect 80 per cent of the sale proceeds.

However, it is possible to benefit from general property price rises. For example, Norwich Union offers a house price inflation guarantee. If you die or leave the property because you need long-term care and the value of your home has increased by more than 7.5 per cent per annum above inflation, as measured by the Retail Prices Index (All Items), you will receive some of the reversion provider's share of this growth.

Other plan providers may pay an income which can be linked partly to house price growth.

What happens if I die shortly after taking out the plan?

This is a drawback of these schemes. In theory, you (or, more precisely, your estate) lose because you did not receive the full value of the percentage of the property sold and there is no way to get this back.

However, some plan providers do offer guarantees to protect you (or your estate) against this possibility.

Norwich Union, for example, offers an inheritance protection guarantee. It pays out not only in the event of death but also if you have to leave the home permanently because you need to move into long-term care. However, if you change your mind or simply want to move, you will not benefit from this guarantee.

A couple's property was valued at £200,000 and they sold 50 per cent to the reversion provider. In this example provided by Norwich Union, based on their age and gender they received 40 per cent of the share they sold – £40,000 as a cash lump sum. So although they sold £100,000 of their property they received only £40,000 as a cash lump sum.

Should the plan end after only nine months, their guaranteed minimum payment would be 80 percent of the reversion provider's share, that is £80,000. So the estate would receive a further £40,000.

The percentages of the guaranteed minimum payment vary from 90 per cent (in the first six months) to 55 per cent up to year five. So if the plan ended in the fourth year the estate would receive £15,000 – bringing the amount up to 55 per cent of the £100,000 sold.

Is the lump sum tax-free?

Yes, as you are selling your main private residence.

Will I be able to leave an inheritance?

Yes, but only if you do not sell all of the property. If you sell 50 per cent, for example, to the reversion company, when you pass away your heirs will benefit from the growth in the value of the 50 per cent you own (subject to costs and inheritance tax).

Some homeowners prefer these types of scheme to lifetime mortgages because of this certainty. With a lifetime mortgage the debt continues to roll up, eating into the capital and any inheritance you wish to leave to future generations.

What happens if I want to move?

Things are slightly more complicated with home reversion schemes than with lifetime mortgages. With a lifetime mortgage you simply repay the debt and any rolled-up interest. With a home reversion scheme the amount you received would have been based on an assumption that you remained in the property until you died.

The whole point of a home reversion plan is that it enables you to remain in your home for life. If you think you may want to move, such a scheme may not be ideal.

However, there will be circumstances when you have to move. For example, you may want to move into sheltered accommodation. Depending on your plan provider, you should be allowed to move as long as the new home meets the reversion provider's conditions. You will be responsible for paying valuation and legal fees for the reversion provider as well as yourself.

If you are moving to a cheaper property the difference between the selling price of the old property and the purchase price of the new property will be divided between you and the reversion provider according to your share in the property. The share owned by the reversion company will remain the same.

What happens if I need more cash later on?

If you did not sell 100 per cent of your property, you may be able to sell a further percentage later on – usually subject to a minimum of £10,000.

Who offers home reversion plans?

Providers include Norwich Union, Cardiff-based Hodge Equity Release, Epsom-based BPT Bridgewater and Bedford-based

Home & Capital Trust. All these firms, along with Key Retirement Solutions, are members of Safe Home Income Plans (SHIP), the trade body for the industry. It is recommended that you buy only from a SHIP member until home reversion schemes are regulated by the FSA.

Does it matter where I live?

Yes, because home reversion companies in effect buy your property, they tend to operate only in certain geographical areas. Even Norwich Union offers its scheme only in England and Wales, so if you live in Scotland, Northern Ireland, the Isle of Man or the Channel Islands you will not be able to take out its plan.

What if I own a flat, not a house?

If you own a flat, you will need a long lease to be able to sell it to a home reversion provider. Norwich Union, for example, requires the lease to be at least 145 years less the age of the younger applicant (so, for instance, if the younger applicant is 70, you will need at least a 75-year lease).

What if I live with someone else?

You will have to jointly own the property and make a joint application for the home reversion scheme.

Are these plans safe?

Home reversion plans are not yet regulated by the FSA (but they should be by 2007 or so depending on how quickly legislation is passed through Parliament), so in theory you are out in the cold if you have a problem.

However, because of previous problems with these schemes, the more reputable providers formed SHIP in 1991.

SHIP members must abide by a code of practice which includes the following assurances.

- SHIP members must undertake to provide a fair, simple and complete presentation of any home income plan they may offer you.

- You will be given full details of your own obligations, commitments and rights under the plan, including security of tenure on your home for you and your partner (if applying jointly) for the rest of your lives.
- You will be told what costs are involved, your tax position and the possible effect on your plan of moving house and of changing house values, as well as the effect of the transaction on the value of your estate on death.
- Your own solicitors will act on your behalf and look after your interests at every stage. Before your SHIP scheme can be finalized, they will be required to sign a certificate confirming that the principal terms of the contract have been fully explained to you.
- A SHIP plan guarantees that you cannot lose your home – whatever happens to the stockmarket or to interest rates.

Contact SHIP to check if the firm you are dealing with is a member and abides by the code of practice and also request or download a brochure called Safe with SHIP.

What if I am not happy?

Home reversion schemes are designed for life. In theory there is no way back although some providers may allow you to buy the reversion provider's share of the property in full. However, this will be very costly.

If you are not happy because you feel you were mis-sold the reversion plan, SHIP has a formal procedure for handling complaints. In future the FSA will provide a complaints service and can in certain circumstances offer compensation if you were mis-sold a plan.

Opting for equity release

The types of scheme and their benefits and pitfalls have been explored in detail earlier in this section.

Whether or not equity release is an ideal solution to your

Lifetime mortgages *vs* home reversion schemes

Everyone should seek independent financial and legal advice before taking out any type of equity release scheme. These are complex financial products and taking one out can have implications for your tax, benefits, the inheritance you leave to future generations and your financial well-being.

Lifetime mortgages account for over 90 per cent of the equity release market. There are several very obvious reasons why.

Main advantages of lifetime mortgages

- You benefit from the future growth in value of your property.
- You can release extra cash when you need it (using flexible drawdown).

Possible disadvantages of lifetime mortgages

- Your debt continues to grow and could – if property prices fail to rise significantly, or even fall, and you live a long time – grow to exceed the value of your home. A negative equity guarantee will prevent the debt exceeding the equity, but you will be left with no capital to pass on as an inheritance.
- The limit on how much equity you can release may be low – just 15 per cent or 25 per cent depending on your age.

The main advantage of a home reversion scheme

- You can – in theory – raise far more capital than with a lifetime mortgage by selling 100 per cent of your property. The maximum loan-to-value rate of a lifetime mortgage is around 50 per cent (although a few lenders will let you borrow more). However, with a home reversion scheme because you do not receive the full value of your home you may find that the amount of capital you receive is roughly the same with both types of scheme.

The main disadvantages of home reversion schemes

- You no longer benefit from the full increase in value of your property. If you sell 100 per cent of your home to the reversion company you will lose out entirely on any future house price growth. However, note that some companies will give you a house price increase guarantee.
- You will not receive the full market value of your property and may only receive 40 per cent of what you have sold.

income problems (or the need for capital) depends on a wide range of factors including your age, the value of your home, how much you need to raise, your other savings and investments, and the impact releasing equity will have on tax and means-tested benefits. This is why equity release is one of the most difficult financial products on which to advise.

There is no central information source for all the schemes on offer, and advisers need to be able to calculate how any income or capital raised will affect state benefits, which can involve lengthy investigations.

Getting advice

To get advice on equity release you can go directly to an equity release provider. However, you are advised to seek independent financial advice and independent legal advice before taking out a scheme.

Look for an adviser with specialist qualifications in this field. The Institute of Financial Services (IFS) has introduced the Certificate in Lifetime Mortgages (CeLM), a supplement to CeMAP, which covers all aspects of selling and recommending lifetime mortgages.

Opt for a specialist firm, preferably a member of SHIP. To find an independent financial adviser, contact IFA Promotion* and ask for a list of advisers in your area who specialize in equity release.

The sales process

It is important that you know what to expect when seeking advice about equity release so that you are sure you are getting good quality advice. Unfortunately, many homeowners are not getting the quality of advice the regulators require.

A mystery shopping exercise by the FSA in May 2005 discovered that more than 70 per cent of advisers were not gathering enough information about their customers before offering them advice on equity release.

The regulator also found that once the lifetime mortgage was sold consumers were being advised to invest some of the equity released in products that were not suitable for their needs and sometimes unnecessarily exposed them to risk.

Also, more than 60 per cent of mystery shoppers reported that their adviser had not explained the downsides of equity release.

The three main problem areas identified by the FSA were:

- **investing for growth** The FSA identified that in some firms advisers were encouraging customers to release more than they required and reinvested the surplus cash in products such as investment bonds
- **investing for income** There are equity release products on the market that allow the consumer to draw down an income from their lifetime mortgage. Instead of recommending this route, advisers were recommending that consumers release a lump sum and reinvest it in, for example, an investment bond and take 5 per cent withdrawals to provide a regular income stream. As well as being more expensive for the consumer, reinvesting capital in equity-backed investments unnecessarily exposed the consumer to risk
- **inheritance tax (IHT) mitigation** Using equity release for IHT mitigation is a very finely balanced arrangement. A number of the cases the FSA reviewed were likely to leave the customer's estate worse off than if they had not taken any action to mitigate their IHT liability.

How can I protect myself against poor advice?

If the chief financial watchdog is concerned about the quality of some of the advice being offered, so should you be. Therefore, it is vital that you are properly advised.

The best way to protect yourself is to be well informed. The FSA has produced guides to help consumers understand the risks and lists key questions to which they must have satisfactory answers before making a decision.

The FSA has distributed 120,000 leaflets entitled *Thinking of Raising Money From Your Home?* to GP surgeries, libraries,

Citizens Advice Bureaux and other not-for-profit agencies across
the UK. A free factsheet providing more detail for consumers is
also available from the FSA.

The cost of poor advice

Being advised to take out an equity release scheme when it is not
the best solution to your financial needs can result in huge financial loss:

- Any income or capital raised may simply wipe out the means-
  tested benefits you may have been entitled to, so you are no
  better off.
- If you change your mind or decide to move it can be costly to
  get out of these schemes.
- You will be depriving the next generation of some if not all of
  their inheritance.
- Even if a scheme is the best solution, selecting a lifetime
  mortgage with a slightly higher rate – for example, opting for
  a 6.74 per cent rate compounded on a monthly basis instead of
  a 6.75 per cent rate – can result in thousands of pounds of
  extra interest once this is compounded over 20 years. The 6.74
  per cent rate has an actual annualized rate of 6.95 per cent,
  which is why it is more expensive.
- The difference between the lowest and highest rate on a
  lifetime mortgage over 20 years on a £40,000 loan is almost
  £20,000 in additional interest.
- Releasing too much equity – money you do not need – will
  result in unnecessary interest payments. Again, these could
  amount to thousands of pounds.

The questions you should be asked

The Council of Mortgage Lenders'* notes on good practice
concerning the sales process for lifetime mortgages (which can
be found on its website) look at the sort of questions you should
be asked and the checks that should be made. Although this
list is relevant mainly to lifetime mortgages, because advisers
should check whether home reversion schemes are more

suitable for the client the checklist covers both types of equity release scheme.

- **Property location** Not all lenders lend in all locations.
- **Age** You will have to be a minimum age to qualify (usually 60 but as old as 70 with some lenders).
- **Property value** There is a minimum value that will be lent against.
- **Loan amount required** Again, there is a maximum (as well as a minimum) in relation to the value of the property, known as the MLV (maximum loan to value).
- **Purpose of loan**
- **State of your health for your age**.

This will determine whether or not these types of mortgage are suitable.

The adviser will then delve deeper and look at the following.

- **Type of property** Usually the property will need to be a freehold house or a flat with a long leasehold.
- **Ownership and occupancy** You will generally need to own and live in the property rather than owning a property you rent out. Also, the property will need to be vacant when sold so that the mortgage can be repaid.
- **Income** This is to determine the impact on your benefits and tax.

If you are entitled to means-tested benefits you should be advised on the impact equity release will have on your financial situation. The extra £50 a week you can raise from equity release could simply wipe out £50 of benefits, so you will be no better off.

Then the adviser should look at what you want to do with the money. If you want a lump sum you will be asked how this will be spent/invested. If you want an income the adviser should tell you about monthly drawdown products and annuities.

The CML warns: 'It is generally inadvisable to borrow money

purely to invest it. A realistic rate of return on the investment is most certainly going to be less than the lifetime mortgage interest rate and this can only be justified in exceptional circumstances.'

The CML also cautions: 'Customers should not be encouraged to borrow more than they need to. However, where there are one or more additional items of expenditure intended in the short/medium term the adviser will need to consider whether it is better to take a larger initial loan. A larger initial loan will result in higher interest costs but might be better than incurring the additional costs associated with a series of loans or drawdowns/further advances.'

To assess whether lifetime mortgages (and equity release plans generally) are right for you, you should be asked:

1. Have you considered moving to a cheaper property?
2. Do you have access to other funds? If you have savings/investments or even have family prepared to lend the money, a lifetime mortgage may not be best *and* you will save on interest costs.
3. If you are raising money to pay for home improvements are you eligible for a grant? Maybe you do not need a lifetime mortgage at all.
4. Are you eligible for benefits which you are not currently claiming? You may not need – or may reduce the need – for a lifetime mortgage.

Advisers should also assess the individual's attitude to risk and look at whether a reversion plan may be better by considering the following.

1. **Attitude to house price inflation** If the customer has an unoptimistic view, then a home reversion plan may be more suitable.
2. **Maximum loan required relative to age** Elderly homeowners may be able to obtain a larger release from a reversion plan.
3. **Attitude to leaving an inheritance** If the customer wants certainty that there will be something to leave as an inheri-

tance, then a reversion plan or a protected lifetime mortgage may be more suitable.

4. **Views of future interest rates** This will help ascertain whether a fixed or capped product will be more suitable.
5. **Whether the customer can afford interest payments** The adviser should compare and contrast the merits of paying interest or rolling it up and also look at affordability.
6. **Other factors** The adviser should look at the implications if the purpose of the loan is for debt consolidation. Set-up fees, ease of moving, ability to drawdown further advances, early repayment fees, portability and service reputation should also be considered.

Note Even though these questions may lead the adviser to believe the customer will be better off with a reversion plan, some advisers may not have access to these plans so will not be able to advise on the relative merits of different products. So the customer will be given information only on the most suitable lifetime mortgage. However, they should be told that they should get advice on home reversion plans from a different adviser.

Once a product has been recommended the adviser should then detail the reasons for this decision. Advisers should tell customers to seek the involvement of their family in making their decision and should also, once again, look at the income tax and benefit implications.

The impact of equity release on one's finances

Equity release and means-tested benefits

Nearly half of all single pensioners are reliant on state benefits (See Chapter 1 for details). Even those who have additional private pensions or savings are now often entitled to some means-tested help in the form of Pension Credit.

It means that one-third of pensioners are now entitled to some

An advice checklist
The Actuarial Profession has set out seven key steps consumers should take before signing up to an equity release scheme.
Go through this checklist before signing on the dotted line.

1. Consider all the other options to equity release, for example, have a 'benefits check' to see if there are any state benefits which you are entitled to but not claiming; investigate trading down, use savings, or sell other assets.
2. Consider the inheritance you will leave. Talk things over first with your family.
3. Take advice from a properly qualified adviser, who has considered other alternatives and has explained the impact an equity release scheme can have on any means-tested benefits.
4. Make sure both mortgage schemes and reversion schemes have been investigated, and you fully understand what the future repayments will be.
5. Ask for an illustration of what repayments will be if you live ten years beyond the average life expectancy, and consider what impact this would have on any inheritance.
6. Fully understand the legal contract, and go to an independent solicitor to have it explained before making a final commitment.
7. Be aware of what happens if you make repayments, or if you move, trade down or go into care? Or if you remarry, or perhaps have a family member move in at some time in the future?

form of means-tested benefits and it is these homeowners who need to take particular care when considering equity release.

However, even those who do not currently qualify should be aware of the implications because they may, in future, qualify for state help should their financial circumstances change.

Attendance Allowance, the state retirement pension and Carer's Allowance are *not* affected by equity release. Pension Credit, Council Tax Benefit (CTB) and health benefits (help with the cost of glasses and dental treatment) *may* be affected by equity release.

Anyone considering equity release should ensure they are in receipt of all the benefits to which they may be entitled. It is also a requirement of the FSA that anyone advising on lifetime mortgages should consider the implications of equity release on benefits – so some of this work may be done for you, provided your adviser is doing his or her job properly.

Tip One way to avoid equity release impacting on benefits is to consider flexible drawdown if opting for a lifetime mortgage. This will release capital as you need it. So instead of releasing the maximum possible and investing what is not needed for immediate expenditure, you phase the release of capital. This will either affect the capital test (a maximum of £16,000 for CTB) or the income test (both Pension Credit and CTB assume you earn £1 for each £500 or part thereof above the lower limit).

How will equity release affect my Pension Credit?

Pension Credit is a means-tested benefit. That means it is affected by any additional income or capital that you have.

Equity release will have an impact on Pension Credit because it is likely to release at least £10,000 of equity (the minimum amount). When calculating Pension Credit:

- the first £6,000 of capital is ignored. Capital includes shares, investments or other savings and the value of second homes, but not the value of your main home
- any capital over £6,000 will be treated as producing an assumed income of £1 for every £500 (or part of £500). In a residential or nursing home the threshold is £10,000.

So if equity release means that your income – or assumed income – takes you over the guarantee credit limit of £174.05 for a couple (the 2006/7 limit), you will miss out on this benefit. Although you may still qualify for savings credit, the cost of the loss of the guarantee – which could be £50 a month particularly if Council Tax Benefit is also lost – needs to be weighed up against the additional income you will receive from equity release, which may be roughly the same.

When equity release may not be appropriate
Should equity release be used for essential home improvements?

Possibly not. Although essential improvements will get around the means-tested benefits rules, equity release may not be the best way to fund these improvements.

This is because there is a statutory Disabled Facilities Grant scheme in England and Wales (there are similar schemes in Scotland and Northern Ireland) which provides means-tested assistance with the cost of adaptations required because of disability (for example, a stair lift). These schemes are operated by local authorities, which also have discretionary home improvement grants and loan schemes that can provide help with the cost of essential repairs.

So you may be able to get other forms of help to pay for essential home improvements and may not need equity release after all.

Financial advisers are required to consider other forms of funding including grants when assessing whether equity release is the most suitable way to raise extra income.

Are there any other circumstances where equity release may not be the best option?

Yes, in addition to thinking twice before taking out equity release to improve your home, think carefully if you are taking out a scheme to repay a mortgage.

This is why it is so vital for advisers to really understand why you need an equity release scheme. Often, there are more obvious or cost-effective solutions.

For example, if you receive Pension Credit and you use this to pay some of your housing costs (say, interest on your mortgage), there may be no need to take out an equity release scheme to repay this mortgage.

Also, if you take out a loan to effect 'repairs and improvements to the dwelling taken out with a view to maintaining the fitness of the dwelling for human habitation', the interest costs of any loan you take out for this work may be met by Pension Credit.

If you take out an equity release scheme to pay for vital home improvements – and the money goes straight to pay for that work – it should not affect your means-tested benefits, so that is one way of avoiding losing your Pension Credit.

There is provision within means-tested rules to ignore any capital or loan taken out to 'make essential repairs and improvements to the dwelling', that is, with a view to maintaining the home 'fit for human habitation'. Sadly, this means that conservatories are excluded. Repairing your leaking roof, on the other hand, will qualify.

Many of those taking out equity release plans do so to improve their homes, so they should think carefully about the type of improvements they plan.

How will equity release affect Council Tax Benefit?

Council Tax Benefit (CTB) is another means-tested benefit. Operated by local authorities, it provides help with your Council Tax bills. It usually runs alongside Housing Benefit, which provides help with rent and other housing costs.

It is calculated slightly differently to Pension Credit. For those aged 60 and over, the first £6,000 of capital is ignored. The maximum amount of capital you are allowed is £16,000. Those with capital above this figure will not be entitled to the benefit unless they also get the guarantee credit element of Pension Credit.

If you receive Pension Credit guarantee credit you will automatically be entitled to full help with Council Tax costs.

If your income level (or capital) means you do not qualify for guarantee credit, you may still get some Council Tax benefit. The amount tapers off as your income rises.

As Council Tax bills can easily amount to £1,000 a year, the full CTB is very valuable. You would need to release £25,000 of equity and earn 4 per cent on this after tax just to match the loss of CTB. And you would still be no better off.

The rules regarding CTB are very confusing, which is why so many pensioners fail to claim the credits and benefits to which they are entitled.

The Council of Mortgage Lenders produced the following example which illustrates how these complex rules work in practice.

A pensioner who qualifies for CTB and receives a lump sum If he or she had no capital at all, and the lump sum they acquired was only £6,000, then there would be no effect on his or her CTB provision.

If the lump sum was larger and took the capital above £16,000, he or she would lose entitlement unless he or she was receiving state pension guarantee credit.

If, instead, the pensioner took the money he or she had generated from equity release as income, the receipt of the income would decrease the amount of CTB payable (because CTB entitlement reduces as income rises) but would not necessarily prevent entitlement altogether.

Note Within Pension Credit and CTB there is a specific provision that where a lender is making payments at regular intervals under an equity release scheme such amounts shall be treated as income, not capital.

Mark, a single pensioner aged 75 and receiving £82.05 a week in state pension, pays £20 a week in Council Tax. As a result of taking capital from an equity release scheme he would still receive CTB until his capital reached £19,500, at which point it would sharply drop. Some entitlement to savings credit would continue until the capital reached £39,000 at which point it would stop completely.

A pensioner who qualifies for CTB and receives additional income *Ben is also a single pensioner aged 75, receiving £82.05 a week in state pension and paying £20 a week in Council Tax. He would – as a result of taking out an equity release scheme – lose some entitlement to guarantee credit with a small amount of additional income. (Remember that even if you take a lump sum with equity release, it is assumed that this produces an income.) However, there would be a small gain in savings credit.*

Only once the private income from equity release exceeds £120 a month would Ben lose all entitlement to guarantee credit. Savings credit would continue to be paid until his private income reached £300 a month. CTB would stop only once the private income reached £700 per month.

In the example of Mark, there is a sharp reduction in CTB once his capital reaches £19,500. So releasing, say, £19,500 – rather than £18,500 – could mean more than a £70 reduction in monthly income, a loss of £840 a year for the sake of an additional £1,000 lump sum.

In terms of income from equity release the loss of benefits is much more gradual (there is no sharp decline at a certain point) but the gain from equity release still needs to weighed up against the loss of benefits.

How do home income plans affect benefits?

Home income plans are far less popular today following the advent of lifetime mortgages. Even so, it is still possible to take out a loan and use the capital to purchase annuities. Some of the income from these will be used to service the interest repayment and the remainder will provide additional income for the homeowner.

Any income that is used to pay the interest is ignored for both Pension Credit and CTB provided the loan was:

- made to someone who was aged 65 or more (and whose partner was 65 or more if a couple)
- made as part of a scheme under which not less than 90 per cent of the proceeds of the loan were used to purchase an annuity; and
- secured on a dwelling in which the annuitant(s) owns an interest in the dwelling and occupies it as his (or their) home.

When I release equity, how quickly will this affect my means-tested benefits – and who do I need to tell and when?

Means-tested benefits are assessed in Assessed Income Periods (AIPs). The aim of these is to spare the over-65s from informing the Pension Credit helpline (run by the Department for Work and Pensions, DWP) or local authority (in the case of CTB) every time there is a small change in their circumstances or they receive extra income from savings or a lump sum.

Not all changes in circumstances have an immediate effect on benefit entitlement, so you could, for example, continue to receive CTB until the AIP ends.

However, in certain circumstances there is an immediate effect. To avoid having to make a large repayment of benefit it is vital that you know what needs to be reported – and when.

For example, if you receive savings credit and CTB you have to report only any increase in capital above £16,000 to your local authority. Otherwise no change will be made until the end of the AIP.

If no AIP has been set, you need to report changes in retirement provision immediately.

If you are in the middle of selling a property when applying for Pension Credit its value will be disregarded for 26 weeks.

If you had an AIP set at the time you applied for Pension Credit it could be for up to five years if, at the time, you had no plans to take out equity release.

So you could, for example, release £20,000 of equity and then spend this in the meantime so that when your AIP ends your circumstances are, in effect, unchanged. However, if you are asked to provide details of increases in income or capital, you must do so.

If I spend the money I have released can I claim benefits when my money has run out?

There are rules to prevent benefit claimants from squandering cash simply so that they can claim money from the state. These rules are known as 'deprivation of resources'.

So if you release a cash lump sum, spend it and make a claim for benefit you may find that the DWP refuses your claim.

However, this rule is unlikely to affect most of those with equity release schemes because it:

- has to be shown that at least one reason why 'deprivation' took place was so you could gain entitlement to state benefits, and
- that you spent the money on something that was not reasonable. Home improvements, a new car or holiday will probably

be considered reasonable although a luxury car or private jet would probably not be.

So to be safe you should keep records of sizeable items of expenditure as Pension Credit staff may want to look at the changes in the level of your savings/capital over the AIP.

What if my circumstances change?

The difficulty in assessing state benefits – and their impact on equity release – is that benefits change and so do people's circumstances. If the homeowner becomes severely disabled, for example, they could then qualify for additional benefits. It is more likely that one partner will pass away, affecting entitlement to benefits for the homeowner and possibly the need for additional income.

So future life events also need to be taken into account when assessing whether equity release is – and will continue to be – the right solution to meet your needs.

Equity release and tax

The good news is that any equity released is usually tax-free (there is no capital gains tax to pay). The bad news is that once you invest this money, any interest or dividends you earn could be liable to tax.

If you are a non-taxpayer this additional income is likely to push you into the basic- or lower-rate tax bracket. So if your total income exceeds the tax-free personal allowance, you will pay tax for the first time.

These were the allowances for the 2005/6 tax year (they usually rise each April).

Personal allowance for those aged 60   £4,895
Personal allowance for people aged 65–74   £7,090
Personal allowance for people aged 75 and over   £7,220

In addition, some older pensioners (those born before 6 April 1935) qualify for married couple's allowance.

Married couple's allowance for people born before
    6 April 1935   £5,905
Married couple's allowance for those aged 75 or more   £5,975

What if I am not a taxpayer?

If you are currently not a taxpayer you need to check that the income you generate after equity release will not exceed the personal allowance (and married couple's allowance) thresholds.

If, as a result, you do – and remember taxable income includes the state pension and any savings interest – you will be liable for tax on the income that *exceeds* the personal allowance (not the full amount).

The tax rate for the 2005/6 year was:

10 per cent on the first £2,090 of taxable income
22 per cent on the next £30,310 of income

Note However, if you are liable for the 22 per cent basic tax rate, savings interest is taxed at only 20 per cent and UK dividends at 10 per cent.

What if I am still a taxpayer?

If you are still a taxpayer, you first need to ensure that your income – including that from any equity release scheme – does not exceed £19,500, the 2005/6 threshold.

If it does, you will lose some or all of your age allowance until it is reduced to £4,895 (the basic personal allowance).

The loss of this allowance will increase your overall tax bill. This loss needs to be taken into account when calculating the benefits of equity release.

You also need to look at the tax implications of an increased income. Although many pensioners do not fall into the higher-rate tax bracket, if their income starts to exceed this limit (which was payable on taxable earnings – those above the personal allowance – over £32,400 in the 2005/6 tax year) they will pay 40 per cent tax on some of their earnings.

Those paying the low 10 per cent starting rate of tax – payable on the first £2,090 of taxable income (again, the 2005/6 figure) – will find that they suffer a 20 per cent (on savings interest) or 22 per cent (on other income) rate of tax.

How does equity release affect inheritance tax (IHT)?

The IHT threshold for 2006/7 is expected to be £300,000. Anyone whose estate (the figure includes other assets not just your home) is likely to exceed this threshold needs to consider ways to mitigate the tax.

Equity release is a valuable tool to avoid paying IHT. However, before you get carried away and opt for equity release, investigate the alternatives to avoiding IHT: there are plenty of other, less risky and less expensive, ways around the problem. For more information see Chapter 25.

However, if equity release is a solution for you, you will find it an effective way to reduce – or eliminate – an IHT liability. This is because your property will be worth less when you pass away and, as the main home is usually an individual's biggest asset, it will probably have a large effect on the value of your estate.

Should I be worrying about IHT?

Yes. One in ten of those taking out equity release products is doing so to reduce or eliminate an IHT liability.

The tax is expensive – charged at 40 per cent of the value of the estate above the threshold. So if your estate is worth £600,000, the IHT due will be 40 per cent of £300,000, which is £120,000.

That is a lot of money to leave to the Inland Revenue – particularly as you have already paid tax on this money when you earned it and when you invested it.

Although the tax is not payable on assets left to your spouse, it will then become an issue for the surviving partner.

Equity release and long-term care

Financial assistance for long-term care fees is means tested. Those with more than £20,500 of capital (in England and Wales only) in the 2005/6 tax year receive no help with their care bills.

As your main home is usually exempt from means-testing, if your spouse still lives there equity release can work against you – because your income will be higher than otherwise and the equity you own will not affect your entitlement to free long-term care.

However, if your home will form part of the means test and you have released equity which has then been used up, when you come to requiring long-term care at a later age you may find that as you have little capital left in your home you qualify for much more help from the state. So equity release can still help you financially.

It can mean that you enjoy a better standard of living today and do not have to see your capital eroded later in life to pay massive long-term care bills. So rather than giving your money away, you can enjoy it.

Further information

IFA Promotion, the organization which promotes independent financial advice, has produced a free guide called Equity Release – Unlocking Money From Your Home. For a copy call (0800) 085 3250 or download it from www.unbiased.co.uk

The Financial Services Authority has produced a free guide to releasing money from your home. For a copy call (0845) 456 1555 or download it from www.fsa.gov.uk

Age Concern has produced a leaflet called *Releasing Income or Capital from Your Home*. For a copy call (0800) 009 966.

The Council of Mortgage Lenders (www.cml.org.uk) has produced a guide to equity release. For a copy call 020-7440 2255.

Safe Home Income Plans (SHIP) (0870) 241 6060; www.ship-ltd.org

Chapter 6

Making money from your home

Releasing equity from your home – by downsizing, moving abroad or using a specialist equity release plan – is not the only way to make money from your property. A home can be an asset in many other ways and provide an income without you having to sell up and move. You can either rent all or part of it or turn it into a business or a base for a business.

Renting out your home

Rent out a room tax-free

If you already have a lodger or are thinking about letting furnished rooms in your home, you can receive up to £4,250 a year tax-free (£2,150 if letting jointly). This is known as the 'rent-a-room' scheme.

Taking in a lodger is not just for young first-time buyers trying to cover some of their mortgage costs. Even older homeowners who may have a property too large to meet their needs – and which they want to keep but perhaps cannot afford to – rent out rooms. The extra income from the rent-a-room scheme can make a big difference to their income. Often single (many couples resent the intrusion of another person in their home), these empty nesters may enjoy having the company of another person as well as the extra income – up to £81.70 a week (£354 a month) tax-free.

Remember that this income will affect any means-tested benefits you may be receiving. However, unless you receive in excess of £80 in benefits you should be better off. Also – depending on how much income you have from other sources – you may still be entitled to a reduced amount of benefit.

These are the scheme rules:

- the room (or part of your property) you rent out must be furnished
- it must be in your only or family home
- if you do not want to share too many facilities you can rent out an entire floor.

However, the scheme does not apply if your home is converted into separate flats (this is covered later in this chapter).

Note You don't have to be a homeowner to qualify for the rent-a-room tax break.

Rent a room as a business

If the rent you are likely to receive from renting out one room is more than £81.70 a week – as may well be the case in London or parts of the South East – it may still be worthwhile. Although all the rent will not be tax free under the rent-a-room tax break, there are tax breaks on offer.

You can:

A opt out of the rent-a-room scheme and rent the room as a business. You can then deduct expenses relating to the letting including insurance, repairs, heating, lighting and wear and tear (for a full list see below), or

B you can claim the rent-a-room allowance of £4,250 and pay tax on any amount over this but cannot deduct any expenses. So if your rental income is £5,200 (from £100 a week rent) you will add only any other income you receive from laundry services, meals etc. and pay tax on the difference – around £1,000.

You need to do your maths. In some cases it may be better to opt out of the scheme and claim more expenses.

However, as most homeowners have very low levels of expenses relating to the room they rent out, they will probably be better off opting for the second option and claiming the rent-a-room allowance.

To choose which method is better for you, you will need to work out how much profit you are making – how much rent you are left with after your expenses – then compare that figure with the amount of rent over £4,250.

The examples below are included in the Inland Revenue leaflet IR87, *Letting and Your Home*.

Susan lets a room for £110 a week.
Her total letting income (rent) for the year is £5,720.
Method A   She has expenses of £1,000, so her profit is £4,720
Method B   The amount of rent over £4,250 is £1,470
Using method A, she would pay tax on a profit of £4,720.
Using method B, she would pay tax on £1,470.
In Susan's case, method B is better.

John also lets a room for £110 a week.
His total letting income (rent) for the year is £5,720.
Method A   He has expenses of £4,500 so his profit is £1,220
Method B   The amount of rent over £4,250 is £1,470
Using method A, he would pay tax on a profit of £1,220.
Using method B, he would pay tax on £1,470.
In John's case, method A is better.

Can I change the method from year to year?

Yes. But each time you want to change you must tell your Inland Revenue office by 31 January, 22 months after the end of the tax year.

Method B will automatically cease if the rent you get drops below £4,250. If, in the following year, your rent goes up and you want to use method B again, you must tell your Inland Revenue office by 31 January, 22 months after the end of the tax year.

What happens if I provide meals and a laundry service? Do I pay tax on this income?

Providing meals and a laundry service does not affect your entitlement to rent-a-room-relief, but any payment you get has to be added to the rent for rent-a-room purposes.

If the income you receive from total rent and services is more than £4,250 a year, even if the rent alone is less, you will have to pay tax. Your choice will be between methods A and B shown on the previous page.

What about the cost of furnishings?

If you are not part of the rent-a-room scheme you will be classed as running a business – or trading. Businesses can claim what are known as 'capital allowances' – a deduction of part of the cost of investing in equipment and furniture to reduce their tax liability. You cannot claim capital allowances within the rent-a-room scheme. However, if you are running a furnished lettings business you can.

See the Inland Revenue Help Sheet IR223, *Rent a Room for Traders*.

Will I have to pay capital gains tax (CGT) when I sell my property?

If you are part of the rent-a-room scheme you do not have to pay CGT when you sell your home if you are the owner (or co-owner) of the property and you occupied the whole of it (apart from the room let out) as your main home throughout the time you owned it.

This is called 'private residence relief' and it is not affected if you have a lodger who is treated as a member of your family, sharing the living rooms and eating with you, even if he or she has a separate bedroom.

Special rules apply if you have let part or all of your home as residential accommodation.

You may have to pay some CGT on a proportion of your property's rise in value. There are many ways to reduce your CGT liability and you are advised to seek professional accounting advice.

What happens if I live abroad?

If you let your own home in the UK while you live abroad you will not normally be within the rent-a-room scheme.

What are the rules if I am running a bed and breakfast?

If you run a bed-and-breakfast business or a guesthouse, or provide catering and cleaning services as part of a letting business, the rent-a-room scheme can still apply to you. You will need to complete the relevant parts of the self-employment pages of your self-assessment tax return (see Turning your home into a business, below).

Rent out part of your home

If, for example, you have a self-contained flat – or can afford to invest a few thousand pounds in converting the basement, say, into a studio flat suitable for renting out – this will provide not only the most income, but also the least intrusion on your life.

The advantages are that you can keep an eye on the property you are renting out and that you do not have to suffer living in the same house as a tenant.

How do I decide whether the let accommodation is part of my home?

This has important implications for CGT because you may or may not qualify for lettings relief (which can reduce your capital gains by up to £40,000). This is a relief given to those letting out their main home (as generally your home is free of CGT).

For example, if you let part or all of a single dwelling which has been your home, without making structural alterations or with only minor changes, the part let out will not be treated as a separate dwelling-house. This applies even if the let part has its own areas for washing and cooking. You will receive the lettings relief in these circumstances.

If you occupy a self-contained flat as your home within a building and let all or part of the rest as residential accommodation you will not get the lettings relief because the rest of the building will not be treated as part of your home.

If the building is altered so that the let part of it becomes a fully self-contained flat (whether or not it is treated as a separate dwelling-house), you will not get the lettings relief because the self-contained flat will not be treated as part of your home. So you will have to pay CGT on the profits when this property is sold.

Rent out the whole home/a second home

In the main, this will be an option if:

- you own a second home that you are prepared to let out for all or part of the year
- you are planning to try before you buy either abroad or in a different part of the UK
- you have a large property that will attract a high rental income and this income will easily cover the rent on a cheaper property in possibly another part of the country – a cottage by the sea – as well as providing you with an additional income.

Those moving abroad could find this option particularly appealing. Many of those who have moved overseas find that when they want to return to the UK, they can no longer afford to buy a property, so renting out their house in the UK would get around this problem.

High rental yields from UK homes can easily fund a much more lavish lifestyle abroad, where the cost of living tends to be much lower – without the need to sacrifice the capital in your property.

This option does have drawbacks and can be risky. However, the advantages are that you earn a living without having to work, you continue to benefit from growth in the property's value and you have the freedom to move elsewhere – possibly abroad – with the knowledge that you can return home to the home you love at a later date.

Income tax

Rental income is taxable, although some expenses can be offset against the rent (for a full list see pages 139–40). If you own the property jointly with a partner, you can split the income for tax purposes – this may mean that one of you may pay tax at a lower rate than the other.

Unless you come under the rent-a-room scheme you will need to work out your net profit by:

- adding up all your rental income
- adding up all your allowable expenses
- taking away your allowable expenses from your income.

If you let furnished property, you can then deduct either:

- a wear and tear allowance – based on a percentage (roughly 10 per cent) of your rent
- a renewals allowance – the cost of replacing old items with a new equivalent (but not for improving the property).

Generally, you cannot deduct the cost of furniture. However, you can deduct some or all of your mortgage interest.

Your taxable profit from property letting is added to your overall income. If this is more than your tax allowances you'll pay tax on it at your normal income tax rates.

What records should I keep?

You must keep a careful note of the rents you receive and any expenses as they arise. You must retain these records, together with back-up records such as receipts and invoices, for six years after the tax year in question. These will help you if your Inland Revenue office decides to make enquiries into your tax return.

Capital gains tax

Some of the profits on the sale of the property may be liable to CGT. However, there are several ways to avoid paying tax, including letting out the home for only a few years and then returning there to live in it at a later date. It is vital that you receive professional accounting advice on the ways to minimize or eliminate CGT.

CGT is not paid on the whole amount you sell your property for, but on the gain you make in selling it.

Ask for Inland Revenue leaflet CGT1, *Capital Gains Tax: An Introduction*, and Help Sheet IR283, *Private Residence Relief*, for more information on this.

The Inland Revenue rules states that if you let:

- part of your only or main home while you owned it, or
- all of your home for part of the time you owned it

to someone who is not treated as a member of your family, or to more than one lodger, you may have some CGT to pay when you sell it.

In other words, the amount of private residence relief will be affected depending on how much of your home you let, and the length of time you let it.

In addition, you may be entitled to a **special lettings** relief, which means the gain will be reduced by as much as £40,000.

If you qualify for private residence relief on any part of your property at any time, you will also qualify for this relief for the last three years in which you owned it.

The Inland Revenue publishes the following example showing how these CGT rules work.

John Smith sells his house in 2004 after owning it for eight years. During that time he occupied one-sixth (1/6) of the property as his home and let the other five-sixths (5/6). His gain is £60,000.

John occupied 1/6 of the property, so the proportion of the gain which qualifies for private residence relief is 1/6 x £60,000 = £10,000.

John also qualifies for the lettings relief because he let part of his house. The lettings relief is the lower of the principal private residence relief due to him (£10,000) or the gain from letting (£50,000) or £40,000. So he gets lettings relief of £10,000.

His total gain of £60,000 is reduced by £10,000 for private residence relief and £10,000 for lettings relief, giving him a charge-able gain of £40,000.

Mary Jones sells her house in 2004 after owning it for ten years. She occupied the whole of her property for two years before letting the whole of it for the remaining eight years. Her gain is £140,000.

In this case she is treated as occupying the whole property for the last three years of her ownership (even if she did not).

The proportion of her gain which qualifies for private residence relief is

> *first two years + last three years = five years.*
> *This is half the ten-year period of ownership*

So her £140,000 gain is halved to £70,000 for private residence relief (reflecting five years of exempt ownership) and £40,000 (this is lettings relief, which is the lower of £70,000 or £40,000), leaving a chargeable gain of £30,000.

Benefits

Receiving an income from your property will affect any entitlement to means-tested state benefits such as Pension Credit or Council Tax Benefit.

What expenses can I claim?

The expenses you can deduct from letting/rental income (unless you have opted to be part of the rent-a-room scheme) to reduce your income tax liability include:

- letting agent's fees
- legal fees for lets of a year or less, or for renewing a lease for less than 50 years
- accountant's fees
- buildings and contents insurance
- interest on property loans
- maintenance and repairs (but not improvements)
- utility bills (such as gas, water, electricity)

- rent, ground rent, service charges
- Council Tax
- services you pay for, such as cleaning or gardening
- other direct costs of letting the property, such as phone calls, stationery, advertising.

If your annual income from the letting is less than £15,000 (before you have taken off expenses), you include the total expenses on your tax return; if it is £15,000 or over you need to provide a breakdown.

Bear in mind that you can claim only expenses that are solely for running your property-letting business. If the expense is only partly for running your business (or if you use the property yourself) then you may be able to claim only part of it.

You can claim the expenses for the let part of your home. For example, if your house is in three storeys and you let the top floor, you can claim:

- one-third of the expenses incurred on the whole house, plus
- the full amount of the expenses incurred solely on the let part of the house, such as the cost of advertising for tenants.

Payments made by members of your family towards household expenses are not taxed.

The risks of renting out property

Renting out your property is not risk-free: there is always the chance that you might have a bad tenant.

Fortunately, most older people do not have a mortgage to worry about so there should be no risk of the mortgage going unpaid because the tenant has run off without paying the rent.

Becoming a landlord

Should I let my property furnished or unfurnished?
This will depend on:

- whether you need to take your furniture with you
- the rental market for your type of property
- how expensive your furniture is (you will probably not want to leave valuable antiques)
- how much rent you will receive.

Generally, a property offered as 'fully furnished' would come with all the main fixtures, furnishings and fittings, white goods etc., plus the standard crockery, cutlery, glassware, pots and pans etc., that a reasonable tenant would normally use on a day-to-day basis.

At the other end of the scale, an unfurnished property would normally be provided only with such basics as carpets, curtains and light fittings. You can also have part-furnished properties.

What about the cost of furniture?
You cannot claim the cost of furniture when you first buy it, but you can choose to claim the actual cost of furniture when you replace it (after deducting the cost of any improvements and anything you receive for the old furniture), or a wear-and-tear allowance.

The wear-and-tear allowance is 10 per cent of the annual rent after deducting any part of the occupier's Council Tax, water rates and any other service charges which are normally paid by a tenant, but which are paid by you.

Once you have chosen between the wear-and-tear allowance and the cost of replacing items you cannot change your mind.

What regulations do I need to know about as a landlord?
There are specific legal obligations and responsibilities on a landlord with regard to fire safety for furniture and furnishings;

gas supply and appliances; plus electrical wiring and appliances.

The Association of Residential Letting Agents (ARLA)* produces a leaflet called *Let's Make it Safe*, which explains these more fully.

What about insuring my home?

Renting out all or even part of your home will affect your household insurance. For example, if your lodger steals from you without forced entry you will probably not be able to claim on a standard household contents policy.

It is important that both the landlord and tenant should be aware of what is covered by your respective insurance policies.

As a homeowner you should buy cover for the building – and inform the insurance company that you are renting out the property. There may be restrictions on cover as a result. A failure to inform your insurer that you are renting/letting a property could invalidate any subsequent claim. You should also insure your own contents, fixtures and fittings.

However, the tenants need to buy their own contents cover for their own possessions.

There are various specialist insurance products designed for landlords and tenants and rented property: buildings, contents, legal expenses, emergency repair cover and rental guarantee cover. A regulated insurance broker should be able to advise you on which of these you need.

Protecting yourself as a landlord

A tenancy agreement You will need a legally binding contract setting out legal and contractual responsibilities of both the landlord and tenant.

You can buy sample agreements from legal stationery shops. A reputable letting agent will generally organize the agreement.

The most common form of tenancy that provides the greatest protection for the landlord is an **assured shorthold tenancy.** It includes straightforward ways of bringing the tenancy to an end and a special accelerated possession court procedure if the tenants do not leave when required to or fail to pay the rent.

According to ARLA, if certain specific conditions are met relating to the proposed letting, a 'contractual' non-housing act tenancy must be created. One example of this would be what is commonly referred to as a 'company let', in which the tenant is a *bona fide* registered company; another would be where the annual rent equates to over £25,000.

Assured tenancies are not generally suitable for landlords as they give long-term security of tenure to the tenant.

Where there is to be more than one (adult) person living in the property, the tenancy will say the tenants are 'jointly and severally' responsible, which means that individually each tenant is responsible for the rent.

Inventory/schedule of condition This is an absolutely essential document that provides a written benchmark and which should be amended, updated and recreated before the beginning of each new tenancy. A properly constructed inventory/schedule of condition details the fixtures and fittings and describes their condition and that of the property generally. Landlord and tenant often share the costs involved in preparing and checking the inventory; such costs should be seen as a necessary investment that helps protect the interests of both landlord and tenant.

Deposit Tenants normally pay a deposit that is equal to between four and six weeks' rent. The landlord can then retain some or all of this if rent is not paid or when the tenant leaves the landlord needs to pay for work or repairs as a result of damage or breakage by the tenant. The letting agent (if you have one), or sometimes landlord, can hold the deposit. You can agree to pay interest on it and there should be an agreement as to when it is refunded. If you are using an agent, check that he or she is signed up to the Tenancy Deposit Scheme for Regulated Agents (TDSRA), which ensures that in the event of an unresolved dispute or stalemate over the allocation of the deposit, it can be referred to the scheme for a prompt, independent, third-party adjudication.

Break clause Usually included in the tenancy agreement, this will allow you to break the agreement – for example, if you want to return to your property. Usually two months' written notice is required.

Landlord's right to check on the property You have the right to view the property to assess its condition and to carry out necessary repairs or maintenance at reasonable times of the day. The law says that a landlord or agent must give a tenant at least 24 hours' prior notice in writing (except in an emergency) of such a visit. Naturally, if the tenant agrees, on specific or odd occasions to allow access without the 24 hours' prior written notice, that is acceptable.

Know your responsibilities Renting out your home may be an easy way to earn an additional income, but you cannot sit back and do nothing. Landlords are responsible for keeping the property in good repair (that means clearing drains and gutters and getting leaks in the roof fixed) as well as ensuring that gas, electricity and water installations are kept working. Tenants are expected to undertake day-to-day things such as changing a light bulb and keeping the property and garden tidy.

What is the landlord responsible for?

The landlord is responsible for:

- repairs to the structure and exterior of the property, heating and hot water installations, basins, sinks, baths and other sanitary installations
- the safety of gas and electrical appliances
- the fire safety of furniture and furnishings provided under the tenancy
- ensuring that the property is fit for habitation
- repairing and keeping in working order the room- and water-heating equipment
- the common areas in multi-occupancy dwellings.

What is the tenant responsible for?

The tenant is responsible for:

- paying the rent as agreed and taking proper care of the property

- paying bills for gas, electricity, telephone, etc., if this was agreed with the landlord
- in most cases, paying the Council Tax, water and sewerage charges.

How do I get my home back?

Once the tenancy ends (if it is shorthold) or you have given the required notice (two months), your home should be vacated by the tenant. If the tenant will not leave, you need to apply to the courts for a possession order. Under the accelerated possession procedure for shorthold tenancy this should be quick and inexpensive.

It is also vital to have the inventory and condition of property checked (ideally by an independent third party) in the presence of the tenant, who can then agree any items of damage.

How much will using a letting agent cost?

A lot of the hard work in finding a suitable tenant, drawing up a tenancy agreement and having the inventory checked can be done for you by a letting agent.

Generally, you can expect to pay 16 per cent of the rental income (plus some initial costs) for a full management service.

How much rent could I receive?

This will depend on the location and type of the property and its general state of repair and furnishings. According to ARLA, average rents achieved in early 2005 ranged from £2,604 a month for a house and £1,663 for a flat in prime central London to £828 a month for a house and £583 for a flat outside London and the South East.

You have to bear in mind that your property might not be continuously inhabited: you could have a long gap between lettings. The average 'void periods' remain at around a month a year all over the country. The longest empty periods are to be found in prime central London, where the period between lettings averages 32 days. In the rest of the South East the average is 27 days, and away from London and the South East the average void period drops to 25 days.

If I live abroad can I receive my rent tax-free?

You have to pay income tax on the rent if you let your previous home in the UK while you live abroad.

Your letting agent, or your tenant where there is no letting agent, should deduct tax from your rental income and pay that tax to the Inland Revenue. You can then set off that tax against your personal tax bill when you complete your tax return.

The deduction of tax will not apply:

- where there is no agent and the rent paid is less than £100 per week, unless the tenant has been told to deduct tax by the Inland Revenue
- where the Inland Revenue has issued a notice confirming that rents may be paid without deduction.

You can apply to receive rental income without deduction of tax on the grounds that you do not expect to be liable to UK tax for the year in which you make your application, or your UK tax affairs are up-to-date.

To find out more, ask for Inland Revenue leaflet IR140, *Non-resident Landlords, Their Agents and Tenants*.

Rent out a home overseas

If you are fortunate enough to own a second home overseas, this can – instead of being your retirement home – become a second pension.

Renting a home overseas has similar pitfalls to letting a home in the UK, only there is the added problem that the property will probably be thousands of miles away.

Paying tax on overseas rents

Just as you have to declare any income you get from renting your home in the UK, the same applies to rents from overseas. However, how much tax you will pay will depend on whether you are:

- resident – if you are in the UK for 183 days or more in a tax year, you are a 'resident' for that year
- ordinarily resident – if you are resident in the UK year after year you will be treated as 'ordinarily resident', or
- domiciled – if you intend to make the overseas country your home for the rest of your life (and intend to be buried there).

If you are resident, ordinarily resident and domiciled in the UK you will have to pay tax on the income from the letting whether or not that income is brought into the UK. This is known as the 'arising basis' of assessment.

If you are resident but either not ordinarily resident or not domiciled in the UK you can claim to be taxed only on the income received in the UK in the year. This is known as the 'remittance basis'. (This does not apply if the property is in the Republic of Ireland.)

When calculating your net profit, which you will need to know if you are being taxed on an arising basis, you can include the same expenses as for a UK let with the addition of some travel costs (provided they are solely for the running of your property-letting business and not for a holiday).

If you have already paid tax on your rental income abroad you can usually claim credit against the UK tax you will have to pay on it. Or you can deduct the foreign tax from your overseas rental income when you work out the profit on which you will pay UK tax.

Once you sell your home you may have to pay foreign tax. You may also have to pay CGT in the UK if you are resident or ordinarily resident in the UK, whether or not you bring the gains into the UK.

Running a business from home

More than 2.1 million people work from home and around 8 million spend at least some of their working week in the house instead of at the office, according to the Office for National Statistics.

Basing your business at home or turning your home into a business such as a bed-and- breakfast is a way to use your biggest asset – your property – to help you earn an income. However, it is not always an easy option. Many small businesses fail to make money, so you have to research your ideas well before launching into it.

Homeworking

If you do not have a business idea or a skill that you can turn into a business – for example, tutoring if you are a teacher or home typing if you are a secretary – you can consider a ready-made business.

There are many so-called homeworking business opportunities on offer from sewing and assembling kits to selling cosmetics or home improvements. However, some are scams. You must, therefore, be careful in choosing one. Never pay an upfront fee to join a homeworking business opportunity (only businesses classified as a franchise will need some form of advance payment). Homeworkers are often paid very low wages (the minimum wage does not usually apply as they are self-employed) and it can be quite isolating.

Setting up your own business

Working from home is a popular, low-cost way of launching a business as there are no premises costs – and you do not have to commute.

Information technology means that anyone's spare bedroom or living room can be used for a business. However, some businesses cannot operate from home. You will need planning permission for some and it is likely to be refused for others: for example, setting up a car repair workshop in your front garden would probably not be allowed.

Working at home has many advantages: the flexibility, low operating costs, the fact that you can run your business round family needs and the opportunity to work when and in the way you like (say, in your pyjamas at midnight).

But there are also disadvantages: isolation and lack of social contact, the fact that you never get away from the office and family needs that could intrude on your business.

Businesses that work best from home include:

- freelance and consultancy work – building on your existing skills or profession. This could include tutoring, journalism, auditing, design and even dressmaking
- trades and domestic services – for example, home ironing, or work which is carried out at the customer's home such as plumbing, decorating or gardening, which requires only a storage area (such as the garage) at your home
- craft-based businesses
- direct selling – for example, party-planning.

Will my business be allowed?

There may be planning and legal issues to consider, particularly if the business generates noticeable smell, noise or traffic. Talk over your plans with Business Link, or in Scotland, a Small Business Gateway adviser* and your local authority planning department.

How do I start a business?

Most first-time entrepreneurs start off as self-employed. However, even though you can set up as a one-man (or woman) band from your spare bedroom, you still have to understand that every business – however small – needs to meet certain rules and regulations.

Choose a name If you are a sole trader you can simply trade under your own name, which is often the easiest option. If you are setting up a limited company, you need to register your business and its name at Companies House,* which produces a guide to choosing a company name.

Tell the Inland Revenue The taxman needs to know when you are starting in business so that you can either register as self-employed or as a company, which means you will pay corporation tax.

Also, if you start to employ staff you will have to deduct pay as you earn (PAYE) and National Insurance Contributions (NICs) from their salaries and pay this over to the Inland Revenue – along with employer's NICs. Call HM Revenue & Customs* to register as self-employed and to receive an easy-to-follow guide to starting up in business.

If you fail to register within the first three full months of self-employment, you may be liable to a penalty of £100. Fortunately, there is a lot of help for those with no tax expertise – HM Revenue & Customs is a good place to start. It produces a number of very useful publications on self-employment.

Start paying NICs If you are under state retirement age and are becoming self-employed, you will need to pay self-employed flat-rate Class 2 NICs. Only those with very modest earnings (below £4,345 for the 2005/6 tax year) or who already pay contributions in another job can avoid paying what is a very small amount – just £2.10 a week.

Register for VAT This is a requirement only if your business turnover (that is, the total amount of money coming into your business from goods or services you sell) is over £60,000 a year (the 2005/6 limit).

Purchase insurance If you employ staff you must have at least £5 million worth of employer's liability insurance – it is a legal requirement and insures your legal liability for injury, death or disease suffered by employees. There are numerous small business packages that cover this, insurance for your office equipment and a limited amount of cash and business interruption insurance (compensation if, for example, your business is flooded). You should also consider legal expenses insurance (in case you are sued) and credit insurance against bad debts. Contact the Association of British Insurers* for a guide to insurance for small business.

Register under the Data Protection Act If you store information on customers and staff you will probably have to register with the Data Protection Registrar.*

Get to know employment law If you plan to employ staff, learn about employment law or get to know someone who does. There are many regulations to do with the minimum wage, maximum working week, equal opportunities legislation and the Health and Safety at Work Act, and it is easy to fall foul of the law.

Expenses you can deduct if you work from home

The items of expenditure the self-employed can claim include the following.

1. A proportion of the costs of running your home – if you use it mainly or even only part-time for business use. Generally, the self-employed can deduct a proportion of the following:

   - heating
   - lighting
   - cleaning
   - insurance
   - mortgage interest or rent
   - Council Tax, although this is open to interpretation – check with your tax office as current understanding is that only if a room is entirely used for business purposes can a proportion of Council Tax be deducted.

The proportion should be agreed in advance with the tax office and should reflect actual usage.

Harry Homeworker uses the dining room of his home as an office. His three-bedroom house has five rooms excluding kitchens and bathrooms and as he uses one exclusively for business he has agreed with his tax office that he can deduct a fifth of the household running costs as an allowable expense.

Mortgage (interest only)	*£9,200 p.a.*
Council tax	*£800 p.a.*
Gas	*£600 p.a.*
Electric	*£300 p.a.*
Insurance	*£250 p.a.*
TOTAL	*£11,150*
Business proportion 1/5th x £11,150 =	*£2,230*

Plus

Telephone (used only for business)	*£1,000*
TOTAL	*£3,230*

So he can deduct £3,230 p.a. as the cost of running his office from home.

2. The running costs of your own car if you use it (even only occasionally) for business – you can deduct a proportion relating to the amount of business usage. Costs that can be claimed include motor insurance, road tax, maintenance and fuel. Costs can be deducted even when a car is hired.
3. Bank charges, loan interest and overdraft fees on business accounts but not any capital repayments of loans.
4. Interest on loans from friends and relatives who have helped start the business (provided they do not have a say in how the company is run and the loan is covered by a written agreement).
5. VAT – those who are not registered for VAT can still claim it back by including it in the cost of any items of allowable expenditure.
6. Insurance – to cover business premises and equipment (including a proportion of household insurance bills if working from home, but check with your insurer if business equipment is covered).
7. Wages – paid to others.
8. Legal fees for debt collection and preparing trading contracts and employee service contracts and accountancy and audit fees.

Would I have to pay CGT when I sell my home?

Increasing numbers of people use their home as their office. However, working from home – and claiming part of the costs of the home against tax – could mean that the profits made on the sale of the property are liable for CGT. Only the proportion of the home used for business will be liable for CGT, so if a home has four rooms (excluding kitchens and bathrooms) and one room is used exclusively for business, one-quarter of the profits could be subject to CGT.

To get around this rule, those working from home can use a room almost exclusively for business. They will still be able to claim for some of the running costs such as heating, light and telephone bills. If the house has four rooms (excluding kitchens and bathrooms) and one is used mainly for business, instead of claiming a quarter (25 per cent) of the running costs of the home as an allowable expense, the home worker can claim, say 75 per cent of this 25 per cent. The self-employed should agree these proportions with their local tax office when starting to work from home.

How will my business affect my means-tested benefits?

It all depends on how much profit – if any – you make. Your pre-tax profits (that is, all your income minus your expenses) will be added to other income when calculating how much you are due by way of benefits.

Turning your home into a business

A popular business is to run a bed-and-breakfast. It may seem like an easy way to make money, but you need to do your research and be prepared to work extremely hard. You will spend hours washing bed linen and cleaning, and you will be sharing your home with complete strangers.

Other factors to bear in mind include the following.

- Locations close to tourist attractions are generally the most popular.

- Check with your local town hall about the process for getting planning approval – some areas prohibit them.
- If you plan to renovate your home (for example, to include en-suite bathrooms) have a contractor confirm compliance with local building codes.
- Find out whether there are any restrictions on the types of food that can be served, such as a full breakfast.
- Work out your numbers – profit margins are modest. Check out competitors' prices to see how much you can charge.
- Decide how you will market your B&B.
- Do not forget insurance – buildings, contents, public liability and possibly employee liability.

What are the tax implications of running a business at home?

A bed-and-breakfast is a business and you can therefore deduct certain expenses to reduce the amount of tax you pay. As with the self-employed running a business from home you can deduct a proportion of the costs of running your home in line with actual usage (see the list above).

However, you cannot deduct the cost of your own time spent cleaning or washing (although you can deduct the cost of cleaning materials you use as part of your business) or the cost of buying your property (other than mortgage interest) or improving it.

There are also CGT implications. The rules are complex and as you still live in your home there are several ways to avoid paying – or to reduce the amount of – CGT when you sell the property.

Remember, any income you receive will affect your entitlement to means-tested benefits.

Further information

HM Revenue & Customs (www.hmrc.gov.uk 08459 154 515) produces useful leaflets, including:

SE1 *Thinking of working for yourself?*

SA/BK3 *Self Assessment – A Guide to Keeping Records for the Self-Employed.*

For help when employing staff call the New Employers' Helpline on (0845) 607 0143

HM Revenue and Customs also produces the following leaflets you may find useful (0845 9000 404):

CGT1 *Capital Gains Tax: An Introduction*

COP1 *Putting Things Right: How to Complain*

IR20 *Residents and Non-Residents: Liability to Tax in the United Kingdom*

IR140 *Non-Resident Landlords, their Agents and Tenants*

IR223 *Rent a Room for Traders*

IR283 *Private Residence Relief*

Association of British Insurers (ABI) 020 7600 3333; www.abi.org.uk

Association of Residential Letting Agents (ARLA) (0845) 345 5752; www.arla.co.uk

Companies House (0870) 333 3636; www.companieshouse.gov.uk

Data Protection Registrar www.dataprotection.gov.uk

Small Business Gateway adviser 0845 609 6611; www.sbgateway.com

Business Link 0845 600 9006; www.businesslink.gov.uk

Part Three
REDUCING YOUR OUTGOINGS

Introduction

The difficulty of living on a fixed income is exactly that – it is fixed. If you have made the most of your capital (or spent it) and maximized your investment returns, there may be little choice but to reduce the amount you spend.

This does not necessarily mean turning off the heating so that you freeze or subsisting on boiled cabbage: there are often far larger savings to be made by simply shopping around for the best deals, not just on groceries and petrol but on major household bills. The average household can save about £1,000 a year just by signing up for the best deals.

Chapter 7

Household bills

Utility bills

How much can I save?

Households can easily save up to £100 a year on their combined energy bills by switching supplier – yet half have never bothered to change electricity or gas provider. In addition, they can save a further £200 by being energy-efficient. Even those reluctant to move supplier can save an average £20 a year by simply moving to payment by direct debit from standard credit terms.

However, the biggest savings are made by moving to combined fuel (or dual-fuel) packages, where the household buys both gas and electricity from the same supplier. This cuts up to £120 a year off bills. With some suppliers, such as npower, those switching to a dual-fuel package and paying by direct debit get a larger discount. Signing up to pay your bills online will save a further £10 with some energy companies.

How do I find the best deal?

Finding the best deal is comparatively easy. Energywatch,* the gas and electricity watchdog, publishes comparisons of the different prices charged by suppliers in each area. In addition, Energywatch has a code of practice for domestic energy comparison websites, with nine so far signing up to the code.

To find out how much you can save, you simply need to compare the cost of your usage from different suppliers. Although you can do this by keying in the amount you spent the previous year on energy, sites that compare the cost of actual kilowatt hours used may provide more accurate figures.

There are more than 6,000 different tariffs listed on comparison websites, so it is worth using a service to do the hard work (the most well-known of these sites are listed at the end of this chapter). These sites earn a small commission for each customer signed up, but they should be impartial and independent of any one gas or electricity supplier.

However, these sites have one drawback: they are unlikely to recommend one of the newer fixed or capped price deals, which will probably not come up as a best buy, although these offers could provide the biggest savings in the long run.

Should I opt for a price freeze?

Price freezes keep the price static for as long as the deal lasts. Price caps mean that bills will not rise, but if energy costs fall, these savings will be passed on to the customer.

Some deals are better than others so it will pay to read the small print. Customers of a few energy companies will be charged if they switch to a different provider during the offer period. British Gas could charge up to £50.

Longer-term price fixes tend to come at a premium so you need to weigh up the risk of further price increases against any extra you may pay initially. For example, British Gas was charging a premium of 2.8 per cent on gas bills in exchange for a guarantee that prices would not rise until 2010. As electricity bills are expected to fall, it was giving a discount of 4.8 per cent for freezing your electricity bills until April 2010. The price promises change regularly so it is worth taking up offers quickly.

So should you opt for instant savings or for peace of mind? If energy bills rise as fast as they have since 2004, these deals make financial sense. However, if prices rise more slowly over the term of the deal, you could pay more than if you shop around and move to a cheaper supplier. It is a gamble.

How do I find a supplier?

When switching suppliers, Energywatch recommends households compare prices and complaint levels using its website or a price-comparison service. They should also compare like with like – not, say, paying by cheque with paying by direct debit.

When considering switching to a dual-fuel package they should compare the cost of all their existing services to get a more accurate saving.

Internet tariffs and 'green' tariffs (for example, npower's Juice tariff, which generates electricity from offshore wind farms) can add further savings, and some suppliers have special rates for older people so investigate these as well. Those who run a lot of appliances (such as dishwashers and washing machines) at night and who have electric storage heaters should consider Economy 7.

Energywatch also recommends that households cut their bills by being more energy-efficient. All white goods and light bulbs are now marked with a rating of A–G, with the most energy-efficient given an A-rating. One low-energy lightbulb can save up to £10 a year, and turning heating down by just 1 degree centigrade can cut gas bills by up to 10 per cent.

How do I switch suppliers?

1. Get in touch with the new supplier and agree a contract with it. The transfer process should take about six weeks to complete.
2. Give the old supplier 28 days' notice of the changing to a new supplier. Do this initially by telephone and follow it up with written confirmation.
3. Pay any outstanding bills owed to the existing supplier (it could prevent the transfer if this is not done).
4. Take a meter reading on the day of the change. This will be needed to work out the final bill with the existing supplier and the starting point for the first bill with the new supplier.

How do I find out about special deals for those on fixed incomes?

Ask suppliers if they offer any special tariffs for pensioners (there is no central list).

If you are of pensionable age, have a long-term disability or suffer from ill-health you may also qualify for free services if you join the Priority Service Register.* These services include free gas safety checks and free movement of controls if you find it hard to operate your central heating or hot water boiler.

How do I find out more about energy efficiency savings?

By being energy-efficient you could save up to £200 a year on your bills, as well as helping the environment.

Here are some good examples of how to save.

- **Televisions, stereos, computers** To cut down on wasted energy avoid leaving appliances on standby.
- **Lightbulbs** If you use any light for four hours or more a day, replacing it with an energy-saving equivalent will use a quarter of the electricity and last 12 times longer. Energy-saving light-bulbs cost around £5 each, but will give you a saving of £10 over the year.
- **Boilers** Replacing a 15-year-old model could save you over 20 per cent on your fuel bills.

For more tips on saving energy and for advice on choosing and fitting energy-saving measures, contact the Energy Saving Trust.*

Can I get help improving my boiler and central heating system?

You might get help in improving your boiler or heating system, which in turn will lead to lower energy bills. The Energy Saving Trust provides an up-to-date source of grants and offers from the government, energy suppliers and local councils.

These are some of the schemes available.

Warm Front This provides free grants of up to £2,700 to households who may be receiving benefits and who want to improve their home's heating and energy efficiency.

In Northern Ireland it is known as Warm Homes, in Scotland as Warm Deal and in Wales the Home Energy Efficiency Scheme.

Those over 60 and in receipt of one or more of Pension Credit, Income Support, Council Tax Benefit, Income-based Jobseeker's Allowance and Housing Benefit could benefit from a package of energy-efficiency and heating measures, including central heating specifically tailored to the needs of your property. Energy-efficiency advice, tailored to each household, is provided by Eaga Partnership's Home Visits team in accordance with the Energy Savings Trust's Code of Practice. However, this grant is subject to available funding.

If you think you could be eligible for assistance under the Warm Front grant contact Eaga.*

Local authority grants Most local authorities offer some form of grant. For example, Wandsworth Council in London offers 'Coldbusters' heating and insulation grants of up to £4,000 to homeowners in receipt of a means-tested benefit to improve central heating, replace a boiler or provide loft and cavity wall insulation as well as draught-proofing.

Energy Smart This gives big discounts on boilers (supply only or fully installed), heating controls or full heating systems. You could save £80–£120 off your fuel bills each year.

Contact your local authority and your energy supplier for further details of grants that may be available.

Telephone bills

Over 20 million households could cut up to a fifth off their phone bills by taking just a few minutes to switch telephone provider. Only a quarter have so far switched to take calls from a fixed-line supplier other than BT, and of these many could make further savings by shopping around in what is now a highly competitive market with over 170 service suppliers.

What is deterring many from making these easy savings is the difficulty in comparing services to find the best deal, according to the telecoms regulator, Ofcom.

Ofcom is looking at ways to improve information and simplify switching for consumers and has introduced mandatory guidelines on the selling of fixed-line services, replacing what had been a voluntary code of practice. This should reassure customers that they will not be mis-sold services in the way some have been in the past.

How do I find the best deal?
Calculating which call-provider is cheapest is complex and involves comparing not only the total spend on calls but also when calls are made, how long they last and the balance between local, national and international calls.

Ofcom has launched the PASS logo to reassure consumers that comparison websites, which do the hard work of comparing the hundreds of different telecom packages, comply with a strict code of practice and provide independent, accurate and up-to-date price information.

However, at the time of writing only one website – www.uswitch.com – had so far been awarded this PASS logo.

How do I switch suppliers?
If you are switching only calls, it is simple. Nobody has to visit your house. All you have to do is call a supplier and give it your phone number, postcode and direct-debit details, and ten days later you have a new supplier.

BT will continue to maintain your line and the new call provider bills you for the calls.

How much could I save?
You could save £30 or even £60 a year – more if you are switching line and calls.

What options are open to me?
In addition to switching calls (the most popular choice to date) there are several other options.

Cable companies Some 14 per cent of households have so far switched to cable companies. These can provide the line and calls as well as cable television.

Indirect access For those wanting cheaper calls, for example, to overseas numbers, indirect access (IA) could be useful. Users must dial a short code (or sometimes a freephone or other phone number) before they dial the number of the person they wish to contact. Or, they can have an adaptor plugged in between the socket and their phone and the adaptor will dial the code automatically. These calls will then be charged by the IA phone company. BT will continue to charge for line rental and any calls made with it.

Call-only providers This is known as carrier pre-selection (CPS), and more than four million users have taken up this option. The BT line is used and no access codes have to be dialled. Instead, calls (or various types of calls – for example, all national calls or all international calls) are automatically routed through the CPS supplier. In addition, the household continues to receive a bill from BT for line rental. BT will still carry emergency calls (999 and 112), calls made to the operator (100) and calls to certain number ranges used for unlimited Internet access. These calls will appear on the bill from BT.

Line and calls The telephone company rents lines wholesale from BT and the household stops being a BT customer (although BT still maintains the lines). Once the price of wholesale line rental comes down, a large number of call-only suppliers are likely to offer this package. The Post Office has launched HomePhone, promoting it as a scheme that combines you having the same phone, same line, same number and a single bill. It claims that savings average 12 per cent compared with BT's Together Option 1 tariff (see below).

Broadband When shopping around for the best fixed-line deals households should also compare broadband offerings. Often these can be bought as a bundle – for example, 1MB of broadband plus free evening and weekend calls for £14.99 a month. Broadband can provide savings for those with high Internet usage who want the added benefit of keeping their phone line free while they spend hours surfing the internet.

What savings can BT offer me?
For those not comfortable switching landline supplier, the first step should be to ensure they have the correct BT tariff.

In addition to a 'lower user' scheme' and a 'Call Mobile' scheme, which, for £1.50 a month, gives a 25 per cent discount on calls to mobiles, BT offers three 'Together' packages.

- Option 1 costs £11 a month and enables customers to talk evenings and weekends for 5.5 pence an hour.
- For an extra £6.50 a month, Option 2 gives free evening and weekend calls up to one hour.
- And for £25.50 a month, Option 3 gives all calls, including daytime calls, free (up to one hour).

Note Calls over an hour long, calls to Internet providers and to 0845 and 0870 numbers are not included in the package, so actual bills may be higher.

Before considering switching from BT check that you are making the most of the friends and family discount. If you rarely make calls, join the 'lower user' scheme.

How do I go about switching?

1. Look at your telephone usage – what sort of calls are made, when and how often.
2. Use this information to compare prices at the uswitch website. This is complex, as different types of call cost varying amounts and some are worked out per second or per minute and some have a minimum call charge.
3. If possible sign up online and pay by direct debit – this will give the biggest savings.
4. If you are considering signing up for a package that includes a phone service and another service, for example, gas, electricity, or a supermarket loyalty scheme, compare your combined current payment for all the separate services with the cost of the package that is being offered.
5. Read the small print in the contract. Check the term of the contract, how you can end it and if there are any penalties for ending the contract before the end of its minimum period.

How do I find out more?

The regulator, Ofcom,* produces consumer leaflets explaining what telephone services are on offer and how to switch provider.

Water rates

While households cannot switch water supplier to save money, there are other options to cut bills, which are set to rise by as much as 18 per cent by 2010. This means that the average household bill will increase by £46 over five years (before inflation) to £295.

One option is to switch to a water meter. However, this will bring savings only for those with low usage. Households can visit www.uswitch.com to find if a water meter could bring any savings or contact their water and sewerage company to enquire about water metering.

How much does it cost to switch to a meter?

You should be able to switch to a water meter free of charge. However, it may not be possible to fit a meter if, for example, you have a shared water pipe supply.

Who already has water meters?

Properties built after 1989 are automatically fitted with a meter by water utilities companies, as the 'rateable value' system, which unmeasured water bills in England and Wales are based on, was scrapped in 1990.

If you move into one of these properties you cannot then switch to an unmetered water supply.

How is my water bill calculated?

England & Wales There are two ways that water utilities companies can calculate your water bill. If it is **unmeasured**, you pay a set amount for your water and sewerage service, regardless of how much you use, based on the rateable value (RV) of your home. This RV cannot usually be changed and may appear on your bill. Unmeasured bills also include a standing charge to cover services such as billing. If it is **measured**, you are charged for the number of units of water you actually use, based on readings taken from a meter. Your measured bill will also include a standing charge to cover services like billing and meter reading.

Scotland There are two ways that water utilities companies can calculate your water bill. **Unmeasured** bills are based on the Council Tax rate of a property, plus a standing charge for services such as billing. **Measured** bills charge you for the number of units of water you actually use, based on readings taken from a meter. Your measured bill will also include a standing charge to cover services such as billing and meter reading.

Northern Ireland Domestic customers will pay for water utilities and sewerage services from April 2007. Those on pensions are expected to pay as little as £60 a year, rising to £180 in 2010.

How much could I save?
According to the industry regulator, Ofwat, the average annual household bill for water and sewerage utilities in 2004/5 in England and Wales was £249 (£117 for water utilities and £132 for sewerage) and in Scotland £272. It says that on average an unmetered customer who switches to having a meter saves 5 to 10 per cent (that is, around £20–£25) on their bill.

Will a meter be cheaper for me?
If your property has a high rateable value but you have low usage (like many pensioners), you might find that having a meter is a better option for you. Once you switch, make the most of water efficiency to cut your bills further.

Get to know your water usage. According to uswitch.co.uk on average each person will use 150 litres of water every day.

- Flushing the toilet uses 7–10 litres each time.
- Drinking/cooking uses 10 litres.
- A bath or power shower uses 80 litres.

- A washing machine cycle uses 70–120 litres.
- A dishwasher uses 25–60 litres.
- A dripping tap wastes 25 litres a day.
- A running tap uses 10 litres a minute.
- Hosepipes and sprinklers use 1,000 litres per hour.

Household insurance

Buildings and contents insurance premiums are sometimes cheaper for the over-50s who may qualify for discount because they are often at home all day (so there is less risk of burglary) and they are considered more careful homeowners (so they are less likely to claim for accidental damage).

How can I save money?

You might be able to make a saving by shopping around. The average buildings insurance bill of £208.65 can be reduced by £76.28 by switching to the best deal, and the average contents insurance premium of £151 can be reduced by £64.02, according to AA Insurance. That is a total saving of just over £140 a year.

However, do not consider saving money by:

- not buying cover – the premiums may seem high, but if your home burnt down you would be left with nothing
- skimping on the amount of cover – if you are under-insured you may find that when you come to claim the pay-out is reduced to reflect the level of under-insurance
- not covering valuables separately or individually itemized on the policy – check the cash limits on individual items and money in the home. Antiques worth £1,000, for example, may not be covered.

Other ways to cut costs

- Buy the correct amount of cover. Ensure that you are not over-insured. Many policies provide a level of cover based on the number of bedrooms in your home. This takes into account the contents of the average household. If your home has few electronic gadgets and the furniture is not expensive, you may find that you need less cover. Buying a set amount – for example, £15,000 of contents – may save you money.

- Join a neighbourhood watch scheme – you may qualify for a discount.
- Improve your home security – this may be a requirement of your insurance policy in some areas. In others it leads to a reduction in your premiums.
- Forgo accidental cover if you have few breakages and never claim.
- Opt for a no-claims discount. Some insurers now offer these as a reward to those who do not make claims.
- Pay annually – some insurers charge up to 30 per cent APR to pay monthly.
- Increase your voluntary excess (the amount you pay towards each claim – for example, the first £250).

How do I find the best deal?

You can visit an insurance broker or flick through *Yellow Pages* and contact a few insurance companies direct. Buying direct can often be cheaper.

There are also dozens of Internet web sites which will do this hard work for you.

When shopping around, you will find that some companies offer policies specifically for the over-50s or 60s. They do not always offer the best deals.

The following survey from online price-comparison site www.insurancesupermarket.com shows just how much it is possible to save.

Buildings and contents insurance for a 3-bedroom detached house built in 1968, based in Coventry (CV3), market value £175,000, rebuild value £100,000, contents value £35,000, £100 excess & no accidental damage cover.

Provider	Individual aged 70 Annual premium	Excess
Cheapest – Budget	£165.29	£100
Saga	£182.75	£100
Help the Aged	£286.40	£100
Most expensive – Egg	£411.45	£100
Average premium	£261.47	

Television licence

Do not forget that you do not have to pay for a television licence if someone you live with is aged 75 or over. Also, if you are retired, disabled or aged 60 or over and live in a care home or sheltered housing you may qualify for a concessionary licence.

Average annual savings
This is how the savings can quickly add up.

Household bill by switching to a best-buy deal Average annual saving

Mortgage
Average £55,000 repayment loan
at standard variable rate   £876

Energy bills
Average family of four in a semi-detached house   £80
spending £700 on fuel

Buildings insurance
On an average bill of £208.65   £76.28

Home contents insurance
On an average bill of £151   £64.02

Telephone bills
On an average fixed-line bill of £328   £39.36

Total annual saving   **£1,135.66**

Sources: Charcol, Ofgem, The AA British Insurance Premium Index,
NAO, Post Office.

Further information

Age Concern has produced a leaflet called *Help with heating*. For a copy, call (0800) 009 966 or download it from www.age concern.org.uk

Free energy price-comparison services include:

www.energyhelpline.com	(0800) 279 4546
www.energylinx.co.uk	(0800) 849 7077
www.moneyexpert.com/energy	01942 710910
www.saveonyourbills.co.uk	(0870) 005 2095
www.theenergyshop.com	(0845) 330 7247
www.ukpower.co.uk	(0870) 458 4200
www.unravelit.com	(0800) 279 4091
www.uswitch.com	(0845) 601 2856

Eaga England (0800) 316 6011; Northern Ireland
(0800) 181 667; Scotland (0800) 072 0150; Wales
(0800) 316 2815; www.eaga.co.uk
Energy Saving Trust (0800) 915 7722; www.saveenergy.co.uk
Energywatch (0845) 906 0708; www.energywatch.org.uk
Ofcom 020-7981 3000; www.ofcom.org.uk
Priority Service Register (0845) 906 0708

Chapter 8

Home maintenance and repairs

While running a home may be expensive, most people can budget to cover their regular bills. It is the unexpected costs of events such as a boiler breaking down or a roof leaking that can scupper financial plans. In addition, as people get older there are other costs to consider – for example, installing a chair-lift if they can no longer use the stairs.

This chapter looks at ways to protect against unexpected costs and ways to get help or raise finance with repairs to your home.

Protection against high repair bills

It is possible to buy insurance cover for almost every eventuality.

Accidents Your home insurance policy can include accidental damage cover, which will protect your pocket against expensive repairs if, for example, you put your foot through the ceiling while looking for something in the attic. Accidental cover does bump up your premiums so you need to weigh up the additional costs against the chances of making a claim.

Boiler problems Many homes in the UK suffer weather-related breakdowns each winter, with central heating failure the most common home emergency. Insurance to protect against boiler breakdown has now become one of the fastest-growing areas of insurance.

However, it does not come cheap. Premiums vary from £90 to £180 a year – comparable to the £151 average cost of home contents insurance. While the latter covers the entire contents of your home against theft, floods or fires, boiler breakdown insurance may not even cover the full cost of repairs and it could take days for heating and hot water to be restored.

While the marketing literature may promise service of 365 days a year, 24 hours a day, that does not mean the engineers operate round the clock, and there can be limits on the amount of cover. Policies with no financial limits – such as British Gas's Central Heating Care or Home Service's Gas Boiler Breakdown Cover – offer more comprehensive coverage.

British Gas will offer you a replacement boiler (not necessarily the same make) if yours is uneconomical to repair provided it is less than seven years old. But if it is older than that you will only get a 5 per cent discount on the cost of a new one if British Gas fits it.

To sign up for some policies such as the one offered by British Gas your boiler needs to pass an inspection. Some major insurers such as Domestic & General do not require an inspection, and there is no age limit on repairs to boilers. The policies offered by Seeboard and SWALEC also require a pre-inspection.

In general, boilers should be under 15 years old (eight years if a combination boiler) for you to find cover.

Some policies include a yearly safety inspection (British Gas), while others, such as the more expensive Domestic & General policies, provide a more comprehensive annual maintenance, which should help to avoid problems and prolong the life of your boiler.

It is worth shopping around on price. British Gas's Central Heating Care costs £16 a month or £192 for the first year, which is expensive, but it has no limit on the cost of call outs. There is a lower price of £12 a month for boiler and controls only at www.house.co.uk.

A cheaper alternative may be home-emergency cover from your household insurer. Esure, for example, charges £33.60 a year on top of your existing household insurance premium and will pay up to £500 including VAT for the call-out charge and up to two hours worth of labour costs. It will also pay out for parts and materials to a maximum of £100 including VAT. While this will not pay for a new boiler, it will cover you for emergency costs.

Help with repairs to the home

If you are an older homeowner, and your house needs work on it, you may be able to get either help with the work or help finding funding to pay for the costs.

The Home Improvement Trust* has set up a scheme called Houseproud which helps older homeowners repair, improve or adapt their homes so they can live there safely and independently.

Houseproud has links with a number of lenders – all regulated banks and building societies – which provide low-cost equity release loans to older people, secured against the value of the home.

The Home Improvement Trust acts as an impartial go-between and arranges property valuation, as well as liaising with the bank or building society on your behalf.

A number of different equity release schemes are available through Houseproud, but all the banks and building societies involved provide a written guarantee of no repossession while the original borrower remains in the house.

As a safeguard, the Home Improvement Trust arranges for the borrower to receive advice from an independent financial adviser free of charge, and provides a full written analysis of all the costs involved, before any financial commitment is made.

Home Improvement Agencies (HIAs)* in England, Wales and Scotland provide older people with help and advice on repairs, improvements and adaptations, and are often known as 'Care and Repair' or 'Staying Put' schemes. As well as providing advice and information, these agencies will organize and supervise the work being done, and can offer more guidance on your financial situation.

There are 227 HIAs in England, most of which receive some support from the government. They are small, not-for-profit, locally based organizations which provide advice, support and assistance to elderly, disabled and vulnerable people to help them to maintain an independent lifestyle and continue living in their own homes. Each year they deal with almost 100,000 enquiries and over 80 per cent of those helped are:

- 75 years old and over
- registered or registerable disabled
- from a low-income household.

What HIAs can do for you

HIAs cannot help you financially, but they can give you advice on the best ways to raise finance to improve your home. They can also help you deal with builders and ensure that work is completed satisfactorily.

Many clients of HIAs are apprehensive about housing repairs carried out to their own home. Jobs undertaken can range from the very small (such as minor plumbing repairs) to major renovations or the construction of adaptations or extensions for a disabled person.

The building work is specified, competitive estimates are sought from good-quality, vetted contractors and the whole work is overseen by the agency's technical staff in order to ensure that the finished result meets the needs and wants of the client.

Home Improvement Agencies can also help with the following.

- **Hospital discharge projects** These provide a rapid-response team to enable older people to be safely discharged from hospital into their own home by carrying out essential repairs and adaptations.
- **Handypersons schemes** These schemes provide people to carry out small repairs to the homes of mainly low-income, older and disabled people to enable them to maintain their properties and live in greater comfort and security.
- **Aids and adaptations** These schemes organize the fitting of a range of small adaptations in the homes of older and disabled people to assist independent living.
- **Home security schemes** These organize the installation of measures such as door and window locks, door chains, viewers, external lighting and related security features in the homes of vulnerable people.
- **Energy efficiency projects** These schemes help vulnerable

people to identify measures that can be taken to improve energy efficiency in their homes and provide practical help and assistance to implement them.

- **Home safety schemes** These schemes offer HIA clients the option of having a detailed check carried out to identify 'risk factors' that could result in an accident in the home and recommend remedial action.
- **Disabled persons' housing service** This service aims to achieve appropriate and affordable housing solutions for people with disabilities through the provision of a range of services which help with access to adaptable rented and owner-occupied housing, and adapting properties to meet the needs of people with disabilities.
- **Home maintenance project** This aims to emphasize the importance of regular maintenance work in order to avoid emergency or major works at a later date.
- **Free Government help** The December 2005 pre-Budget announced that all pensioners in receipt of Pension Credit will receive free installation of central heating and loft insulation if they do not have a system; others will receive a £300 discount if they do not have central heating.

Further information

Home Improvement Trusts 0115-934 9511;
   www.improvementtrust.fsbusiness.co.uk/
Home Improvement Agencies (01457 891909);
   www.cel.co.uk/foundations/

Chapter 9

Mortgages and other debts

Your mortgage

If you are still paying off a mortgage it could pay to shop around for a better deal than the one you have. However, bear in mind that your income may be lower than it was previously and you may not be seen as such a good financial bet by lenders as you were when you were younger. As a result, you may find it hard to switch and/or to get a better rate.

Around half of all homebuyers have switched mortgage at some stage. However, the older you are the less likely you are to do so.

What happens if I still have a mortgage when I retire?

If a repayment mortgage has still not been repaid or the debt on an endowment policy is not fully covered by the maturing policies, most people usually repay the mortgage using a lump sum taken from a pension fund.

Lenders do offer loans that extend into retirement but most borrowers take out loans with the aim of repaying them well before then.

Even so, according to research by the Abbey National published in November 2004, 47 per cent of homeowners now have a mortgage that extends into retirement. It is not surprising, therefore, that 55–64-year-olds are far less optimistic about using the housing market as an investment to fund their retirement compared to younger homebuyers.

According to the Abbey's research, people retiring see an average drop of 41 per cent in monthly income when they stop work. For some people who reach retirement age with no long-term savings or income other than a state pension and the equity in their home, the prospect of a few more years' work could be a necessity rather than a choice.

Should I repay my mortgage?

Not only are increasing numbers of borrowers still saddled with a mortgage once they reach retirement, the endowment scandal has also taken its toll.

If you do not want to – or cannot afford to – make up for shortfalls in your endowment policy, it may not repay your mortgage on time. Therefore, the term of your mortgage may be extended until you reach, or even get past, your intended retirement age.

For most borrowers, repaying a mortgage makes sense for many reasons. The amount you can earn on savings is usually far less than the interest you pay on the same amount of money borrowed as a mortgage. Earning 4 per cent on £20,000 in the bank while owing £15,000 on a mortgage with a rate of 6 per cent does not make financial sense.

Also, in the past tax relief (MIRAS) on mortgages often made keeping a small mortgage worthwhile. However, this scheme was scrapped long ago. Another reason is that inflation is at a historic low so it will not erode the value of your debt. In the 1970s inflation would have halved the value of what you owed in just a decade in real terms so it often made sense to have a debt. What seemed like a large mortgage at the start of the decade shrunk to a much more affordable amount by the end of it. You can no longer rely on inflation to erode your debt.

Moreover, repaying your mortgage will reduce your monthly outgoings – possibly by a significant amount.

However, there are several reasons why older homebuyers should think twice before clearing their mortgage debt.

- You may need any savings for a rainy day – once you have used them to repay the mortgage you may have little or none left.
- It may be a bad time to cash in investments to repay your mortgage because the stockmarket is now recovering from its

slump and your investments could rise in value by a greater percentage than the interest you are charged on your debts. Also, you may still have investments that have failed to recover and by cashing them in you may suffer a loss from which you cannot recover.

- Your mortgage repayments are likely to be relatively low and affordable.
- If you repay your mortgage and need to borrow money against the value of your home in future – for example, using equity release – the cost of borrowing will be far higher.
- Having a mortgage debt reduces the value of your home for inheritance tax purposes.

So although, on balance, most older homeowners may be better off clearing their mortgage debt once and for all – if only for peace of mind – if you feel that you will probably need your savings, a better option may be to remortgage to a cheaper rate (if you can) and/or to repay your mortgage more quickly out of income rather than using up your capital.

Another option is to use your savings to reduce your mortgage debt – while still keeping these savings intact. By investing them in an account linked to your mortgage (known as an offset or all-in-one account) you can save interest and clear your mortgage debt more quickly. This is because your savings 'earn' the mortgage rate of interest, which is generally higher than the rates paid on savings accounts. Moreover, this sum is tax-free because you do not actually receive any interest – you save it. These accounts work by using your savings and any money in your current account to reduce your overall debt. As you owe less, you pay less interest. So this option will preserve any savings and leave you mortgage-free at an earlier age as well as saving you money in total interest costs.

What if I have an endowment mortgage?
If your endowment is unlikely to repay your mortgage debt you may find that you still have a mortgage at retirement even though you had thought you would be mortgage-free much earlier.

Generally, advisers recommend that you do not bother to top up an endowment so that it repays the mortgage. Instead consider remortgaging some of the loan to a repayment mortgage which is guaranteed to repay the mortgage at the end of the term, or move to a cheaper mortgage rate and use the monthly savings to build up a savings reserve (to meet the endowment shortfall) or to overpay on your mortgage each month so it is repaid more quickly.

Compensation

If you were sold an endowment that has a shortfall you may be entitled to compensation – often several thousand pounds. Contact the insurer for details.

How do I get a mortgage if I am near to retirement?

So-called granny loans are now offered by a range of lenders, including Halifax, Nationwide, Cheltenham & Gloucester, Abbey and HSBC. They will lend money to homeowners who are nearing retirement or already drawing their pension.

Older borrowers at Halifax can apply for loans that last for up to 40 years while Nationwide customers are eligible for 35-year loans that are extended upon request. Borrowers must generally be aged at least 55 and there is no age limit on when the mortgage can be taken out.

Payments on such mortgages are low because only interest is paid: there is no repayment element to the mortgage. Instead, the debt is repaid when the property is sold either because the homeowner moves or dies.

The drawbacks of such mortgages are:

- you may never be mortgage-free
- if interest rates rise you may have difficulty paying the mortgage interest
- borrowing money over such a long period means that the total interest paid is higher
- if one of you dies, the surviving spouse may not be able to afford the payments on a reduced income.

How can I remortgage?

1. **Find out if you can remortgage** If you are near retirement or already retired you may find it hard to get a lender to advance you a mortgage – unless it is an interest-only age-related mortgage. These advance between 50 per cent and 75 per cent of the property value. You may need to visit a mortgage broker for advice. The sale of mortgages is now covered by the Financial Services Authority so all advisers should now be authorized and regulated.

2. **Check whether you can make savings** It is worth remortgaging only if you are going to cut your borrowing costs (unless you plan to increase your monthly repayments to reduce the term of the mortgage. See *How to be mortgage-free*, below).

3. **Take into account other costs** Even if your monthly mortgage bills are lower, once you take into account the costs of valuation fees, arrangement fees and any redemption charges on the existing mortgage, you may be no better off.

How to be mortgage-free

Use capital/savings to repay some or all of your mortgage debt The chances are that you are paying a higher rate of interest on your mortgage than you are earning on savings. If you are repaying only part of the debt, you will need to consider some of the other options as well. Before taking up this option check that there are no penalties or charges for doing this. Also, some lenders impose a minimum amount on how much can be repaid as a lump sum.

Increase your monthly repayments If and when you can afford to repay more each month, you should do so. This will clear your mortgage debt more quickly. Once again, check that there are no penalties for doing this. Also note that some lenders will not let you do this unless you have a flexible type of loan and that there may be a minimum additional amount that you have to pay.

Remortgage to a cheaper rate – and use the savings to overpay each month This has the same benefits and pitfalls as above but is an option for those who cannot afford any additional monthly mortgage payments but who can remortgage.

Use your savings to offset your mortgage debt – without losing your savings Offset and open plan accounts enable you to use money in your current and savings accounts to help pay your mortgage off more easily – and reduce your total interest bill. Rather than earning interest on the money in their current account and savings accounts, customers do not pay interest on the equivalent amount of mortgage. As their monthly mortgage payments stay the same, the interest saved each month goes to repay their mortgage early.

With a £90,000 mortgage and an average current-account balance of £1,000 and £5,000 savings, a customer would not pay interest on £6,000 worth of mortgage. Over 25 years, he or she would save £16,327 in mortgage interest and pay off the mortgage 2 years and 5 months early. Older homeowners who tend to have smaller mortgages and larger amounts of savings can expect even greater interest savings – enabling them to be mortgage-free more quickly without having to use up their savings, which will remain untouched.

As interest is usually calculated daily, every pound in all of your accounts linked to the mortgage means daily interest savings.

Credit cards and other debts

Interest rates are now so low on credit cards (0% for limited periods in many cases) and personal loans that it is not surprising that consumer debt now stands at over £1 trillion.

However, if you are retired or living on a fixed income, you may find it hard to qualify for the best rates as lenders credit score these and offer the lowest rates only to those with the best credit history, long-term job security and a high income.

Don't cut up your credit cards
As it can be difficult to get a new credit card when you are on a fixed income, keep any existing cards you have as they can be useful when paying for larger items.

Remember, provided you pay the balance in full each month, you will pay no interest, and if you keep your account in good order, you should be able to keep your credit limit. Also, think twice about borrowing on the card (instead use it as a payment method). When you are on a fixed-income you may be able to afford only the interest on the debt, but not to repay the debt itself.

Clearing your debts more quickly

If you can afford to, it is advisable to clear your debts as quickly as possible. Pay off the loans, credit cards and store cards and other credit deals with the highest rates of interest first. Always check that there are no penalties for early repayment before doing this.

If you cannot afford to repay these high-rate borrowings, consider a consolidation loan.

- You may be able to combine borrowings with rates as high as 20 per cent into one low-cost loan.
- Paying off the loan more quickly will result in higher monthly repayments but a lower overall interest bill.
- However, if affordability is a problem, repaying the loan over several years will mean lower monthly repayments.
- Unlike with credit cards and overdrafts, loans are repaid by a set date (the end of the loan term). This is a major advantage – often those with other forms of borrowing never repay what they owe and simply service the interest each month. So you can continue to owe £2,000 on a credit card for many years, with this balance rising and falling as you spend more and repay the interest. However, the same amount owed on a loan will gradually reduce each month until, say, after three or five years, the debt is totally repaid.
- Alliance & Leicester has found that a typical consumer with total debts of £5,000 could save £1,213.56 in interest payments by consolidating these to a low-rate loan over three years.

Warning Avoid consolidation loans that are secured on your property. If you fail to keep up with repayments you could lose your home.

Dealing with money problems

Avoid debt-advice companies that claim to be able to eliminate your debt problems. Deal with reputable lenders, and if you run into trouble talk to your local Citizens Advice Bureau.

Always tell a lender if you are going to miss a payment and give a reason why (ill-health, for example). You may be able to arrange a repayment holiday or have your debt frozen (no further interest added).

Make it a priority to pay off those debts that have the biggest impact. If you fail to pay your mortgage your home could be repossessed. If you fail to pay your gas bill, you could be disconnected.

Further information

Age Concern produces a useful guide called *Dealing with Money Problems*. For a copy, call (0800) 009 966 or download it from www.ageconcern.org.uk.

Chapter 10

Motoring costs

Motor insurance

As you get older your insurance premiums drop – to reflect the fact that you are considered a safer driver – before rising as you reach your 70s.

The average car insurance paid by the under-25s in the period to April 2005 was £917.59, dropping to £490.79 for the under-50s. For those over 50 the average premium dropped to £380.45, before rising to £428.63 for the over-65s, according to a survey by Consumer Intelligence done in April 2005.

However, these average premiums can be cut substantially by shopping around. This is how premiums varied in April 2005 according to the online price-comparison site www.insurancesupermarket.com.

Motor insurance for a retired male driving 10,000 miles per year, based in Coventry (CV3), driving VW Golf SE 1.6 16v kept overnight on driveway, registered 2003, £10,000 value, 5 years NCD, 10 years licence, fully comprehensive, £100 voluntary excess.

	Individual aged 70	
Provider	**Annual premium**	**Excess**
Cheapest – Quinn-Direct	£195.45	£175
Help the Aged	£289.80	£100
Saga	£299.48	£150
Most expensive – Asda	£319.99	£100
Average premium	£ 276.18	

Note Different insurers will be best or worst buys depending on where you live, the age and make of your car, and your past driving history.

In addition to shopping around, other ways to cut your premiums include the following.

- Choosing an insurer that rewards safer drivers. Some offer higher maximum no claims discounts than others.
- If you have four years or more of no claims, you can protect your bonus (a discount of up to 70 per cent on your premiums) by paying an extra premium.
- If you only clock up a low mileage each year, find out if you can get a reduced premium as a result.
- Keep your car off the road – in a garage or on your driveway. You can usually get a lower premium as a result.
- Think twice about adding younger drivers to your policy – their premiums may be higher. Also, they may already be insured to drive any car, depending on their policy.
- Opt for a higher excess (for example, £250) as this could lead to a further £20 off your premium.

Motor breakdown cover

Roadside assistance is a competitive market and you can easily cut your cost of cover by shopping around and reducing the amount of cover.

Consider if you really need a replacement car should yours break down and what extras you can do without. Some providers reward those who do not claim – or claim rarely – with a form of no-claims discount. Premiums vary from £28 to over £100, so it pays to shop around.

Driving licences

What happens if I suffer from a medical condition?

You must tell the Driver and Vehicle Licensing Agency (DVLA)* if you have ever had, or currently suffer from, a medical condition or disability that may affect your driving. You must inform the agency immediately and not wait until your licence is due for renewal.

You must also provide details of a medical condition or disability that has become worse since your licence was issued or if you develop a new medical condition or disability, as it may affect your fitness to drive. Failure to do so is a criminal offence and is punishable by a fine of up to £1,000.

You can notify the DVLA by telephone. Remember to quote your full name, date of birth and or driver number (if known). You must also give details of your specific medical condition or disability in order that you can be sent the appropriate medical questionnaire.

What happens if I become disabled?

In addition to informing the DVLA, apply for a disabled badge for parking. You will also become exempt from road-user charges such as the congestion charge in London (provided you register with Transport for London first).

People who fall into one of the following categories automatically qualify for a disabled badge:

- the registered blind (when being driven by another person)
- recipients of the higher rate of the mobility component of the Disability Living Allowance
- recipients of a war pensioner's mobility supplement
- owners of a vehicle supplied by a government health department
- holders of a valid driving licence and having severe disability in both upper limbs and being unable to turn by hand the steering wheel of a vehicle, even if that wheel is fitted with a turning knob.

People who do not fit into one of these categories but who are either unable to walk or who can walk only with very considerable difficulty may be able to apply for a badge under the discretionary category. This will involve an assessment by a social work team member and may require a medical assessment.

If you think that you would qualify for a disabled person's parking permit, then you should ring your local council's social services office (in Scotland the social work department). The staff there will be able to advise you and can send you the application form and, if necessary, arrange an appointment for an assessment.

You will be asked to supply two passport-sized photographs and, if your application is approved, pay a small administrative charge. Currently this is £2.00. Your badge should normally reach you within three weeks of approval and will be valid for three years.

Where is the badge valid?

Badge-holders may usually park on single- or double-yellow lines for up to three hours in England and Wales, (followed by a minimum gap of one hour) and without time limit in Scotland. Supermarkets and public buildings also offer disabled parking bays.

Renewing your licence at 70 or over

You will automatically be sent D46 and D750 forms 90 days before your seventieth birthday. You must complete these application forms and return them with your paper licence, original documentation confirming your identity and a passport-type size colour photograph taken against a plain light background.

If you have a photocard licence you will be sent form D46 every three years. Renewing your licence after the age of 70 is free.

Other motoring costs

It is worth budgeting for these when you are on a fixed income because motoring costs can quickly add up.

According to the AA, the average cost of running a car worth up to £10,000 when new is almost £2,000 a year – before you have bought any fuel. This includes £125 on the road tax, £406 for insurance and £40 for breakdown cover; the rest is made up of the cost of capital and depreciation (over £1,000 a year).

In addition, you need to budget for servicing and labour, replacement parts, an MOT when the car is over three years old, wear and tear of tyres, and parking costs.

Further information

DVLA (0870) 600 0301; www.dvla.gov.uk

Chapter 11

Travel insurance

Older people who wish to travel find that getting insurance can be problematic. Not only can it become very expensive, it can be hard to obtain. Some insurers have an upper age limit while others refuse to cover you if you have a medical condition.

Only half of insurers provide cover for those up to 79, and a tiny number have no age limit at all. The remainder may stop providing cover once you reach 65 or 70.

What do I need to know before buying cover?
Do not travel without cover Filling in form E111 to provide some medical cover in European countries (the form is available from post offices) is no substitute for cover. You will need insurance to pay the costs of being flown back to the UK if you have a serious injury and to cover your possessions against theft.

Save money if you are a regular traveller Opt for an annual policy if you travel abroad two or three times a year – it will be much cheaper.

Do not buy from your travel agent Policies tend to be far more expensive if bought from travel agents than if you shop around.

Buy a policy when you book your holiday A significant number of claims are for cancellation – owing to ill-health or bereavement, for example. If you delay buying cover until you are about to travel, it may be too late to make a claim.

What if I have an existing medical condition?
If you have a pre-existing medical condition, some insurers will simply refuse to cover you. If they will cover you, remember to provide full details of any problem – a heart condition or a bad back, for example. If you have to make a claim you do not want

it turned down because you failed to disclose enough information.

If an old health problem re-occurs you may find that you have to pay all your medical bills yourself or that the cancellation of your holiday is not covered.

When you buy your policy you may not be asked for adequate information so always ring the helpline and check that cover will be provided. Often you find out that you are not covered only when the policy documentation arrives and you read an exclusion clause in the small print.

There are several insurers that offer products specifically for those with pre-existing medical conditions. An insurance broker can help you to find one.

How much can I save by shopping around?

According to the website www.insurancesupermarket.co.uk this is how the cost of insurance varies.

Travel insurance for an individual aged 70. All policies include baggage and cancellation, and are quoted for two weeks to Spain.

Single trip		Annual worldwide multi-trip	
Provider	Premium	Provider	Premium
Cheapest			
Rapid Insure	£18.50	Rapid Insure*	£83.85
Saga	£50.86	Saga	N/A
Most expensive			
MRL Insurance Direct	£89.00	MRL Insurance Direct	£269.00
Average premium	£52.79	Average premium	£176.42

* includes winter sports.

Chapter 12

Private medical insurance

Another cost that rises as you age is private medical insurance. The charity Help the Aged claims that medical insurance premiums for older people increased by 109 per cent over the decade to 2004. The rise will be about the same in the future as premiums continue to rocket, with the average annual premium for a 50-year-old costing more than £1,000 a year.

According to the website www.insurancesupermarket.com, those in their 60s pay about 60 per cent more than policyholders in their 20s, but there are ways to cut costs of premiums.

- **Shop around** Premiums vary by as much as £200 a month.
- **Buy reduced cover** A cash plan which pays out if you need treatment rather than paying for the treatment itself, or a policy that integrates with the NHS paying for cover only if you have to wait for a certain period of time.
- **Opt for a higher excess** Like any form of insurance, you can arrange an excess to keep premiums down. To do this, however, there is the element of taking a certain amount of responsibility for your own healthcare. Some companies offer private medical insurance (PMI) plans that incorporate an excess of £1,500 for those under 60 and £3,000 for the over-60s. Research shows that 80 per cent of all claims are for treatment costs of £1,500 or less.
- **Pay as you go** A large number of people over 60 have stopped paying for PMI because of the soaring costs. Instead, they pay for treatment as they need it – out of their savings. The 'pay-as-you-go' market is the fastest-growing sector of private medical treatment.
- **Don't claim** If you can use the NHS for most of your treat-

ment and therefore can limit your claims on your PMI policy, you may qualify for a no-claims discount of up to 50 per cent.

- **Restrict your cover** Some policies for the over-55s limit treatment to lung, heart and cancer treatments and outpatient consultations, so any physiotherapy or dental treatment will not be covered.

Note There is no longer any tax relief on private medical insurance premiums for older people.

How do I find the best deal?

Shopping around for medical insurance is very difficult because each insurer offers a wide range of policies and costs vary widely. Also, any pre-existing medical conditions will affect the premium you pay so you should discuss your needs with an insurance broker who can find the most suitable – and affordable – package to meet your requirements.

Private medical insurance – along with other forms of general insurance – is now covered by Financial Services Authority rules, so you should expect your insurance broker to give you clear information about the policy and detailed information as to why it is being recommended.

How much can I save by shopping around?

Monthly premium for medical insurance: all providing a superior level of cover, with no voluntary excess and for non-smokers.

Male aged 65		Male aged 25	
Provider	Premium	Provider	Premium
Cheapest			
General & Medical	£90.72	General & Medical	£36.29
Foundation PP Freedom		Foundation PP Freedom	
Most expensive			
InterGlobal HealthCare	£291.00	Secure Health	£60.06
Ultracare Plus		Executive Single	
Average Premium	£190.86	Average Premium	£48.18

Source: www.insurancesupermarket.com.

Part Four
MINIMIZING YOUR TAX BILL

Introduction

Take just two minutes to fill out one simple form and save £53. That is how easy it would be for some 6 million non-taxpayers to save a collective £318 million a year by ensuring they did not pay tax on their savings interest.

On average, UK adults waste £133 each year in tax according to IFA Promotion, the organization which promotes independent financial advice. That is an unnecessary £5.7 billion this year in tax.

Reducing your tax liability does not mean you have to employ an expensive accountant as the following examples show.

- **If you save** Use up your annual individual savings account (ISA) allowance – £127 million in tax could be avoided each year by sheltering investments in ISAs, or moving savings from an ordinary deposit or savings account to an ISA. Also, consider a friendly society savings account or products from National Savings & Investments as additional tax-efficient savings options.
- **If you fill in a tax return** Sort out your self-assessment – £418 million in wasted money could be wiped out by all forms arriving present and correct by the 31 January deadline.
- **All taxpayers** Maximize your personal tax allowances – £431 million goes begging each year, £318 million through non-taxpayers failing to claim tax back on banks and building society savings accounts, and a further £113 million by taxpayers not transferring savings accounts to non-taxpaying spouses, if appropriate, so that the tax liability on the savings is lower, or none.
- **If you have assets over £300,000** Plan your inheritance – an

extra £1.6 billion could go to chosen heirs by planning properly to avoid inheritance tax (IHT) liabilities. This is lost through not writing life assurance policies in trust, not thinking about IHT allowances and, worst of all, by not making a will at all.

- **If you save for a pension** Top up your pension pot – £613 million could be spared by optimizing contributions to personal or company pension schemes, or by making Additional Voluntary Contributions.
- **If you have capital gains** Use your allowance efficiently, perhaps by transferring assets between spouses to make the most of the lower-rate taxpayer – £333 million could be saved in this way.
- **If you give to charity** Some £691 million more could go to good causes by using tax-efficient means of charitable giving, such as Gift Aid.

Read the chapters in this section to find out more about easy ways to minimize your tax bill.

Chapter 13

Income tax

Income tax is an annual tax based on an individual's income for a tax year, which starts on 6 April and ends on 5 April. It is charged at different rates on different bands of taxable income, which is income above the individual's personal tax allowance (in other words, the amount that can be earned before paying tax).

Tax rates and tax bands

2005/6 tax year

Starting rate	10 per cent	First £2,090 of taxable income
Basic rate	22 per cent	next £30,310 of income
Higher rate	40 per cent	on income over £32,400

These rates and thresholds (which often change at the start of each year) apply to non-savings and non-dividend income. So they are the rates that apply to earnings for employment and self-employment, for example, but not to savings interest.

Each rate of tax applies only to income that falls within that tax band. So an individual can be taxed at the lower rate, basic rate and higher rate. If, for example, taxable income (that is, income above the level of the tax allowance – see below) is £10,000, then the first £2,090 is taxed at 10 per cent giving a tax bill of £209, and the remaining £7,910 is taxed at 22 per cent, giving a tax take of £1,740.2. The total tax paid would be £1,949.20. Higher-rate taxpayers pay tax only on taxable income over £32,400 – not on all their income.

Tax rates on savings and investments

Tax rates for savings income are charged at 20 per cent (basic rate) and 40 per cent (higher rate).

Dividends are charged at 10 per cent (basic rate) and 32.5 per cent (higher rate).

Savings income is added to other income to determine the rate paid. So an individual who pays tax at the basic rate may find that savings income is taxed at the higher rate as it pushes his taxable income into the higher tax band.

Tax on savings income is usually deducted at source at the rate of 20 per cent. This lower rate is the rate paid by basic-rate taxpayers, even though they pay 22 per cent on their other income.

Tax-free income

Although most types of income – and even payments in kind – are subject to income tax, some are exempt.

- income from tax-free savings schemes including individual savings accounts (ISAs), National Savings Certificates and the first £70 of interest from the National Savings Ordinary Account
- grants – home improvement grants etc.
- redundancy payments (up to £30,000) and certain other payments on loss of job
- some employee benefits such as a subsidized canteen
- some social security benefits including: Child Benefit and allowances, housing benefits, Council Tax Benefit, maternity allowance, Christmas bonus for pensioners, Bereavement Benefit, Incapacity Benefit paid for the first 28 weeks of sickness, Incapacity Benefit paid to someone who was receiving invalidity benefit paid before 13 April 1995, provided there has not been a break of more than eight weeks in the claim, Attendance Allowance, Disability Living

Allowance, war disablement pension, war widow's pension, working families' tax credit and maintenance payments from a former spouse
- Premium Bond, National Lottery and gambling prizes.

While state benefits paid to those unable to work owing to illness or unemployment (statutory sick pay and Jobseekers' Allowance) are both taxable, people who take out insurance policies to cover them against unemployment, accident, sickness, disability or infirmity will find that these benefits are tax-free if the policy is:

- a mortgage payment protection policy, which pays the mortgage interest
- permanent health insurance, mainly taken out by the self-employed
- creditor insurance, which meets loan or bill payments
- long-term care insurance, but only if the policy is taken out before the need for care becomes apparent.

Taxable income

All other income, including the following, are subject to income tax:

- income from employment – including salary, bonus, overtime, tips or gratuities, holiday pay, maternity leave pay and sick-pay
- many benefits in kind/employee perks (individuals are generally taxed on the value of these)
- income/profits from self-employment or partnership
- savings interest and investment income/dividends
- pension income (pensions from employers, personal pensions and state pensions)
- income from property
- certain state benefits including Jobseeker's Allowance, statutory sick pay, statutory maternity pay and invalid care allowance.

Tax allowances

Taxpayers do not have to pay income tax on all of their income. Everyone is entitled to what is called a tax allowance – the amount that can be earned before paying tax.

In most cases, individuals receive these allowances automatically. The allowances are usually included in their Pay As You Earn (PAYE) Tax Code and are used to reduce the amount of tax deducted from salaries and company pensions. Alternatively, people can claim allowances when filling in their tax returns and deduct the allowances from income when calculating the amount of tax that needs to be paid.

The basic personal allowance

Everyone is entitled to the basic personal allowance. It is the amount that everyone can earn before paying tax. The allowance usually rises at the start of each tax year in line with inflation and is announced in every new Budget.

The allowance can only be used once. Those who have more than one job or more than one source of income – an occupational pension and part-time earnings, say – can set the personal allowance against only one lot of income (usually their main source).

The personal allowance for the 2005/6 tax year was £4,895.

Tax allowances for pensioners

The personal allowance is increased for older people. Those aged 65 to 74 had an allowance of £7,090 in the 2005/6 tax year; for those over 75 the figure rose to £7,220. This allowance usually rises at the start of each new tax year.

Therefore, pensioners can earn much more than those below the age of 65 before having to pay tax. However, there is an allowance restriction which means that those on higher incomes benefit less than those on lower incomes.

Those whose taxable income exceeds £19,500 for the 2005/6

Tax Tips
- To qualify for an age allowance individuals must have reached the required age by the end of the tax year, not the start. Even those born on 5 April (the last day of the tax year) can still claim age-related allowances for the entire tax year once they reach 65.
- Pensioners who earn more than the allowance restriction limit of £19,500 should plan their investments carefully. If they can defer income to later years or switch to investments that produce capital gains rather than income, they can reduce their taxable income to below the threshold and make full use of their age allowances. They should also consider tax-free investments as even if these produce an income this does not affect the age allowance.

tax year will see their allowances reduced by £1 for every £2 earned over this limit. The allowance stops being reduced only when it is cut to the basic personal allowance of £4,895. So the more a pensioner earns, the less tax savings he or she makes.

This is how earnings reduce age allowances.

Arthur Pensioner is 69 and had a total income from pensions and investments of £22,000 for the 2005/6 tax year. This exceeded the £19,500 threshold by £2,500.

His age increased personal allowance is £7,090. However, this will be reduced by £1 for every £2 in excess of £19,500, so in his case his allowance will be reduced by £2,500 divided by 2, which is £1,250. His allowance will therefore be £7,090 - £1,250 = £5,840.

Married couple's allowance

This is no longer given to married couples unless they were born before 6 April 1935.

For the 2005/6 tax year the allowance was £5,090 for those aged 65 to 74, and £5,975 for those over 75.

Note It is in addition to the basic personal allowance.

Once again, this allowance may be reduced if earnings exceed £19,500 for the 2005/6 tax year.

Tax tips

- When calculating total income (to see if an individual exceeds the £19,500 earnings threshold) not all income needs to be included. Only income that is assessable for tax needs to be added up. Income not assessable for tax, which includes interest credited to an ISA, dividends paid into an ISA, the growth in value of National Savings Certificates, amounts withdrawn from insurance bonds (up to the 5 per cent limit) and income received under the rent-a-room scheme, is excluded. Pensioners with earnings reaching or exceeding the threshold should therefore consider the alternative sources of income listed above. That way their age allowances will no longer be reduced because of their earnings or at least they will be reduced by a lower amount.

- Another way to reduce the assessable income so that earnings do not exceed the threshold is to increase the amount of outgoings that qualify for tax relief. This could include making a gift to charity under the Gift Aid scheme. Donations through the scheme are treated as tax-allowable deductions and can be used for the purpose of reducing total income for the age allowance. To donate £100 to charity, taxpayers only need to donate £78 – the remaining £22 is claimed by the charity from the Inland Revenue. Even so, when calculating their income pensioners can reduce it by the full £100.

  Note Each spouse qualifies for his or her own personal allowance. So if one spouse is over 65 and the other under 65 only the older partner will qualify for the increased age allowance. Likewise, if one partner is aged 75 or over that partner will qualify for an even higher age allowance.

- It will pay to put income-generating investments and assets in the name of the older spouse as he or she will qualify for a higher age allowance and therefore be able to earn more before paying tax. Just as individual partners each qualify for their own age allowance, when calculating whether or not their allowances should be reduced because their income exceeds the earning threshold, they need to do separate calculations. So if one partner has an income above the threshold he or she will suffer a reduction in the age allowance even if the other partner has earnings below the threshold. This is why it pays to split the ownership of assets – and therefore the income they generate – so that neither exceeds the threshold.

However, the personal allowance will be reduced first and only after that has been reduced to the level of the basic personal allowance will the married couple's allowance be affected.

The rate of relief for the married couple's allowance for people born before 6 April 1935 is 10 per cent. So the maximum benefit is only £597.50.

The married couple's allowance is given if either spouse has reached the required age at the end of the tax year. It is given even if one partner is much younger.

The married couple's allowance is made up of two parts:

- a minimum amount (of £2,280 in 2005/6). This is restricted to 10 per cent, so it is worth only £228
- a second amount dependent on your or your spouse's age bracket:

£3,625 (if you or your spouse was born before 6 April 1935 but is under 75)

£3,695 (if you or your spouse is over 75).

Again, these allowances are restricted to 10 per cent so are worth only £362.50 and £369.50 respectively.

When these two parts are added together they come to:

- £5,905 (if you or your spouse was born before 6 April 1935 but is under 75)
- £5,975 (if you or your spouse is over 75).

This gives a maximum tax saving of £590.50 and £597.50 respectively.

The minimum amount will always be due whatever the level of the husband's income (although you can change who receives the allowance, see below). The age-related amount can be reduced if the husband's income exceeds certain limits, whatever the level of the allowance. So even if the husband has a very high income, he will still receive at least £2,280 of married couple's allowance.

Can we change who receives the allowance?

Couples can opt for the minimum allowance to go to either spouse (if they both agree) – or to be split between them (a wife can elect to receive half the allowance without her husband's consent). However, if no choice is made, the allowance will always be given to the husband.

The choice must be made (using Inland Revenue Form 18) before the start of the tax year for which it is to have effect. There is no need to make a new election at the start of subsequent tax years unless the couple wishes to change the way the allowance is given.

Even if an election is made, if the wife then has insufficient income to use her part of the married couple's allowance she can transfer the excess back to her husband. Similarly, if a husband cannot make full use of the allowance he can transfer any unused amount to his wife.

How can we save tax if the wife is the higher earner?

If the wife is a higher earner than the husband, she should consider asking for all of the minimum allowance to be used to offset her income rather than his. This is particularly important if the husband has insufficient income to use up his allowances.

The husband gets an allowance of £2,280 – but that allowance is restricted to 10 per cent, so it is worth only £228. If he has no income or very little income, then he will not make any tax savings. This is because the allowance reduces the amount of tax you pay – it is not a cash payment to you.

How do earnings reduce age-related allowances?

As discussed in the previous section, if those in receipt of an age allowance earn more than a certain threshold – £19,500 for the 2005/6 tax year – their allowances are reduced by £1 for every £2 of income in excess of this threshold. In the first instance, the higher age-related personal allowance is reduced.

However, this cannot be reduced to below the personal allowance of £4,895 for the 2005/6 tax year. If there is any unused reduction this will be used to reduce the married couple's allowance. However, once again this cannot be reduced to below the minimum of £2,280.

What happens when one of us dies?

If the husband dies first, the married couple's allowance is set against his income in the year of his death, even if the couple had elected to share the allowance. If the wife dies first, the husband will continue to receive the married couple's allowance for the whole of the tax year in which she dies. However, if a couple marries, the husband and wife are entitled to only a proportion of the married couple's allowance, reflecting the number of months in the year they have been married.

Note Even though the married couple's allowance is set against the husband's income in the year of his death, any unused part can be claimed by the wife.

How do I find out more?

The Inland Revenue produces a leaflet called *IR121 Income Tax and Pensioners.*

Blind person's allowance

This is given to those who are registered blind. In England and Wales this means the person's name appears on the local authority's register of blind persons. In Scotland and Northern Ireland taxpayers need to be so blind that they cannot perform any work for which eyesight is essential.

The allowance for the 2005/6 tax year was £1,610.

If both the husband and wife are blind they can each claim a separate blind person's allowance. If the husband has insufficient income to use all his blind person's allowance he may be able to transfer the allowance or part of it to his wife (or *vice versa* if she is blind).

Using allowances effectively

Each year millions of pounds are wasted by those who fail to use up their allowances or use them effectively. Anyone who earns less than their allowances cannot carry these unused allowances forward to another tax year, so they are lost forever.

Couples should therefore ensure that both partners use up their allowances by transferring income-generating assets to the spouse with no or a low income.

The same applies to couples in which one spouse is a higher-rate taxpayer and the other falls well within the basic-rate tax band. By giving income to the lower-earner or putting assets in joint names, more income will fall into the basic rate rather than the higher rate, leading to overall tax savings for the couple.

Note It is not possible to transfer unused basic personal allowances to a spouse. However, the whole of the higher age-related married couple's allowance may be transferred to the wife if the husband has insufficient income to use it himself. In addition, the blind person's allowance can be transferred.

Tax codes

Tax codes apply only to those paid income under the PAYE scheme (that is, employees and those in receipt of occupational pensions). These codes tell employers how much tax to deduct. The Inland Revenue issues a code for each employee or pensioner, and sends them a note explaining what their code means. Those who have not received one should find their coding notice on their payslip or pension notification.

Some taxpayers receive several coding notices a year, and others, who have straightforward tax affairs, may not receive one at all. Most notices are sent out in the spring, giving details of what will apply from the next tax year.

Anyone who receives a PAYE coding notice should check it thoroughly. It is not unknown for mistakes to be made – particularly if the individual's circumstances have changed. A leaflet should be enclosed telling taxpayers how to correct any errors. An incorrect amount of tax could be deducted if the code is wrong.

Tax codes are made up of a letter and a number, for example, 489L.

The number tells the employer how much tax-free pay or pension each employee or former employee is allowed in each tax year, but with the last digit deleted. So, for example, those with a personal allowance of £4,895, should find the number 489 on their tax code.

Note This allowance is spread evenly throughout the year. It does not mean that the first £4,895 earned in any one year is tax-free, which would mean a tax-free April and May and a heavily taxed February and March. Those who are paid monthly will be able to earn one-twelfth of their allowances each month before paying tax.

PAYE tax code letters

These are easier to check than the tax code numbers.

L   This is given to taxpayers who get the basic personal allowance.

HP   This is given to taxpayers who get the full higher age-related personal allowance for those aged between 65 and 74.

V   This is given to taxpayers who get the full higher age-related personal allowance for someone aged 65 to 74 and the full married couple's allowance for those born before 6 April 1935 (these taxpayers are usually basic-rate taxpayers).

Y   This is given to taxpayers who get the full age-related personal allowance for someone aged 75 and over.

T   Tax will not be adjusted by the employer but by the tax office. These codes are issued if the tax office needs to review the tax code.

DO   This is given to taxpayers who have earnings elsewhere and tells the employer to tax all earnings from this source at the higher rate and that allowances have been allocated elsewhere.

BR   This is given to taxpayers who have earnings from elsewhere and tells the employer to tax all earnings from this source at the basic rate and that all the allowances have been given elsewhere.

NT   No tax is paid on this income.

Those aged 65 or over may see an estimate of their total annual income on their tax code. This is listed as 'estimated income'. The reason for this is that age-related allowances depend on income. Check that the Inland Revenue is not overestimating the amount.

Chapter 14

Tax-saving for the over-65s

Retirement may be a time when most people want to put their feet up and take life easy, but the Inland Revenue does not see it that way. Tax gets more complicated for the over-65s: they are entitled to tax allowances not available to younger taxpayers (these were detailed in the previous chapter), but they also lose some or all of these allowances if they earn more than a certain threshold.

Pension income

Most pension income is taxable, including:

- the basic state pension – which, although paid gross (without tax deducted), is taxable if, once it is added to all other income, the individual's total taxable income exceeds his or her allowances
- the State Earnings-Related Pension Scheme (SERPS) – or any other additional state pension such as the graduated pension or the age addition for those over 80
- occupational or employers' pensions – these are paid net of tax through the Pay As You Earn (PAYE) scheme.

However, the war disablement and widow's pensions are not taxable, and neither are cold weather payments.

Those about to retire should contact their tax office to tell them that they plan to draw a pension. They should give their tax office an estimate of income after retirement, including income from the state pension and from savings. This is so the Inland Revenue can issue a PAYE code.

The tax deducted from an employer's pension using this PAYE code may seem higher than when the individual was an employee. This is to reflect the fact that the retiree now receives untaxed income (such as the state pension). Tax due on this income is collected through the PAYE code.

On retirement, the PAYE code should be adjusted automatically to reflect the fact that the individual has reached 65 and now qualifies for higher age-related tax allowances. Even so, individuals should check that their PAYE code is correct.

- A code ending with a V means the pensioner is receiving the married couple's allowance for those born before 6 April 1935 and pays tax at the basic rate.
- A code ending with a P means the individual receives the higher age-related personal allowance for those aged 65 to 74.
- A code ending in a letter Y means the individual receives the higher age-related personal allowance for those aged 75 or over.
- A code ending in a T means the individual does not receive the full age allowances because his or her income exceeds the threshold (£19,500 for the 2005/6 tax year).

What happens if I decide to work past state pension age?

Those who work past state pension age will have their state pension added to other taxable income when determining the amount of tax they need to pay. However, they will not have to pay any more National Insurance once they reach state pension age. (Those who are self-employed will continue to pay Class 4 contributions until the end of the tax year in which they reach state pension age.)

Those who want to work past state pension age can defer taking the pension for as long as they want. As a result they will receive a higher pension when they do retire. It will be increased by 7.5 per cent for each year retirement is put off.

Non-taxpaying pensioners

Pensioners who are non-taxpayers can register to receive any savings interest paid gross (without tax deducted) by filling in form R85 available from banks and building societies. Any tax already deducted can be reclaimed.

Those who need to pay tax at the starting rate of 10 per cent can also claim a tax refund.

Pensions from employer pension schemes will be paid without tax deducted if the pensioner's income is less than the personal and age allowances (the amount that can be earned each year before paying tax). So no tax should be paid, and no tax should need to be reclaimed.

Pensions paid by retirement annuity contracts are usually paid after basic-rate tax has been taxed off. Pensioners whose total taxable income is less than their tax allowances can ask for this income to be paid without tax deducted. Ask for form R89 from the retirement annuity provider.

Those who need to pay some tax, but who can also receive some annuity income free of tax, will need to claim a tax refund from the Inland Revenue.

Tax and death

The married couple's allowance is not reduced in the year of death of either spouse.

In addition, both are entitled to the full personal allowance and any age-related allowance for the entire tax year in which they die.

The bereavement payment is also tax-free. This £2,000 payment is paid as soon as an individual is widowed but is only paid if the late husband or wife was not entitled to the state retirement pension when he or she died or the surviving spouse was under state pension age at the time of death.

Benefits paid on death – the Widowed Parent's Allowance and Bereavement Allowance – are both taxable.

Tax tip

As mentioned in Chapter 13, if the husband's income does not exceed his allowances, then any unused married couple's allowance can be transferred to the widow. However, unused personal allowances cannot be transferred. The married couple's allowance will first be used against the husband's income – even if the couple shared the allowance. If the couple shared the allowance any unused part can be transferred to the wife upon her husband's death.

Maintenance relief

Provided one spouse (either the payer of maintenance or the recipient – a divorced or separated spouse) was born before 6 April 1935, then tax relief on qualifying maintenance payments can be claimed. Individuals can claim 10 per cent tax relief on payments up to £2,280 for the 2005/6 tax year (giving maximum tax relief of £228).

Tax relief is not given on maintenance paid to, or for, children. The spouse receiving maintenance does not have to pay tax on this amount.

Chapter 15

Charitable donations and tax

This chapter sets out ways to minimize the tax you pay when you make charitable donations.

It is possible to give to a good cause – and at the same time save tax. However, putting a few pounds in a collection box will not help you save tax: you must make your donations through one of the Inland Revenue's approved schemes. By using tax-efficient schemes for charitable giving, some £550 million more could go to good causes each year, according to IFA Promotion.

Gift Aid

Donations to charity through the Gift Aid scheme qualify for basic-rate tax relief. The scheme has no minimum donation.

Higher-rate taxpayers can claim higher-rate tax relief on any donations they make. Although the charity they donate to receives the basic-rate tax relief, it is the donor who gets an 18 per cent tax relief (the difference between the basic- and higher-rate tax rates). This must be claimed through the taxpayer's tax office.

Other donations

It is also possible to give listed shares (shares in stock-market-quoted companies) and units in a UK-authorized unit trust or shares in an open-ended investment company to a charity and obtain tax relief. Tax relief is based on their market value (inclusive of any costs of disposal).

For more information ask for Inland Revenue leaflet IR178 *Giving Shares and Securities to Charity.*

Tax Tips

- Non-taxpayers or starting-rate taxpayers should think twice about using Gift Aid as it could cost them money. They may have to repay tax reclaimed by the charity (in part or whole depending on their rate of tax).
- Pensioners whose income is close to or slightly above the maximum allowed before age-related allowances are reduced (£19,500 for the 2005/6 tax year) can keep their income within the limit by deducting the gross amount of gifts made during the tax year.

Tax Tip

Those facing a hefty capital gains tax (CGT) bill – or wanting to reduce their gains to below the threshold of £8,500 for the 2005/6 tax year – can consider giving some shares to charity. No CGT arises on these gifts. So, in addition to receiving income tax relief at 40 per cent, higher-rate taxpayers can make CGT savings too.

Chapter 16

Tax relief

There are very few ways to get tax back from the Inland Revenue now that most forms of tax relief including MIRAS (mortgage interest tax relief) have been scrapped. Investing in a pension is one of the few options (apart from a few more high-risk investment schemes).

Even if you have retired you can still contribute to a pension and receive tax relief.

- **Non-taxpayers** do not have to pay tax to qualify for tax relief.
- **Non-earners** do not have to earn money to save in a pension and receive tax relief.
- **Higher-rate taxpayers** can receive tax relief at the top 40 per cent rate, so investing £1,000 costs only £600.
- **You can take 25 per cent as a tax-free lump sum** once you have received your tax relief. This is known as immediate vesting.

How much can I contribute?
If you have already retired or left an occupational pension scheme, your main option is a stakeholder pension.

Everyone can contribute up to £3,600 a year and receive basic-rate tax relief. This means that you need pay in only £2,808 – the remainder will be invested by the Inland Revenue.

Contributions over £3,600 can be made based on your earnings. However, even those with little or no earnings may be able to get around this rule as contributions over £3,600 can continue to be made for up to five years after an individual's earnings have ceased.

The rules are due to be changed from April 2006. However, for pension contributions up to that date the maximum that could be paid in based on age was:

Age	Percentage of earnings
51 to 55	30
56 to 60	35
61 to 74	40
75 and over	nil

Under the new rules, there is a lifetime limit on pension funds of £1.5 million, with a maximum annual contribution limit of £215,000.

Why pay into a pension when I already (or am about to) receive one?

Paying into a pension is a highly tax-efficient way to invest because:

- contributions attract tax relief
- the money grows tax-free
- lump sums taken on maturity can be up to 25 per cent of the fund and are tax- free.

However, the new pension rules from April 2006 do not require those whose funds are less than £15,000 to buy a pension (before that date there was a cap of £2,500) and you may therefore be able to take the entire amount as a cash lump sum rather than buying a very small pension.

When can I take my pension?

You can take your pension from any age from 50 (rising to 55 from 2010) to 75 – although there are proposals to increase this to 85.

You do not have to retire from work or reach state pension age to take your personal or stakeholder pension.

Chapter 17

Tax rules for people living abroad

Thousands of UK residents each year go to live abroad, often to retire to a sunnier climate. However, this does not always mean that they escape UK tax.

Even if an individual is not resident in the UK he or she is still liable for tax on any income 'arising' in the UK. If the individual is classed as a UK resident for tax purposes he or she will be liable to UK tax on all of his or her worldwide income.

Those planning to live overseas should ensure that they are no longer classed as UK residents for tax purposes. That way they escape UK tax on their worldwide income. However, they may have to pay tax in their new country of residence, so they should check that the tax regime there is more favourable than in the UK.

Non-resident rules

Generally, an individual will be taxed on any money earned overseas as well as any UK income, unless he or she is absent from the UK for an entire tax year.

However, trips home are allowed, provided the non-resident:

- spends fewer than 183 days in the UK in any tax year
- spends fewer than 91 days a year over a four-year average in the UK.

Note that days of arrival and departure are not normally included in this test.

Those who fail to meet these requirements may find that they are taxed in the UK on their worldwide income and taxed in the country where they live. As a result they will be taxed twice.

There are treaties in place to ensure that this does not happen and that any double payment of tax can be reclaimed.

Can I still claim my personal allowance?

Non-residents may be able to continue to claim the UK personal tax allowance (of £4,895 for 2005/6) against any income subject to UK tax.

The rules covering residency relate to entire tax years. However, this does not affect personal allowances. Those arriving or leaving the UK partway through the tax year can still claim the full personal allowances (they are not apportioned depending on the number of months spent in the UK).

How can I keep my income free of UK tax if I live abroad?

Non-residents should transfer investments overseas so that income can be earned free of UK tax in the years they are non-resident for UK tax. A bank in an offshore tax haven will pay interest gross (without tax deducted).

Tax Tips

- Those non-resident in the UK should make the most of their tax status by selling assets to generate tax-free capital gains in the years they are overseas.
- Those planning to rent out their UK property when they move overseas should note that rental income is subject to UK tax even if the individual is not a UK resident for tax purposes. Tax should be withheld at the basic rate by the tenant or managing agent. However, if the landlord is registered for self-assessment and has up-to-date tax affairs he or she can apply to receive rent gross. The Inland Revenue's leaflet IR140, *Non-resident Landlords, Their Agents and Tenants,* is useful.
- Non-residents can also apply to receive interest from savings gross (without tax deducted).

Chapter 18

Capital gains tax

Capital gains tax (CGT) is the tax on gains made when an asset is sold. So, while income is subject to income tax, profits are subject to CGT.

CGT is quite complex. A potential CGT liability can occur when an asset is disposed of – and that can include being given away. In addition, if a loss is made on the disposal of an asset, this loss can often be used to offset any gains to reduce a CGT bill.

As with the income tax personal allowance, everyone is entitled to a personal CGT allowance each year. It is the amount that can be earned before paying tax. For the 2005/6 year it was £8,500, which means everyone could make this amount of gain without suffering any capital gains liability.

The allowance, which usually increases every year following the Budget, applies each tax year. Any unused allowance cannot be carried forward to future years. However, losses made in one tax year can be carried forward to offset against gains made in future years.

Assets given away on death are not subject to CGT and instead may be liable to inheritance tax (see Chapter 25 for more information).

Tax Tip

Millions of investors fail to use up their CGT allowance each year and as a result they are missing out on a valuable tax break. By selling assets each year to create a gain that is below the annual allowance, investors can ensure that they do not build up a substantial CGT liability in future years.

The essentials

Why you should invest for capital growth, not income

The CGT allowance is much higher than the basic personal allowance for income tax and is therefore more valuable. So it is worth considering investments that create a capital gain rather than ones that generate income.

For example, you could sell part of an asset (say, a bundle of shares) when you need more income and, if you time it right, you can receive it free of tax.

CGT is fairly simple to avoid. As a result, fewer than 100,000 taxpayers actually pay the tax each year.

What is subject to CGT?

The gain on the disposal of most assets (for exceptions see *What is likely to be tax-free?* below) is potentially liable to CGT.

The assets most likely to be subject to CGT include shares, unit trusts and other investments, businesses or business assets, second homes, land and property, antiques and works of art, and most assets held for personal or investment purposes (unless they are chattels, see page 227).

What is likely to be tax-free?

Certain assets are exempt from CGT. These include:

- private cars
- a main home (principal private residence) provided it has not been let out or used for business, and also any grounds if they are sold with the property
- gifts between husband and wife
- personal possessions or chattels with a predicted useful life of 50 years or fewer when they are first acquired (see page 227)
- Individual Savings Accounts
- National Savings products
- betting, lottery or pools winnings
- gilts (government stocks) and corporate bonds

- Enterprise Investment Scheme (EIS) and Venture Capital Trust (VCT) shares
- proceeds of most life insurance policies (but not those bought from a third party, known as second-hand or traded endowments)
- financial compensation – for personal injury, for mis-sold personal pension plans – and damages including those for defamation
- foreign currency for personal use
- gifts to charities and certain national institutions/heritage bodies
- most cashbacks
- money or assets which are taxable as part of income or would be subject to income tax.

When is a gain made?

A gain is made when an asset is disposed of. This generally means when it is sold, but it can also mean when an asset is given away, destroyed and an insurance company pays out, sold for less than its market value, or exchanged for another asset.

The date taken for the disposal is the date of sale, when the gift was made or when a capital sum was received (such as an insurance payment).

How the tax is calculated

CGT is based on how much an asset has increased in value during the time the taxpayer has owned it minus certain allowable expenses.

Tax Tip

When a gift is made to charity – or shares transferred to one – no capital gain is made. So those facing a large tax liability could instead donate their shares to a charity and give to a good cause rather than to the Inland Revenue.

So the gain is how much it was sold for (or its value on disposal) minus the initial value when it was bought (or acquired). Investors can then subcontract any allowable expenses when calculating the profit.

Allowable expenses include:

- costs incurred in buying and selling, including valuer's/surveyor's fees and auction fees, as well as advertising costs – but it is not possible to claim the costs/interest on a loan used to purchase the asset
- the cost of legal advice
- stamp duty
- stockbrokers' fees (if only part of an asset is sold, such as part of a block of shares, you can claim a proportion of the costs)
- costs of enhancing the value of the asset – restoration etc; but not maintenance or repairs
- inflation (only if the asset was acquired before 1 April 1998, see pages 229–31).

If an asset is given away, valuation costs needed to work out a chargeable gain can be deducted.

Once the gain has been calculated, any losses made on the disposal of other assets can be deducted to arrive at the total chargeable gain for the tax year. This is then reduced the longer the asset is held, using taper relief (see pages 229–30).

It can sometimes be difficult to get an accurate valuation for an asset (for example, if it is not sold but is destroyed). Those who want the Inland Revenue to check their CGT valuations can ask for form CG34. All they need to do is complete the form and return it to their tax office with any supporting information and documents.

How much tax will I have to pay?

Taxable gains are taxed at the highest rate of income tax an individual pays. The gains are treated as the top slice of an individual's income, which means that the rate depends on which tax band the individual falls into once taxable gains are added to other taxable income.

As with income tax, CGT is charged at three rates:

- 10 per cent starting rate – only if taxable income (income exceeding personal tax allowances) and taxable gains (exceeding the CGT threshold) when added together do not exceed £2,090 (the 2005/6 threshold)
- 20 per cent basic rate – if total taxable income and gains fall in the basic-rate tax band (£2,090 and £30,310 in 2005/6)
- 40 per cent higher rate – for gains that fall into the higher-rate band (this was over £30,310 in 2005/6).

Note A chargeable gain is the amount of gain made before applying the tax-free allowance, losses and any taper relief, whereas a taxable gain is what is made after taking into account these items.

What happens if I make a loss when I sell an asset?

If any losses are made on the disposal of an asset, they can be used to offset or reduce the profits made on the disposal of other assets.

Are my personal possessions exempt from CGT?

The legal term for these personal possessions is 'chattels', meaning tangible, movable property. Chattels cover a range of everyday items, including household furniture, paintings, crockery and china, antiques, first editions of books and silver.

Most chattels will be exempt from CGT because when they are sold no gain is made (they are worth less than when you first bought them). Taxpayers need to include gains on their tax return *only* if the chattel was sold for more than £6,000. If the amount exceeds that, the gain is the amount by which the disposal proceeds exceeds £6,000 multiplied by 5/3. So a gain of £10,000 is calculated as £10,000 - £6,000 = £4,000 multiplied by 5/3 = £6,666. Note that this is the maximum chargeable gain before taper relief. The Inland Revenue leaflet IR293 *Chattels and Capital Gains Tax* gives further details on how to do the calculation and which chattels may be liable for CGT.

Tax tips

- Investors who face a hefty CGT liability may want to consider divesting themselves of any assets that are proving poor investments. By creating a loss on the sale of one asset they can reduce the CGT liability on another. The rules require that losses must be offset against any gains made in the same year; and that if, after using current-year losses, there are still taxable gains above the tax threshold, losses made in any previous years must be used to reduce gains to the level of the tax-free amount.
- It is vital that losses are reported to the tax office – they will not be allowable unless the Inland Revenue has been informed that the taxpayer has made a loss. This must be done within five years and ten months of the end of the tax year in which the loss arose.
- Investors who made a CGT loss that they cannot use to offset gains and who want to carry this forward to use in future tax years must notify their tax office of their intention. However, they have up to six years from the end of the tax year in which the loss is made to do this. So any investor who has only just realized that they have unused CGT losses for past years have plenty of time in which to make use of this tax-saving tip. Note that losses made before 6 April 1996 do not have to be notified to the Inland Revenue within a certain time limit.
- Investors can claim as a loss anything that is destroyed or that no longer has any value (or negligible value) including shares in companies that have gone into liquidation.
- Losses cannot normally be carried back to earlier tax years. However, there is an exception – when someone dies. Their personal representative can carry back any unused allowable losses arising in the tax year in which they die and deduct them from total chargeable gains of the three preceding tax years.

Tax tip

Do not try to get around chattel rules by selling sets of items separately so that each is sold for less than £6,000. The rules require that if, for example, a set of four dining chairs were sold separately for £3,000 each, the proceeds should be taken as being £12,000 and would therefore exceed the £6,000 threshold. If they are sold one at a time to the same person, they may still be regarded as a single asset, even though the sales may have take place at different times, and you could be charged CGT because the total value exceeds £6,000.

I have owned my investments for a long time. Does that mean I will have to pay more tax?

The longer you own an asset, the larger the gain (profit) is likely to be when you sell it. However, the Inland Revenue does give a concession – called taper relief – to take this into account.

Taper relief reduces the amount of capital gain that is charged to tax on the disposal of an asset. The longer the asset has been held after 5 April 1998, the larger the reduction.

Introduced in the Finance Act 1998, taper relief applies to the capital gains of individuals, trusts and the personal representatives of deceased persons, but not to the capital gains of companies.

Different tapers apply to business assets and non-business assets.

The taper reduces the effective CGT rates for a higher rate CGT payer from 40 per cent to 10 per cent for business assets, and from 40 per cent to 24 per cent for non-business assets.

As taper relief cuts the chargeable gain the longer the asset is owned (after 5 April 1998), it may pay to hold on to assets for longer periods as the proportion of any gain on which tax is payable reduces.

How taper relief reduces the tax

Gains on non-business assets

Complete years after 5 April 1998 the asset was held	Percentage of gain chargeable (taper)	Equivalent basic-rate taxpayers	CGT rate higher-rate taxpayers
0	100	20	40
1	100	20	40
2	100	20	40
3	95	19	38
4	90	18	36
5	85	17	34
6	80	16	32
7	75	15	30
8	70	14	28
9	65	13	26
10+	60	12	24

A whole year refers to any continuous period of 12 months – it does not have to coincide with a tax year. Fractions of a year are ignored.

As is evident from the table, investors must own a non-business asset for at least three years before taper relief reduces their tax bill.

What happens to assets I have owned for even longer?

The indexation allowance, which enables those disposing of assets to deduct the effects of inflation so they do not pay tax on gains that are purely caused by inflationary price increases, was abolished in 1998.

Only assets acquired before 1 April 1998 – and from March 1982 onwards – come under this scheme. The initial value and allowable expenses are linked to the retail price index (RPI), which measures inflation. They will increase in line with this index.

The indexation allowance can either reduce or eliminate a taxable gain, but it cannot be used to create or increase a loss.

When calculating gains or losses, individuals need to take into account the rise in value of any assets held only since 31 March 1982. Assets held before that date can have the gain calculated

assuming the market value on 31 March 1982. So any appreciation or profit made before that date will not be taxed. This can
make life simpler – and can lead to substantial tax savings.

In order for assets to have the March 1982 value taken as the
initial value, you need to make an election to 'rebase' your assets.

However, once an election is made to rebase assets, it is final
– you cannot change your mind – and it will cover all assets. In
addition, no expenses incurred before 31 March 1982 can be
deducted when calculating a taxable gain.

Should I rebase or not?

Those unsure as to whether they will be better off rebasing
should not make an election to rebase and they can then treat
each asset differently. They will have the flexibility to use the
calculation that will result in the lowest CGT liability for each
asset.

If no election to rebase is made, two calculations must be
performed:

1. Calculate the gain using the market value on 31 March 1982.
2. Calculate the gain using the original acquisition cost (in this
   case expenses incurred before 31 March 1982 can be
   claimed).

As indexation (the factor that adjusts for inflation) did not start
until March 1982, it can be included in both calculations.

- If both calculations show a gain, the smaller of the gains is the
  chargeable gain.
- If both calculations show a loss, the smaller of the losses is the
  allowable loss.
- If one calculation shows a gain and the other shows a loss,
  there is neither a chargeable gain nor an allowable loss.

CGT and married couples

It is important that both spouses make the most of their CGT allowances to either reduce or eliminate their CGT liability. However, many older couples fail to do so, keeping all assets in the name of the husband and suffering a higher tax bill as a result.

Shares – and other assets – can be transferred between spouses without incurring a CGT liability, so both members of a couple can use their CGT allowance against shares originally owned by just one of them.

When calculating a capital gain on an asset given by a spouse the acquisition costs used in the calculation should be the price the partner originally paid for the asset together with his or her allowable costs and the indexation allowance and taper relief.

How much CGT can be saved?

Couples can avoid or reduce a CGT bill by making the most of the allowance given to both the husband and the wife. If they make a profit of £17,000 on jointly held assets, by splitting this (putting half on the husband's tax return and half on the wife's) they will not have to pay CGT.

If all the assets were held by the husband, tax would, potentially, be paid on £8,500 (using 2005/6 figures). If this was at the basic rate it would cost the couple an additional £1,870 in tax.

If, even after splitting the ownership of assets, the couple still faces a CGT bill they can transfer assets to make the most of a lower-tax rate paid by one partner. As CGT is charged at the taxpayer's top rate of tax, it pays to transfer the asset to the spouse who can then sell it, realize a gain and pay tax at only 10 per cent or 22 per cent instead of 40 per cent.

CGT and property

The fact that a main home is exempt from CGT means that what is possibly the largest investment anyone makes is tax-free.

Even if the property-owner spends money and time improving the home in order to make a profit and sells the home shortly after purchasing it, the profits are tax-free.

As with most tax rules, there are exemptions to this rule on private residence relief.

If the property-owner has sold some land, earned money from his or her home (for instance, by renting it out) or used the home for running a business, the profits made on the sale of the home may be subject to CGT.

So, if someone purchased a home and converted it into self-contained flats which were then sold off, he or she would be liable to CGT. The same applies if he or she built a second home in the garden.

If the property has been partially rented, the owner could be liable for tax on the area let for the period of the letting. So, if the home was let for only a few years, he or she will pay tax only on a proportion of the profits made over the total years of ownership of the property and only on the proportion of the home let.

Tax tips

- Homeowners who rent out or let a property can often escape tax as gains up to £40,000 are usually exempt. This is a one-off allowance for those who have rented out their homes.
- The final 36 months of ownership of a main home always qualify as tax-exempt (for private residence relief) regardless of whether the property was let out during this time.
- Taking in a lodger does not jeopardize private residence relief – the home still qualifies as tax-free. Only if the homeowner has more than one lodger could the property become liable to CGT.
- See IR leaflet 283, *Private Residence Relief*, for further details on how to escape CGT or reduce your liability to it, if you want to – or already have – let out your home.

Part Five
MAXIMIZING YOUR INVESTMENT RETURNS

Introduction

There is vast difference between the best and worst savings accounts. However, shopping around to get 3 or 4 per cent more interest is not going to make you rich. Taking on some level of risk may be a better option for most investors who can afford to ride out the rises and falls in the stockmarket.

For older investors and those on fixed incomes this may prove too big a gamble. So much depends on your age, your attitude to risk, how long you plan to invest for and what other investments you have. It is vital to get the balance right.

Whatever you choose to do, make sure you get reliable investment advice.

Chapter 19

Tax-free savings

One of the easiest ways to boost your investment returns – for little or no risk and often at no extra cost – is to make the most of the many tax-free savings and investment schemes on offer.

In most cases investors do not need to use the services of a sophisticated investment adviser specializing in tax planning and do not necessarily need to invest large sums. While the super-rich may need to take advantage of offshore tax havens to escape paying tax, for most investors there are adequate tax shelters at home.

In fact, it is possible to save and invest over £27,000 in tax-free schemes sold in local high streets – more if you already hold existing National Savings products.

Making the most of the capital gains tax (CGT) allowance of £8,500 for the 2005/6 tax year gives further tax-free profits.

How do I keep my savings and investments free of tax?

- If you are a non-taxpayer register to receive interest gross (without tax deducted). Ask for form R85 from your bank or building society. For help in registering to receive interest gross call the Inland Revenue Registration Helpline*.
- If one spouse is a non-taxpayer make sure he or she uses up the personal and age-related allowances by keeping savings in his or her name. That way interest can be earned free of tax.
- Consider a tax-free savings scheme that is free of income and CGT.
- Use up your CGT allowance.

What if I have paid tax unnecessarily on savings?

To claim tax back, savers should contact their tax office, if they know which one deals with their affairs, and ask for form R40. In some cases savers may be sent a Repayment Claim Form R40 or tax return without needing to request one.

Form R40 – along with guidance notes on how to complete it – is also available at any Inland Revenue Enquiry Centre or Tax Office. There are different forms for different tax years, so specify for which year tax is being reclaimed.

For help in claiming back tax deducted on savings income, savers can call the Taxback Helpline* run by the Inland Revenue.

Individual savings accounts

The individual savings account (ISA) was introduced on 6 April 1999 to replace two existing tax-efficient savings schemes – personal equity plans (PEPs) and the tax- exempt special savings account (TESSA).

Designed to encourage people to save more, ISAs enable savers to put their money into cash (savings) and share-based investments. Before 2005 savers could also invest up to £1,000 in life insurance company investments (not to be confused with life insurance policies).

The ISA tax rules are that interest on cash deposits (savings) is free of tax; dividends from UK equities are paid with tax deducted at 10 per cent; corporate bonds (fixed interest distributions) pay interest gross, without tax deducted; and all gains from any investment sold within an ISA are free of CGT.

The ISA provider will claim back all the income tax for investors, who do not have to do a thing. ISA investments do not have to be declared on tax returns.

The rules governing ISAs

As with any tax break, the government limits its generosity. It is important that savers stick to the rules so that they do not lose the tax-free status of their investment.

The rules state that investors must be resident in the United Kingdom for tax purposes (or a Crown employee currently working overseas and treated as resident) and that they must not hold an ISA jointly with anyone else (so couples cannot have a joint account) or hold one on behalf of another person (so grandparents or parents cannot open an account on behalf of their children or grandchildren).

How much can I invest?

You can invest up to £7,000 in each tax year. However, only £3,000 can be invested in a savings account. The limit for stocks and shares investments is £7,000, reducing to £4,000 if you also have a savings or cash ISA.

It is possible to open an ISA with as little as £1. Further investments can be made at any time, either as lump sums or by regular payments. Cash ISAs are offered by banks, building societies and National Savings.

The three types of ISA are maxi, mini and TESSA-only.

For those wanting an ISA for cash savings only, there is little difference between a maxi- and a mini-ISA in terms of the rules. The maximum investment in savings is £3,000 regardless of which type of ISA is purchased. However, for savings only, investors are advised to buy a cash mini-ISA because the rates are often better and there is more choice.

Those who wish to invest in stocks and shares (unit trusts, investment trusts, open-ended investment companies or shares) as well as cash savings can either opt for a maxi-ISA that allows both types of investment or two mini-ISAs.

Can I withdraw my savings at any time?

Yes, you can withdraw your savings at any time. However, if you want the best rates you may have to give some notice or to commit to saving for a minimum period – for example, a year.

Do not put your emergency funds (that is, money you have been saving up for a rainy day) into a cash ISA if you feel you will need them in the near future. Once savers withdraw money from an ISA, that is it. The tax break is lost. The money withdrawn cannot be reinvested. Bear in mind, too, that the tax breaks do not apply just to this tax year: savings will continue to grow free of tax for years to come. So although the tax savings may be only £30 this year, these savings will mount up to £150 over five years.

What can I do if I find I can get a better rate elsewhere?

Investors who are not happy with the performance of their ISA – whether it is a cash or shares ISA – can switch to another ISA provider. However, only the same components can be switched. So an investor cannot move a cash deposit into a share ISA or *vice versa*. Transfers must be made directly from one ISA provider to another: investors cannot cash in their investment and then reinvest this money with a different provider.

How do I go about choosing a stocks and shares ISA?

You should generally seek advice, as any form of stock market-based investment carries risk. If, however, you know what you want to invest in, you can buy directly or from a discount broker. A discount broker will rebate some of the commission most advisers earn from selling you an ISA and as such the cost of investing will be much lower. Most discount brokers operate online as this reduces their cost.

When choosing a stocks and shares ISA also bear in mind the following points.

- **Past performance is no guarantee of future performance** Look for an ISA with a consistently good investment track record rather than the latest investment fad. Sectors that perform spectacularly well often fall back just as fast – remember what happened when the dotcom bubble burst.
- **Charges will eat into your returns** Think twice about investing

in a fund with slightly higher charges than others. You are investing for the long term and even an 0.25 per cent a year difference in charges will add up significantly over ten or even 20 years. There can be two charges – the initial (from 0 per cent up to 5 per cent of the amount invested) and annual (from 0.5 per cent up to 1.5 per cent).

- **Investment choice is important** Some providers only offer basic tracker funds which track a stock-market index. However, if one market dips you may want the ability to switch to a different sector that is unaffected or hit less hard.
- **Diversify your investments** Each year invest the £7,000 you are allowed to put in ISAs in a different fund or sector. You do not want to have all your eggs in one basket. Diversity is important.

Do both husband and wife have an allowance?
Each individual can invest £3,000 a year in a cash ISA. That means a couple can shelter £6,000 a year between them or £14,000 if investing in shares. It is important that couples each use their allowance (remember, joint ISA accounts are not allowed) even if one spouse is a non-taxpayer.

By opening an account for the non-taxpayer, a tax-paying spouse can reduce the couple's total tax bill.

What happened to TESSAs?
TESSAs (Tax Exempt Special Savings Accounts) were scrapped in April 1999. However, anyone who had a policy maturing before April 2004 (they were five-year plans) could reinvest the proceeds in a TESSA-only ISA. These are still available.

TESSA-only ISA limits are in addition to normal ISA investment limits.

If you have a TESSA-only ISA do not cash it in – you will lose the tax breaks for ever.

Where can I find out more?
The Inland Revenue produces a guide, *Individual Savings Accounts*, which will give you more information.

Where can I find the best rates?

For savings account ISAs try www.moneyfacts.co.uk. Stocks and shares ISAs are more complicated as they carry an element of risk and past performance depends on a number of factors. You are therefore advised to seek independent financial advice before investing (contact IFA Promotion) or to visit a fund supermarket which gives performance details of different funds (but does not give advice) and usually offers them at a discount (with much lower charges). Fund supermarkets include www.fundsuper-market.com, www.fundsdirect.co.uk and www.moneyextra.com.

National Savings & Investments

National Savings & Investments has several schemes that are tax-free. However, savers should not be seduced by the tax breaks: some accounts pay very poor rates of interest. In some cases the total return can be beaten by investing in an alternative savings account even where the interest paid is subject to tax.

In addition to offering a cash ISA, National Savings has the following tax-free schemes.

National Savings Certificates

Both the index-linked and fixed-interest savings certificates are tax-free. The minimum investment is £100 and the maximum in any one issue is £15,000. However, as new issues are made relatively frequently, investors have the opportunity to invest further amounts in each one. There is also no limit on reinvesting the proceeds of matured certificates.

Fixed-interest certificates pay a guaranteed income over five years, hence the term 'fixed'. Index-linked certificates, as the name implies, pay interest at a fixed percentage above the annual rate of inflation (the retail price index).

Savers who withdraw their money before the term of the account is up (two, three or five years depending on the certificate) will suffer as reduced interest – or even no interest, in some cases – is paid. No amount of tax breaks will make up for this. So savers need to be sure that they can hold their certificate for the required number of years.

Premium Bonds

Premium Bonds are not savings accounts and they do not pay interest, so technically they are not tax-free savings schemes. However, the prizes paid are equivalent to a competitive rate of interest and all winnings are free of income and CGT. Bonds are included in a monthly prize draw after they are purchased and they can be cashed in at the face value at any time.

The minimum investment is £100 and they can be purchased by parents, grandparents and guardians on behalf of children.

Life insurance policies

Although life insurance policies are included in this section on tax-free investments, they are not technically tax-free.

The proceeds from most 'qualifying' life insurance policies are usually tax-free. However, while the investor need pay no tax, the life company has already paid tax on the underlying investment. This tax is equivalent to the basic rate of tax and cannot be reclaimed.

To be a 'qualifying' policy the investment must last ten years or more. Most regular premium policies such as endowment policies are qualifying. Investors must keep their policy for at least ten years or for three-quarters of the term if they are to escape paying tax on the proceeds. Bear this in mind before cashing in any policy.

Friendly societies and other tax-free investments

Savers could salvage £55 million through friendly society savings schemes, according to IFA Promotion, the organization promoting the benefits of independent financial advice. Friendly societies date back to pre-welfare state days when workers needed to provide for themselves. They offer products similar to life company investments and in the past were mutual (owned by their members, just like building societies) although today many are stockmarket-quoted companies.

Friendly society life policies qualify for tax relief, which means that in addition to any ISAs they may hold, savers can invest up to £25 per month (a total of £300 a year) or £270 as an annual premium in a friendly society and receive a tax-free lump sum when the plan matures.

Only one plan is allowed per saver. Premiums must be paid for seven-and-a-half years on a ten-year term policy, or for ten years on any longer-term policy, to be tax-free.

As they are such long-term policies – and you will lose out substantially if you fail to pay the premiums for the full policy term – they are not suitable for most of those living on a fixed income. However, if you already have a policy weigh up the loss you will suffer if you feel you need to cash in your plan before the full term is up.

Enterprise Investment Schemes and **Venture Capital Trusts** are high-risk investments which come with valuable tax breaks, particularly for higher-rate tax payers. There is a reason for this – many people lose some or all of their investment. They are therefore not suitable for those living on a fixed income.

Further information

IFA Promotion (0800 085 3250); www.unbiased.co.uk
Inland Revenue ISA Registration Helpline (0845) 980 0645
Taxback Helpline (0845) 077 6543

Chapter 20

Savings accounts

The older you get, the fewer risks you should take with your money. Therefore you should use savings accounts for the bulk of your investments.

With hundreds of different accounts on offer, it can – and will – take time and effort to not only find the right account, but to ensure that you continue to earn the best rates on your savings. Often, new high-paying accounts are launched to attract new investors but then as time goes on the rate ceases to be competitive.

Make sure you use up your £3,000 cash individual savings account (ISA) allowance before saving and if you are married that you have made the most of the tax breaks on offer to couples. Married couples should put savings that are held in the name of one spouse in separate names so they can both utilize their personal tax allowances. Savings held in the name of a spouse who pays a higher rate of tax than the other should also be switched – so that the spouse who pays no or a lower rate of tax holds these savings. (These must be outright gifts.)

Current accounts

These are not savings accounts. Rates are often just 0.1 per cent – less after tax. So keep only enough money in your account for immediate needs plus a small buffer.

Shop around: some current accounts pay a lot more interest than others.

Notice/term accounts

Generally speaking, the longer you are prepared to tie up your money for, the higher the rate of interest you get. Some, but not all, accounts require a notice to be given before you withdraw your money.

Do not tie up all your money in notice/term accounts – you will usually lose out if you want access to your money before the term is up or if you do not give the required notice period. Accounts for a set term – known as bonds – can be even longer commitments. If interest rates rise in the meantime you could be locked into an uncompetitive rate.

Bonus accounts

The best interest rates often have a hidden catch. To earn the headline-grabbing interest rate you have to invest for a minimum amount of time (even with a no-notice account) and earn a bonus. This bonus can be as much as 1 per cent if you invest for 12 months. Always read the small print.

Monthly interest accounts

If you need to supplement your savings you can opt for a monthly interest account. This pays your interest on a monthly basis. It can be paid into a nominated account. Some of these accounts include bonuses and many are e-saver (or Internet only) accounts.

Fixed-rate accounts

These are often bonds, which mean you save for a fixed term. The advantage is that you know exactly what you will earn on your savings for some time – often several years – to come. The minimum investments can be high – £2,500 or more – and you will usually have to invest for at least a year. The disadvantage of these accounts is that if interest rates rise in the future you will be locked into what could be an uncompetitive rate.

How to earn more

1. **Pool your money** Instead of having lots of different accounts, invest in just one or two. Although the best-buy accounts often pay a high rate on sums of just £1, in general the larger your investment, the higher the interest rate.
2. **Do not end in tiers** Accounts which pay different rates on different accounts are known as tiered-rate accounts. You may find that once your balance slips below £5,000 or £1,000 the rate of interest drops sharply. A few extra pounds in your account can mean a much higher rate.
3. **Go online** The best rates are often paid to those prepared to open and run their account via the Internet. Withdrawals can be made by transferring savings electronically into a nominated bank account. Deposits can be made by post or sometimes electronically.

Are there special accounts for older savers?

Yes – so-called silver savers are a target market for many banks and building societies. Such accounts:

- are usually restricted to those over 50
- tend to have high minimum investments – as much as £10,000
- may restrict the number of withdrawals or require a minimum withdrawal – £500, for example
- offer very competitive rates.

National Savings also has a product specifically aimed at older savers: the Pensioners Bond, which you can have on a one-, two- or five-year term. The minimum investment is £500 and the rate is fixed. Although interest is paid gross (without tax deducted) this is not a tax-free investment and the interest must be declared.

Pensioners Bonds can be taken out only by people aged 60 and over. If you need access to your cash before the bond's term is up you need to give 60 days' notice and will earn no interest on the amount withdrawn during the notice period. The minimum withdrawal is £500. If you need immediate access, you will lose 90 days' interest.

There are more competitive fixed-rate bonds on offer, so consider these first.

How do I find the best rates?

If you have access to the Internet go to www.moneyfacts.co.uk, which lists the best-buy accounts.

Chapter 21

Stockmarket-based investments

Shares and share-based investments usually come with an element of risk and may therefore be suitable only for a small proportion of your investment portfolio. However, the diversity they offer can be a bonus. When interest rates – and therefore savings rates are low – shares or bonds may be performing well, to compensate.

It is also possible to take a lot of the risk out of investing as there are numerous guaranteed investment products on offer. In the past these have sometimes had a sting in the tail and investors have lost money because the guarantee had conditions.

However, if you know what you are buying and fully understand the risks involved, share-based investments can provide higher returns than savings accounts with minimal extra risk to your capital.

Note Shares and share-based investments are medium- to long-term investments. Always remember that in most cases the value of your investment can fall as well as rise.

Guaranteed investments

With guaranteed investments you are sure to get your money back. In that sense they are like savings accounts. However, you are also guaranteed to share in the growth of the stockmarket, which makes these like share-based investments.

Most are, in fact, deposit-based accounts – even though they are linked to the stockmarket – and are taxed as such. They tend to be offered by banks and building societies. Some, however, are offered by life insurance companies, and are therefore taxed as share-based investments.

Guaranteed equity/growth bonds

A bond is simply a fixed-term investment. Guaranteed equity bonds give you the best of both worlds: all of your capital back (whatever happens to the stockmarket) and a share in the growth of the stockmarket (usually around 70 to 80 per cent of the rise in the value of a share index, such as the FTSE 100 – the index of the 100 leading shares – but as much as 125 per cent of its growth).

In some cases, a minimum return is also guaranteed. For example, you may receive at least 15 or even 25 per cent on your money, whatever happens to the stockmarket. However, in return for this guarantee, you may have to sacrifice some of the share you receive in the growth of the stockmarket. So may receive only 80 per cent of the rise in the FTSE 100.

How long do I have to invest for?
You generally have to invest for at least one to five years. These are set-term investments and there are usually penalties for early withdrawals or encashment.

How much do I need to invest?
You need to invest at least £1,000 but the minimum can be higher – £2,500 or even £5,000. If the bond can be held in an individual savings account (ISA), the minimum may be £3,000.

How are they taxed?
This depends on whether the bonds are equity- or deposit-based. Most bonds are offered by banks and building societies and although they are linked to growth in the stockmarket they are, in fact, deposit-based accounts. So they are taxed like any other savings account. If they qualify to be held within a tax-free wrapper, such as an ISA, the maximum investment will be

£3,000. Some bonds have been launched specifically to be held within mini-cash ISAs.

If the bond pay returns gross, this does not mean the interest is tax-free. The returns must be declared to the Inland Revenue.

If guaranteed bonds are **equity-based** rather than deposit-based, they will usually be based on a life fund and offered by a life insurance company. Their returns are net of the equivalent of basic rate tax so there is no extra tax to pay. This means that basic- and higher-rate taxpayers who are guaranteed an 80 per cent return are in effect getting the equivalent of a taxed 100 per cent growth from the stockmarket.

If the bond is equity-based and qualifies to be held within an ISA, the maximum investment is £7,000. However, this may be a misuse of your ISA allowance. This is because life company investments are taxed at a much lower rate than stockmarket funds. So you may be better off using your £7,000 allowance to shelter unit trusts or shares (which could be taxed at 22 per cent or even 40 per cent) than sheltering a life company fund in an ISA.

Some life company funds are set up as offshore investments. For example, Legal & General's Protected Capital and Growth Plan is a Dublin-based investment taking advantage of the tax-breaks on offer in Ireland. Combined with the ISA wrapper it guarantees (at the time of writing) a £7,000 maxi-ISA investor a return of £8,750 at maturity – more if the stockmarket grows rather than falls.

So I can have tax-free guaranteed returns from the stockmarket?

Yes, you can. You may wonder why you bother keeping so much in the building society. Check, however, if the bond comes under savings or equity investments as this will affect how much you can invest. Also remember that unlike savings accounts these are long-term (usually five-year) investments so you should not tie up any cash you may need in a hurry.

How do I find the best deal?

Guaranteed equity bonds are offered by building societies, banks and life companies as well as National Savings and Investments. The level of guarantee varies widely so it is worth shopping around by asking an independent financial adviser.

For example, in 2004 while some companies were offering a 70 per cent guarantee, NS&I was offering a gross return equivalent to 125 per cent of any growth in the FTSE 100 index over a five-year term with no upper limit on the return.

Guaranteed income bonds

These are often savings accounts and have no link to the stockmarket. However, they are often confused with guaranteed equity bonds and the same organizations – banks and building societies – offer them.

With these bonds the guarantee covers the income. For example, it may be fixed at 5 per cent for the term of the bond or it may be a guaranteed tracker rate that tracks the Bank of England's base rate. Like guaranteed equity bonds, these are not equity investments but are savings accounts and are taxed as such.

In a few cases the guaranteed income bond, in addition to offering a guaranteed fixed income as well as the guaranteed return of your capital, is based on single-premium life insurance investments. Therefore, income is paid net of basic-rate tax which cannot be reclaimable by non-taxpayers and starting-rate taxpayers. While the rates are guaranteed, offering some security, they can usually be beaten by best-buy savings accounts. Savings accounts have added tax advantages (tax-free for non-taxpayers and ISA investors) and do not tie your money up for so long. If you cash in a life-insurance- based bond before the end of the term, you may get back *less* than you paid in even though you think your capital is guaranteed.

Guaranteed with-profits bonds

These are another form of life company investment. 'With-profits' simply means that the investor shares in the profits of the fund. This share is usually given in the form of a bonus but can come in the form of additional units of investment in the fund.

These bonds guarantee to return the original investment on the fifth anniversary of the policy, regardless of investment conditions. The charges are usually higher to reflect this guarantee. Once again, these investments are not flexible and your money is tied up.

Tax-free stockmarket investments

Individual savings accounts

ISAs are tax-free investment wrappers and not investments as such. Everyone over 18 (for share-based investments) can invest up to £7,000 tax free each year using an ISA.

If you also invest £3,000 in a cash (savings account) ISA, your maximum investment will be lower. You can either invest £4,000 if you have a mini-shares ISA and a mini-cash ISA (which has a maximum investment limit of £3,000), or up to £7,000 if you have a maxi-ISA that also allows you to invest in cash. Within a maxi-ISA the investment limits are £7,000 for shares and £3,000 for cash, subject to a total investment limit of £7,000.

Should I have an ISA?

You should have an ISA even if you are a non-taxpayer, as your circumstances may change in the future. Holding assets in an ISA does not usually cost you any more and you are guaranteed that your investment will suffer no additional income tax or be subject to capital gains tax (CGT) for as long as it is held in the ISA. Remember, you get an ISA allowance every year. After ten years a couple could shelter up to £140,000 of assets free of tax. Failing to make the most of this tax break is costing taxpayers over £1 billion a year.

Remember, use it or lose it. If you fail to take up your ISA allowance this year, it is lost.

In addition to individual shares, the following collective

investments can be held in a tax-free ISA. The advantage of these pooled schemes is that they can be low-risk – if you pick the right type of fund.

Unit trusts

Unit trusts are collective or pooled investments that invest in shares. The advantage is that whereas an individual investor would need thousands of pounds to buy a range of shares – and therefore spread the risks of investing – he or she can buy into a portfolio of investments for as little as £50 a month or £500 as a lump sum.

Unit trusts work by pooling together the money of hundreds – if not thousands – of investors and then investing it on their behalf. The unit trust fund is split into units of equal value, which investors can buy – and sell – at any time. The value of these units rises and falls in line with the value of the underlying investments.

There are over a thousand unit trusts to choose from – some with a very general investment remit, such as UK growth funds, and some with a more specific investment, such as technology funds.

You can be taxed on the capital gains (profits when you sell) as well as the income the trust pays out (the dividend). However, invest via a tax-free ISA and up to £7,000 can grow tax-free.

The fund manager levies two types of charges: initial and annual. In some cases there are no initial charges but the usual charge ranges from 3 per cent to 5 per cent of the value of the investment. Annual management charges are around 1 to 1.75 per cent.

Open-ended investment companies

As financial acronyms go, open-ended investment companies (OEICs, pronounced 'oiks') do not exactly sound enticing. However, they are a way for unit trusts to become simpler to understand and, in some cases, cheaper. Instead of being run as a trust, the unit trust becomes a company. Investors purchase shares in this company rather than units in a fund. In addition, OEICs have single pricing. Whereas units have a buying or offer price and a selling or bid price with a spread of about 5 per cent between the two, OEICs have just one price.

OEICs are taxed in the same way as unit trusts. They can also be held in an ISA to keep them tax-free.

Investment trusts

Investment trusts are similar to unit trusts in that they are a collective or pooled investment. However, like OEICs they are companies. Investment trusts are quoted on the stockmarket and rather than buying units in the investment fund, as in the case of unit trusts, investors purchase shares – as they would any other share of a UK quoted company.

The only difference is that instead of the company making a product or selling a service, investment trusts use their shareholders' money to invest primarily in the shares of other companies.

Each trust has a portfolio of investments run by professional fund managers and supervised by an independent board of directors. They offer an easy way into the stockmarket. If an investor wanted to buy a spread of investments, then he or she would need substantial capital to cover the costs. With an investment trust, the investor still purchases a range of shares but from just £40 a month through an investment trust savings scheme.

However, investment trusts are far more complex than other collective investments because there are different types of shares on offer, some of which offer higher returns for much higher risk.

Investment trusts are taxed in the same way as shares. Like unit trusts and OEICs they can be held in an ISA. In addition, there is 0.5 per cent stamp duty to pay, as there is on the purchase of all shares.

Choosing a low-risk ISA

Now that you know what you can buy, how do you make a

choice with over a thousand different options to choose from?

In most cases you will be advised to seek independent financial advice. An adviser should look at your:

- **risk profile** How much risk you want to take. If you are totally risk-averse it is best to avoid share-based investments other than those which come with a guarantee (these are discussed later in this chapter)
- **amount of time you want to invest** This should be at least five years
- **how much easy-access savings you have** You do not want to be forced to sell your shares, unit or investment trusts when the market has taken a tumble because you need the money
- **your asset allocation** In layman's terms how your money is invested. The bulk of your 'assets' should be in low-risk savings if you are an older investor. However, you may be able to afford to put, say, 10 per cent in a low-risk general fund and a smaller amount in something a little more risky but that offers higher potential rewards.

Some guaranteed equity bonds (which are covered earlier in this chapter) can be held within an ISA and are low risk.

In addition, investments which meet the Sandler Commission requirements – known as stakeholder investments (see below) – are lowest-risk (although not guaranteed). These too can be held in an ISA.

Stakeholder investments

Stakeholder investments are sold with basic advice (not the comprehensive, individually tailored advice you should expect from an independent financial adviser) and as such are cheaper products. The new regulations for these schemes were introduced in April 2005.

Reducing the cost of investing can make significant differences to your investment returns – particularly in the current market – but that is not the only advantage.

Risks are also reduced by the type of investments that are held.

For example, the Legal & General Medium Term Investment Plan invests 60 per cent of its fund in corporate bonds. The rules state that the stakeholder must hold a maximum of 60 per cent in equities and property and must be diversified with the remainder in lower-risk assets such as cash or bonds.

Why are bonds less risky?

Bonds are issued by companies and governments. Government bonds are known as gilts. The bonds are used to raise money rather than issuing shares or taking out loans.

The issuer pays interest to borrow money from investors and guarantees to repay the capital at the end of the bond term. Pick sound companies and the risks are very low for a higher return than a savings account. However, the underlying value of the bonds can go down so you may see your fund value fluctuating.

How little can I invest?

You can invest as little as £20 either as a lump sum or as a regular monthly premium.

How cheap are they?

With the Legal & General product there is no initial charge and an annual management charge of 1.25 per cent. The stakeholder guideline ceiling is 1.5 per cent. This drops to 1 per cent after ten years.

With-profits bonds

With-profits bonds are a popular type of life insurance investment. These policies, issued by life assurance companies, enable investors to share in the investment growth of a fund in the form of regular bonus payments.

Investors, known as policyholders, do not see their investment rise and fall in value in line with stockmarket movements, as they do with unit trusts, investment trusts or OEICs.

Instead, with-profits bonds smooth out the rises and falls in the stockmarket by declaring annual bonuses, called reversionary bonuses, so that in years when the performance is good money is held back in reserve to fund bonuses in years when performance is poor.

When added to the policy, the bonuses increase the price of the units. So a 5 per cent bonus added to a 100p unit will bring the new price to 105p.

In addition to reversionary bonuses, investors may also qualify for a terminal bonus when they cash in the policy. They usually need to have held the policy for at least five years to qualify.

The life company invests in a wide variety of assets including shares, fixed interest securities and profits. Typically around 70 per cent is invested in equities, 15 per cent in gilts, 10 per cent in property and 5 per cent in cash.

What are the tax breaks?

Most with-profits bonds allow the investor to make regular withdrawals. Each year up to 5 per cent may be withdrawn as a return of capital and is therefore tax-exempt. Any amount in excess of 5 per cent is a withdrawal of capital but is considered to have had basic-rate tax deducted (so no further tax is paid by basic-rate taxpayers).

There is no personal CGT liability on these bonds and they are therefore attractive for basic-rate taxpayers who are already using their CGT allowances.

So basic-rate taxpayers who have used up their full ISA allowances should consider with-profit bonds for the tax advantages – the ability to withdraw 5 per cent a year tax-exempt and the fact that basic-rate tax is already paid by the fund.

As life companies pay basic-rate tax on the fund this cannot be reclaimed. This makes with-profit bonds less suitable for non-taxpayers.

How long do I have to invest for?

If you cash in a with-profits bond before five years are up there could be a hefty exit penalty to pay. Also, if the stockmarket is falling the life company can introduce a market value adjuster

(MVA), which means it will not pay out the full value of declared reversionary bonuses. Charges can also be high and include a bid-offer spread (the difference between the buying and selling price of units), annual expense costs and allocation rates.

Distribution bonds

These are similar to with-profits bonds in that they are run by life insurance companies and invest in equities and fixed-interest investments. However, while a with-profits bond will generally increase in value, the value of a distribution bond can fall as well as rise. To compensate for the additional risk of a distribution bond, there is additional growth potential.

Offshore funds

Just because an investment is held offshore does not mean it can escape the UK tax authorities. Anyone who is a UK resident is liable to tax on investments regardless of whether they are invested in the UK or in a tax haven.

However, that does not mean there are no tax advantages to holding investments offshore. It is possible to use some offshore investments to delay a tax liability.

This is a good way to save tax for those who expect to be a lower-rate or non-taxpayer in the next few years. Why suffer 40 per cent tax when they can earn the income tax-free in a couple of years' time?

Who should consider these?
Investors planning to retire in the near future or to move overseas should consider investing in one of these tax-delaying schemes.

How do these schemes work?

They are similar to funds in the UK – however, they usually cost more. There are two main types.

Roll-up funds Offshore roll-up funds, which have a minimum investment starting at between £1,000 and £5,000, are like unit trusts and accumulate any income and reinvest it. Investors do not have to declare these earnings until they cash in the scheme. However, as the charges on these funds are often much higher than for ordinary unit trusts, the tax breaks may be worthwhile only for higher-rate taxpayers – provided when they come to cash in the scheme (when the earnings must be declared) they no longer pay tax at the higher rate.

Insurance bonds Offshore insurance bonds work on the same basis, with the added advantage that investors can take out 5 per cent of their investment each year without having to pay any tax until they cash in the bond – usually after five to ten years. They are offered by most of the major UK life companies.

Another advantage of investing in an offshore life fund is that the insurance company does not have to pay capital gains or income tax on its investments. Onshore life insurance investments have basic-rate tax deducted (which cannot be reclaimed by non-taxpayers).

Investment advisers recommend that investors use up all their tax-free investment allowances, including ISAs and National Savings, in the UK first before considering an offshore investment because of the charges involved.

Chapter 22

Where to get investment advice

Only half of those buying financial products take professional advice before making their decision and, of those, only half use an independent financial adviser.

The poor reputation of financial advisers as commission-hungry salesmen pushing unsuitable products on the unsuspecting public to earn fat kick-backs from insurance and investment companies is one of the reasons why.

Your adviser will earn money for advising you even if you think the advice is free. This is because commissions are built into the charges of many products. An adviser can be paid as much as:

- 5.5 per cent of a lump sum investment – that is £550 on a £10,000 investment
- over 100 per cent of each of the first 12 months' payments on the whole of life policy – or over £1,000 in the first year on a £100 a month premium.

Using a financial adviser

Advisers can earn a lot – does that money come out of my pocket?

Yes – in effect. The cost of advice is usually built into the cost of the product. However, even if you do not get advice – for example, if you buy direct – the charges may be no different, so you might as well get advice.

Is there any alternative?

For those investing large sums of money paying a fee could make advice financially worthwhile as the commission (which will be rebated to the investor) may often be worth more than the fees charged by the adviser.

However, according to research by the Association of British Insurers, commission will be a more affordable form of payment than fees for many savers and investors.

Do I need to bother with an adviser?

If you know exactly what you want, you can buy directly from a financial provider.

In some cases you may even get a discount for doing so. For example, individual savings accounts (ISA) investments can be bought through discount-brokers or fund supermarkets. No advice is given – although the broker may offer general investment recommendations – and in return an investor paying in the maximum £7,000 could save over £200 in charges.

This will be an option only for those who know what products they need and which providers they want to buy them from. Buying from an independent financial adviser does have advantages:

- they are experts, you probably are not
- they can find you the best deals
- they may point out areas of your finances that need attention – things you may not have thought about
- if all goes wrong you can claim compensation.

For those who cannot or do not want to make these decisions, there is now an even more bewildering choice of advisers.

How do I know that the adviser is trustworthy?

All financial advisers have to be registered, trained, authorized and regulated by law. The Financial Services Authority (FSA)* is the watchdog responsible. While the FSA checks that the adviser is qualified to give advice and has put in place rules to protect any money that an adviser manages, there are still – now much rarer – cases of advisers giving poor advice or misusing clients' money. In these cases, the FSA can investigate and may give compensation.

The first step is to check with the FSA that the adviser is authorized and to find out what type of advice the adviser is authorized to give. For example, it may be that he or she can advise on the products of only one or a limited number of companies. The adviser should also have specialist qualifications in the areas he or she is advising upon.

The FSA website also has a useful list of scams and swindles that can catch out unsuspecting investors. The Financial Services Compensation Scheme* can pay out if a firm goes bust and leaves you out of pocket, and the Financial Ombudsman Service* can investigate complaints.

How do I know the adviser will recommend the most suitable product?

Only independent financial advisers can – and do – survey the whole market to find you the best deal.

More than half the advisers in the UK, however, work for just one company selling just that company's products whether they are the best buy or not. In most cases, advice from your bank falls into this category.

In the past advisers either worked for one company or were independent. However, advisers can now be multi-tied as well – offering the products of a limited panel of financial firms. This makes the choice even more confusing.

To sum up there are three types of adviser: independent, tied (works for one company) and multi-tied (works for a limited panel of companies).

Several types of advice are also available.

At the same time as the government relaunched stakeholder products and introduced new stakeholder pension rules and a new stakeholder investment, it also introduced 'basic advice'.

The charges on these stakeholder products are capped at a low level so companies offering them cannot afford to offer financial advice. In these cases you may receive only what is known as 'basic advice' instead of a full financial health-check before you are recommended a range of products (not just one Stakeholder product) to meet your needs.

This basic advice will simply tell you if that particular product is suitable for your needs.

In addition, you can buy products on an 'execution-only' basis, which means you do not receive any advice.

So which is the best way to choose an adviser?
Independent financial advice is the best type of advice, as it is advice-led rather than product-led.

IFA Promotion,* the organization that promotes independent financial advice, can provide you with a list of independent financial advisers in your area.

The service was used by some 446,000 people in 2004 to find an adviser. Its website also has a decision tree to help identify which advice is right for the consumer.

You can ask IFA Promotion for an adviser with particular qualifications, who specializes in certain products – and even request a female adviser, if you wish.

IFA Promotion says that most people find their adviser through personal recommendation. But bear in mind that an IFA who is right for one person may not be right for someone else.

Checklist for choosing an adviser

- Ask friends or colleagues for recommendations.
- Search the IFA Promotion website or telephone the organization for a list of advisers.
- Check the adviser is authorized to give financial advice by contacting the FSA.
- Find out if the adviser is tied, independent or multi-tied.
- Ensure that the adviser is in an area convenient for your home/office.
- Check that the initial consultation is free so you can decide if you get on.

- Ask if the adviser charges a fee or commission. (In future all independent financial advisers must give a choice.)
- Find out what product areas if any the adviser specializes in.
- Ask if the adviser has additional professional qualifications.

What a financial adviser could do for you

1. Review your finances and your financial goals – to make sure you can achieve them.
2. Protect your finances and your family – advising you on making a will, ensuring you have adequate life insurance, and critical illness cover and income protection policies.
3. Shop around to get a better deal on your insurance, savings and mortgage – potentially saving you hundreds of pounds a year.
4. Save you tax by investing your money in tax-efficient schemes, getting you tax relief on pension contributions and rearranging your finances to ensure your estate will pay less inheritance tax.
5. Help you make the most of what you have got – investing your money to earn a higher rate of interest and advising you on investing in shares and property.
6. Make sure you are not being ripped off – millions are wasted in poor-performing and high-charging investments.
7. Help you to plan your financial future – ensuring you have the right pension, that your pension is invested in the best place and helping you achieve your dream whether it be paying off your mortgage, or moving overseas.
8. Hold your hand through major life changes. Setting up in business, starting a family, getting divorced and being widowed all impact on your finances and you may benefit from expert advice.

How to complain about poor advice

The Financial Services Act provides investors with protection and, in some cases, compensation.

If you have a complaint about your adviser you should put it in writing to the company you have dealt with first.

According to the FSA problems can arise for many different reasons, for example:

- unexpected or excessive charges
- losing money because of a firm's slow administration
- a dispute over who is at fault if money is stolen from an account
- incorrect or misleading information about a product
- a firm's failure to adequately warn about the risks of a product
- a firm's failure to draw attention to a particularly strict condition in the contract
- a firm's failure to carry out your instructions
- unfairly being offered worse terms than other customers
- not being given adequate notice about changes to a contract.

Only if your complaint is unresolved can you then take your case to the Financial Services Ombudsman. This service and the Ombudsman's role is to be impartial and investigate the dispute between you and the firm. The Ombudsman will try to help you reach agreement by a process of mediation or conciliation. The firm may be asked to make good your losses and the Ombudsman can also award compensation of up to £100,000.

Further information

The Financial Services Authority has a range of free booklets and factsheets including:

- *Choosing a Financial Adviser – How Key Facts Can Help You*
- *You and Your Money*
- *Retiring Soon: What You Need to Do About Your Pensions*

For copies, visit www.fsa.gov.uk or ring the information line on
(0845) 606 1234 or the automated leaflet line on
(0845) 456 1555
Financial Ombudsman Service (0845) 080 1800;
www.financial-ombudsman.org.uk
Financial Services Compensation Scheme 020-7892 7300;
www.fscs.org.uk
IFA Promotion (0800) 085 3250; www.unbiased.co.uk

Part Six
THINKING AHEAD

Introduction

You may not want to think about your own mortality or a time when you are forced to seek long-term care, but it is essential. Without long-term planning you could:

- run out of capital and therefore investment income
- leave a large chunk of what you have worked hard for to the taxman instead of your family
- see your hard-earned savings eaten away by long-term care bills
- leave your spouse or partner with financial difficulties because you have failed to plan your finances properly or not written a will.

Chapter 23

Should you spend your capital?

The generation that is currently retiring has come to be known as the 'SKI' generation – as in 'Spending the Kids' Inheritance'. They are happily spending their money, enjoying retirement to the full, travelling the world and even splashing out on cosmetic surgery and sports cars. While past generations may have been concerned about financial security, this generation – the richest retirees in history – has other priorities.

Capital vs income
Keeping capital intact is important because you need to have something set aside for a rainy day; your capital can generate income; you will have something to leave the next generation and it provides peace of mind.

However, there can be drawbacks to keeping your capital intact. Some people take the attitude that there is no reason to go without a reliable car, a comfortable new sofa, or holidays with the grandchildren when the chances are that some of their capital will be taken away to pay for long-term care or by the taxman to pay an inheritance tax liability. Moreover, if you have a lot of capital, you will get less help from the state. For example, having just a few thousand pounds extra in a savings account can mean that you lose out on free Council Tax bills.

Less can mean more
Some retirees – particularly those with limited amounts of capital – may find they are better off spending their money rather than keeping it for a rainy day.

• **Get to know the means-tested benefits** If your capital limits are just above those allowed to make a claim, consider spending some of your money to improve your quality of life. Invest in a new boiler, for example, to cut your heating bills and avoid worry about being left in the cold when winter comes.

- **Understand the tax implications** Once again, a few extra thousand in the bank can mean the difference between paying only basic-rate tax on savings or – sometimes – paying no tax at all.

- **Assess your liability to inheritance tax** If your estate is likely to be above the £300,000 threshold for 2007/8 (that includes the value of your home) you may want to give away some assets or spend some capital (see Chapter 25 for more on inheritance tax).

Chapter 24

Long-term care

The problems older people face with long-term care bills have been described as a national scandal. Some have been forced to sell homes unnecessarily to pay their care-home bills. Others have moved into care homes only to see the fees rise at well above the rate of inflation, eroding what savings they have. Since 2000 care bills have soared by 33 per cent. Some local authorities have refused to pay towards nursing care bills – even when they are required to by law. As a result, £180 million of compensation will be paid to older people or their families.

The big issue in terms of financial planning is how much – or how little – capital you need to qualify for state help. If you have savings and investments as well as a family home well in excess of the limits, you are unlikely to qualify for state help even if you squander a lot of your capital.

However, if your capital is, for example, £50,000 in excess of the limit, by the time you need long-term care (if at all), you may find that you have used much of this up to supplement your living costs and therefore qualify for help.

Much depends on how the rules change. Long-term care costs are soaring as the population ages and so future governments may be forced to rethink how care is paid for.

Note The rules for state help with long-term care bills vary for those who live in Scotland, Wales and Northern Ireland so this chapter mainly applies to those who live in England. However, where rule changes vary these are indicated.

The essentials

How much could long-term care cost?

In 2004 average fees for care homes were £18,000 and for nursing homes £24,000. These fees vary depending on the location of the home and the facilities. Also, note that care-home fees tend to rise well above inflation.

However, the average person entering long-term care survives only for around 12 months. So the overall cost will depend on how long you (or your spouse, if he or she is in a care home) live.

Will I get help with this?

The law states that if 'your primary need is a health-care need' then you should receive NHS-funded care. However, in the past not all health authorities have applied this rule consistently. Some have been forced to pay compensation to those refused free nursing care, although the problem seems to continue.

The Commons Health Committee has recommended that there should be a single set of national criteria when assessing whether patients qualify for continuing long-term care. Until these criteria are drawn up, long-term care will remain a bit of a lottery.

The maximum amount of state help for nursing care is limited to between £40 and £120 a week, depending on the health of each individual.

In addition, if your capital is below a certain amount – currently £12,700 – you will receive state help with all your care bills, not just the nursing element. If your assets are between £12,750 and £21,000 you will receive some help.

However, you will no longer receive Attendance Allowance or Disability Allowance if your social services department pays your care-home bills.

Your income will also be means-tested. Certain state benefits are excluded from the means test, so these can be kept by you. These include the Christmas Bonus and the mobility element of the Disability Living Allowance. Savings, including the interest paid on them, count towards your capital and not income. Only half of any private pension you receive, if paid to a married couple (and you pay half to your spouse), is taken into account when calculating the means test.

In addition, you are allowed a personal expenses allowance of £19.60 a week.

So if your weekly income is £110 a week in 2006/7, and your care bills are £300 a week your contribution to these bills will be £110 – £19.60 = £90.40. The remainder of the care-home bills should be met by the local authority.

I think I will only go into a care home if I need to for medical reasons, so will that mean it will be free?

Although the law states that if your primary need is a health need all your long-term care should be paid for by the NHS – regardless of your financial situation – this is not always the case.

It can be difficult to prove that your health is so bad that care classed as 'social', such as washing, dressing and feeding yourself, should be funded by the health service.

The first step is to be assessed by your Primary Care Trust. This should be done by a multidisciplinary team, which may include a doctor, psychiatrist and physiotherapist, not just a nurse.

If you disagree with the result, you can ask for an independent review of the assessment by the Strategic Health Authority. If you are still not happy with the answer you get, you can appeal to the Health Ombudsman.

What if I need some nursing help and some residential care?

The nursing part of your long-term care bill should be paid for by your local authority. The bill for residential care – your room, meals, cleaning etc. – will have to be paid out of your capital, income or savings.

There are three bands of nursing care, each corresponding to a level of funding.

- **High band (£129 per week in 2005/6)** People requiring registered-nursing care will have complex needs that require frequent mechanical, technical and/or therapeutic interventions. They will need frequent intervention and reassessment by a registered nurse throughout a 24-hour period. Their physical/mental health will be unstable/unpredictable.
- **Medium band (£80 per week in 2005/6)** These people may have multiple care needs. They will require intervention by a registered nurse on a daily basis and may need access to a nurse at any time. However, their condition is stable and predictable and likely to remain so if the treatment and care regimes continue.
- **Low band (£40 per week in 2005/6)** This band applies to people whose care needs can be met with minimal registered-nurse input. Assessment would indicate that their needs could normally be met in another setting, such as at home or in residential care with support from a district nurse, but they have chosen to place themselves in a nursing home.

Your needs may vary as your health deteriorates or improves so these bands can be subject to review.

If you live in Wales, your care home will receive a flat rate of £107.63 per week in 2005/6 towards your fees. In Scotland the figure is £65 per week. In Northern Ireland nursing-care recipients receive a flat £100 per week. For rules covering Scotland and Northern Ireland see below. These amounts usually increase every April.

If you qualify for help with paying the remainder of your care-home fees from your local authority, the amount will usually be based on its usual or standard rate. Local authorities rarely fund places in the most luxurious retirement homes.

Remember, if you do not qualify for help with your care-home bills you should still be able to receive either Attendance Allowance (if you are over 65) or Disability Allowance (if under 65). This is not means-tested and it not taxable.

Special rules for Scotland
In Scotland you may be able to get help with both the nursing and

the personal care part of your fees if you are aged over 65. First, your needs are assessed by your local authority. If it agrees that you need personal care it will pay £145 a week (2005/6 rates) towards your care. If you require nursing care the authority will pay an additional £65 a week. The payments, which are made directly to the care home, should result in a reduction in the fees you have to pay.

You will still have to pay for normal accommodation costs, which do not involve personal or nursing care, and your finances will be assessed to see how much you should pay.

The rules in Northern Ireland

In Northern Ireland if you pay all or part of your nursing home fees you may be able to get help with the cost of nursing care. You need to be assessed by a Health and Personal Social Services (HPSS) nurse. If the nurse agrees that you need nursing care, your local HPSS trust will pay up to £100 a week (2005/6) towards your care fees, depending on how much help you need. Once again this contribution is paid directly to the nursing home and should result in a reduction in the fees that you have to pay. Nursing care needs are reviewed after three months and then every year.

If I own a home, will that mean I cannot get free long-term care?

The maximum amount of capital you are allowed to own to be eligible for free care in England is currently £21,000 (2006/7 figure). This includes the value of your home and your share of any jointly owned assets such as savings accounts.

However, if you have a spouse or dependant still living in the family home, its value will not be included as an asset and when calculating whether or not you will receive help with your care fees.

The value of your home is also disregarded for the first 12 weeks from the start of permanent admission to a care home (unless the property is sold during this time).

Capital rules

The local authority pays for costs of residential or nursing home care if capital is less than:

England	Wales	Scotland
£12,750 (2006/7)	£14,750 (2005/6)	£11,750 (2005/6)

The local authority still pays for accommodation and personal care, but not fully, if capital is between:

England	Wales	Scotland
£12,750–£21,000	£14,750–£21,000	£11,750–£19,000

What other assets are excluded?

The surrender value of life insurance policies and annuities, personal possessions, money held in trust or administered by a court which derives from a payment for personal injury and capital held in a discretionary trust are all excluded when means-testing you to see if you are eligible for state help with long-term care.

Will I have to sell my home to pay for the cost of long-term care?

Some 70,000 family homes are sold each year to pay for long-term care, so it is a real possibility that you might have to do so. If you do not want to sell the property you can enter into a deferred payment agreement with the local authority, which will put a legal charge on the property to recoup its money when the property is sold. An alternative is to rent out your property and to use the income to help pay for your care fees so you do not need to rely on the state, keeping ownership of the property yours.

What if my assets are over £21,000?

You will have to pay the full fees (minus the nursing element) until your capital is reduced to below £21,000. If your place was arranged by the local authority you will not have to pay more than the standard rate for the home.

What if my assets are under £21,000 but over £12,750?

For every £250 of capital in this £10,000 band you will be assumed to be earning £1 of income. This income will be taken into account when assessing how much help you receive.

Remember, your assessment should change each time your capital drops down to another £250 band.

What other options are there to fund the cost?

Your choices for paying long-term care fees are from your pension income, capital, savings, selling your home or releasing equity from your home, or by buying insurance.

How do most people pay the costs?

Almost half a million elderly people who cannot look after themselves live in long-term care homes, a figure the government predicts could treble by 2051. Currently, some 40 per cent of residents pay most of the bills – an average £2,000 a month – themselves.

Further help and advice

Help the Aged* offers a free Care Fees Advice Service helping you to find the best ways of paying for care. The service is designed to provide peace of mind, keeping you safe in the knowledge that care can be paid for as long as it is needed and that your savings are preserved to leave as an inheritance or spend as you wish.

Insurance for long-term care

There are two main types of insurance you can buy for long-term care.

Immediate-care insurance

This kind of insurance you take out when you need care. The policies are not available to those who simply choose to move into a care home. You invest a lump sum in an annuity which pays out an income for life to cover some or all of the care-home costs. The amount you need to invest depends on how much income you need, if you want this income to rise each year and by how much, your age, gender and state of health.

Insurers use actuarial calculations to work out how long they are likely to have to pay out on the policy and how much it will cost them in total. No tax is payable on a long-term care annuity so long as the money goes directly to the care provider.

The drawbacks of this type of insurance are:

you could lose out on means-tested benefits as a result of taking out a policy

you cannot get your money back

if you die shortly after taking out the policy your estate will be worse off than if you had paid your care bills out of your capital (although some policies provide some death benefits).

How long will I have to survive to make a care-fees annuity worthwhile?

The average yield on a care-fees annuity is about 25 per cent, so it takes four years to pay for itself. For example, if a client needs £25,000 to cover annual fees, the plan might cost £100,000. But it would continue to pay out until death.

Each application is calculated individually so prices vary from one provider to another, even though there are very few to choose from – Norwich Union, BUPA (it offers a FutureCare Product), GE Life, Pafs and PPP. All products are available through only independent financial advisers – you should contact an adviser to help you decide whether one of these plans may be suitable and whether taking out a plan is worth the cost.

Normally, the annuity is designed to cover any gap between care costs and an individual's income, which includes pensions, minus a small amount of spending money.

These plans cover care costs until death. The drawback is that if the person dies soon after going into care, the money is normally lost.

Rates do vary widely so it is worth shopping around.

An alternative is an impaired-health annuity (an annuity that takes into account your poor state of health). There might be income tax to pay on an impaired life plan, but the returns may be higher.

Pre-funded long-term-care insurance

These policies are generally taken out by those in their late 40s, 50s or 60s. You take out a policy that will pay out if you need long-term care. Some policies were linked to investment bonds, which can be more risky. As they failed to provide sufficient returns to cover care bills these have been withdrawn from the market.

Insurance-based plans have been expensive and not popular. As a result many insurers have also withdrawn from this market. However, some do still provide policies.

As ever, premiums depend on your age, gender and amount of cover. Premiums usually rise every five years, when the policy is reviewed, even if you buy a single premium rather than a monthly premium policy. There is usually a 13-week wait before the policy pays out. The policy pays out only in certain circumstances – if you are unable to perform certain activities of daily living (ADLs). So you may find that your condition is not covered. The policy can either pay out until death or for a limited pre-agreed time – for example, three years – after which you must pay your care bills yourself.

The drawbacks of this type of insurance are:

- if you do not need care your money is wasted: you get nothing back
- you may only need care for a short period of time – less than 13 weeks
- your premiums can rise and become much more expensive
- the amount you get may simply mean you miss out on means-tested state benefits
- if you have an investment-linked policy you can cash it in but you may get back less than you paid in premiums
- when you die your estate may get nothing back although some investment funds will pay out the balance of the investment

fund, and a few insurance policies will pay a lump sum to your estate.

Who sells this insurance?

Several players, including Bupa, PPP, Scottish Widows and Norwich Union, have pulled out of the market. Currently only one mutual insurer, Pafs, offers a pre-pay plan. Its policy (Care Prepared) is flexible and covers both care in the home and in a nursing home. The product is available only through independent financial advisers.

Given the drawbacks, why should I buy insurance?

You should buy insurance to preserve your capital, to ensure your partner has enough income (if the bulk of income is going to pay care fees or if you are in receipt of means-tested benefits and the costs of care leave insufficient for your spouse), for peace of mind and to give you greater choice about the type of care – local authorities may not fund places in the most expensive homes.

Will the insurance pay for all my long-term care bills?

Insurance policies generally only cover half the cost of the fees. When deciding the level of cover consider how much you may be able to pay yourself out of savings and pension income, how much the state may pay and how much the care-home bills are likely to be, and then buy insurance to cover the shortfall.

Further information

Age Concern has a range of leaflets covering state help,
    including *Local Authority Charging Procedures for Care
    Homes Fact Sheet 10* and *NHS Continuing Care, NHS Funded
    Registered Nursing Care and Intermediate Care Fact Sheet 20.*
In addition, it has a number of leaflets about paying for care,
    including *Treatment of the Former Home as Capital for*

People in Care Homes Factsheet 38. For copies, call the
information line on (0800) 00 99 66.

The Financial Services Authority regulates long-term care
insurance plans and produces a fact sheet called *Paying for
Long-term Care.* For a copy, call the leaflet line on
(0845) 456 1555.

The Association of British Insurers produces *An ABI Guide to
Long-term Care Insurance.* For a copy, call 020-7600 3333.

Help the Aged Care Fees Advice service (0500) 76 75 76;
www.helptheaged.org.uk

Chapter 25

Inheritance tax and wills

People in the UK waste almost £1.1 billion through poor inheritance tax (IHT) planning, according to research from IFA Promotion, the organization that promotes the benefits of independent financial advice. This figure is set to rise rapidly as more and more homes fall within the IHT threshold, which is £285,000 in 2006/7 and set to rise to £300,000 from April 2008.

The Halifax forecasts that the number of properties valued above the IHT threshold could rise to 4 million in 2015 and 6 million in 2025.

IHT is a relatively easy tax to avoid, with one past Chancellor even calling it the 'voluntary' tax. Yet many believe – wrongly – that IHT planning is just for the rich. It is not: anyone who wants to make sure that as much of their estate as possible goes to the people or charities of their choice needs to plan ahead. With effective planning in advance, it may well be possible to pass on all assets free of tax to the next generation.

Inheritance tax: the essentials

Who pays it?
Anyone living in the UK is subject to IHT on all their property owned worldwide even if they have no assets in the UK and have lived abroad.

What is it paid on?
The tax is paid on the value of the estate upon death. This includes property, bank and building society deposits, shares and unit trusts, investments – including tax-free investments

such as individual savings accounts (ISAs), and cash.

Gifts or transfers made within seven years before a death are also potentially liable to IHT.

What is exempt?

All transfers between spouses, normal expenditure out of income, gifts made more than seven years before death and pension fund savings are exempt from IHT and not included when the value of the estate is assessed.

In addition, the following gifts and transfers are exempt:

- £250 to any number of individuals as small gifts each tax year
- £3,000 per year given to an individual in any tax year
- gifts on marriage, to a maximum of £5,000 from each parent (£2,500 by each grandparent or other relative and £1,000 by anyone else). The gift must be made before the wedding day
- gifts to charities
- gifts for national purposes
- gifts to political parties
- gifts to housing associations.

In addition, the estate of those members of company or occupational pension schemes who 'die in service' may receive the benefits tax-free. Up to four times salary is allowed as death-in-service benefits. The rules state that these payments are exempt from IHT only when the pension trustees have the discretion to decide about paying beneficiaries. However, in practice they follow the employee's statement of wishes.

At what rate is IHT paid?

On death, IHT is levied at 40 per cent on all assets in excess of the nil-rate threshold (£285,000 for 2006/7). This nil-rate band threshold is increased each year in the Budget and is usually raised in line with inflation.

The full amount is not charged on gifts made within seven years before death (those made more than seven years before death escape IHT). The reduced rates are:

Tax tip

Occupational pension schemes are not only tax-efficient in life (contributions qualify for tax relief, the pension fund grows free of tax and a tax-free lump sum can be taken on retirement), they can be tax-efficient in death. Employees should ensure that they update their statement of wishes as circumstances change. After a divorce, they will probably not want their former spouse to receive the death benefit.

The death benefits from personal pensions and other life assurance policies can be 'written in trust' to exclude them from the policyholder's estate for the purposes of IHT. This simply means that a form is filled in stating that the policy is for the benefit of your heirs – not you (but as you will be deceased that will be the case anyway). As a result, the policy proceeds are paid to your heirs, not to your estate and therefore fall outside the scope of IHT.

Number of years before death the gift was made	IHT rate
1–3	100 per cent of the full charge at 40 per cent
3–4	80 per cent of the full charge, giving an effective rate of 32 per cent
4–5	60 per cent of the full charge, giving an effective rate of 24 per cent
5–6	40 per cent of the full charge, giving an effective rate of 16 per cent
6–7	20 per cent of the full charge, giving an effective rate of 8 per cent

Note Even those who are non-taxpayers or basic-rate taxpayers, will suffer 40 per cent tax on their estate if it exceeds the nil-rate band.

There is no upper limit on the amount of IHT.

Who pays IHT?

It is the estate that pays the tax. IHT is deducted from the assets and must be paid before probate is granted (before the will is officially recognized). So any tax liability must be agreed and paid before the beneficiaries receive any inheritance. The tax is due within six months of the end of the month in which death occurred. Interest is usually charged on late payment.

How is it calculated?

All of an individual's assets (other than those that are exempt) at the time of death are added up. Any liabilities, such as debts, a mortgage and bank overdrafts are then deducted from this sum.

Avoiding IHT

This so-called voluntary tax is easily avoided. Just follow these tax tips.

Give assets away

Give assets to your spouse

Transfers between husband and wife during their lifetime, or on death, are totally free of IHT. However, this often lulls people into a false sense of security. If the surviving partner inherits everything, the deceased partner has not made use of the IHT threshold – the facility to leave up to £285,000 tax-free to their children, grandchildren or other beneficiaries.

To ensure that this tax threshold is used to full advantage, any liquid assets such as savings, shares or mutual funds should be split between the two partners so that each can leave up to the £285,000 nil-rate band to their children or grandchildren. This, however, is of use only if the surviving spouse would have sufficient income left, and is not suitable for those whose only or main asset is the family home.

Give assets to the next generation – now

This is the easiest way to escape IHT. However, taxpayers should do this before they get too old. Only if the asset is given away more than seven years before death does it escape IHT and remain outside the estate on death. These are known as potentially exempt transfers (PETs). As a safeguard, those making gifts should insure their life for seven years for the amount of the IHT liability with a policy written in trust for the beneficiaries of the estate.

Some parents wrongly think that they can give away their family home to escape IHT while still living in it. This is called a 'gift with reservation' (see pages 295–6) and it does not count as a PET. However, it is possible for them to give the home to their children, provided they pay a commercial rent to remain in the home. The main drawback with this is that few retired people can afford such a level of rent. Rules introduced in April 2005 have now tightened this rule further. Covering so-called pre-owned assets (known as POATs) they make it far harder to give away assets and retain any form of benefit. You are strongly advised to seek legal and financial advice before making any decision, just in case you then become liable for tax on the perceived 'retained benefit'.

Make use of the annual gift allowances

The annual exemption allows £3,000 to be gifted each year by an individual, and if this has not been used up in one tax year the allowance can be carried forward to the next. In addition, it is possible to make gifts of £250 to any number of people free of tax. However, note that if the value of gifts to one person exceeds £250 all the gifts to that person must be deducted from the £3,000 annual exemption. So consider passing on wealth to children and grandchildren in smaller amounts each year.

Other ways to maximize your gifts:

- note that both husbands and wives have an annual exemption, which means a couple can give away £6,000 between them – £12,000 if they carry forward any unused exemption from one year to the next

- regular gifts from income which do not reduce the individual's standard of living are exempt from IHT. There is no maximum limit on the value of this, but these gifts cannot be made out of capital such as savings or investments and cannot be funded by the sale of assets
- parents who help pay for a child's wedding should ensure that their financial support is tax-free as far as IHT is concerned. They can give up to £5,000 each (£10,000 in total) and this will not be included as part of the estate for IHT purposes. However, they must make the gift at the time of marriage.

Use loans

At the time of writing, it is possible to use a combination of a will, a trust and a loan to reduce IHT. Such schemes can take several forms, and some are offered by life insurance companies, others by solicitors. These schemes are suitable only for those who have assets other than the family home.

For example, both partners could leave everything to their spouses in return for an IOU of the nil-rate IHT band, whatever it may be at the time of death. When the first partner dies, the IOU (loan) is created and held in trust for the benefit of the children or other beneficiaries. However, the surviving spouse can use the assets to supplement income. However, upon the death of the second spouse the value of the IOU is deducted from the estate before IHT is calculated. This means that both partners can make use of their nil-rate IHT band.

With loan trust schemes offered by life insurance companies, the individual makes an interest-free loan to the trust, which then invests this capital for growth. Once the loan is made, it then falls outside of the estate for IHT purposes. If the individual requires an income, pre-arranged repayments of the loan – usually at 5 per cent per annum of the capital advance – can be made. As this money is required to finance expenditure, it will be spent and therefore not added to the estate for IHT purposes.

The minimum value of a trust is usually around £10,000. Loan trusts offered by insurance companies may have share-swap facilities so that the individual can turn an existing portfolio into a loan trust. Generally, loan trusts invest in the insurance company's own bonds (usually with-profits bonds).

Home reversion schemes

These schemes are suitable for those who have a valuable property but few free assets. Part – or all – of the family home is sold to a home reversion company (usually at a discount to the current valuation) and in return the homeowner receives a lump sum and/or an income but continues to live in the home for the rest of his or her life or until he or she sells or moves into a care home. Some or all of the lump sum is then passed on to the beneficiaries. Provided the owners survive for seven years after the gift, it is free of IHT.

By selling only part of the property, the homeowner can still make full use of the £285,000 IHT threshold.

It is also possible to take out a mortgage – an equity release lifetime mortgage – on the property. The debt, which rolls up as no interest is paid, is used to reduce the value of the estate upon death. The cash released can be spent on anything – for example, helping the children on to the property ladder or holidays in the sun.

These schemes do cost money and should be entered into carefully. They are discussed in greater detail in Part Two of this book.

Insure the bill

It is possible to buy life insurance to cover an IHT bill. If you are married this will be written as a joint life/second death policy – as it is only upon the death of the second partner that IHT is usually paid – the life insurance is written in trust for the beneficiaries and is therefore outside of the estate for IHT purposes. It can, however, be expensive and costs around £11 a month for £10,000 of death benefit for a couple aged 60, rising to around £22 a month at 70. So if the potential liability is £100,000, the costs would be £220 a month – which may be too expensive for most retired couples. Single people can also take out a single-life policy to pay their potential IHT liability. Once again, this is usually prohibitively expensive.

Another option is a life assurance bond. These are not life insurance policies, but investments. They can be assigned to a trust and become a PET. However, each year investors can withdraw 5 per cent of the original capital invested over a 20-year period with no immediate tax liability.

Note Although life insurance payments upon death are free of income and capital gains tax (CGT), they can still have an impact on IHT. This is because the lump sum – which will often be used to repay a mortgage – increases the size of the estate by reducing the debts and therefore the amount of IHT that needs to be paid.

Downsize

If the family home is the main asset and it exceeds the nil-rate band threshold, one of the simplest ways to cut a potential IHT liability is to sell the property, buy a smaller one and give the children or grandchildren the surplus. Provided the parents survive for seven years, there will be no – or less – IHT liability. This is discussed in greater detail in Part Two.

Give half your home to your children

It is not possible for parents to give children the family home and then continue to live in it as this is known as a 'gift with reservation' and therefore not exempt from IHT. However, it is possible to leave part of the property to the children on the death of the first spouse.

As the family home is likely to make up the bulk of the estate, this can reduce its value significantly.

First, the parents must change the way in which they own the house from a joint tenancy – in which assets automatically pass to the survivor on death – to 'tenancy in common'. The latter enables the property to be passed on to a third party rather than the other person who owns the property.

However, this will mean that the surviving spouse no longer has exclusive rights to all of the property so before opting for this parents should be sure that their children understand the implications. If the children run into financial difficulties they could be forced to sell the home and leave the surviving spouse homeless.

Moreover, new regulations covering POATs introduced in 2005 make this less advantageous. The spouse continuing to live in the property could get caught out by these rules and may be forced to pay a tax on the benefit of retaining use of the property.

One situation in which POAT rules will not affect the homeowner is co-ownership, where both parties live in the property. For example, an elderly mother living with her daughter could give a share in the family home to her. Provided they both live there and share the outgoings there is no problem with reservation of benefit and this arrangement is also outside the new POAT. If the mother survives seven years then the gift falls out of her estate in the normal way.

Trusts

Discretionary trusts are a legitimate way to reduce an IHT liability. Provision to create a trust can be made when writing a will with the trust coming into existence on death (usually of the first spouse).

The trust enables the first spouse who dies to use up all of his or her nil-rate IHT band while still enabling the surviving spouse to benefit from the assets.

An amount up to the nil-rate band is subject to the provisions of the discretionary trust. Potential beneficiaries should be identified in the will. These beneficiaries will receive income from the trust and can take out loans against the assets of the trust and receive outright gifts of capital from the trust at the discretion of the trustees (which usually include the surviving spouse). However, while the beneficiaries benefit, there is no IHT liability in respect of assets sheltered within the discretionary trust.

This does not mean, however, that no tax needs to be paid.

The trust itself is subject to income tax at 34 per cent and any capital gains are also taxable. Administering a trust can therefore be time-consuming and expensive, so it is important to consult a solicitor and financial adviser before deciding which assets to shelter in the trust.

Life insurance and trusts

Most life insurance or assurance policies can be put in trust if they are intended to provide money for dependants upon death. However, a policy intended to repay a mortgage cannot be written in trust as it is assigned to a mortgage lender.

Both new policies and existing ones can be placed under a trust with forms usually available from life insurance companies. These are standard trusts covering the majority of cases. They can take several forms.

- **Flexible trust** This is a basic type of trust, used for family protection or IHT planning. Everything is left to chosen beneficiaries. The reason why it is called a flexible trust is that the person creating the trust, the settlor, can change the beneficiaries if circumstances change. In addition to life insurance policies, with-profits bonds can be written under this type of trust – although the settlor must survive seven years after setting up the trust for IHT not to apply to the original sum invested.
- **Split trusts** These are for protection policies that include both death and critical illness benefits. The latter pay out a lump sum if the policyholder is diagnosed with certain life-threatening illnesses. The trust enables the death benefits to go to the beneficiaries while still allowing the policyholder to have any critical illness benefits if he or she suffers from a serious disease before death.
- **Family trust** This is a lifetime-interest trust for a single-premium bond (that is, a lump sum bond) or investment such as a with-profits bond. The settlor has access to the policy while still alive but can avoid probate and leave the bond to named individuals when he or she dies. These can be set up as PETS – potentially exempt transfers.

- **Legacy loan trust** The settlor gets access to his or her money because he or she only makes a loan to the trustees, and can ask for this loan to be repaid at any time. The trustees use the loan to invest in a with-profits bond or a capital bond. The estate is liable for IHT only on any of the loan that has not been repaid. Generally, these are suitable for older investors who need the income in the trust. Each year, as an element is repaid, the IHT liability reduces. No IHT is paid on any profits the bond makes.

Reversionary interest schemes

These schemes transfer assets outside the estate for IHT purposes while still giving the individual control over the assets – and the right to receive regular annual payments for them.

When assets are transferred into the reversionary interest scheme, which involves a series of insurance bonds, they are classed as PETs so there will be no IHT liability if the donor (known as the settlor) survives seven years.

As these schemes are based on investments, the assets can continue to grow and provide an income. Different maturity dates of a series of bonds can ensure that one matures each year giving the settlor the option of withdrawing the maturity value as income. Alternatively, the money can be reinvested and remain outside the grasp of the Inland Revenue.

Held within a trust, the bonds will eventually be inherited by the beneficiaries – usually children or grandchildren. These bonds get their name because the settlor has a 'reversionary right' to receive the maturity value of the underlying bonds.

Bare trusts

Returns on investments (such as interest or dividends) made by parents on behalf of their minor children are generally taxed at the income of the parents. This means that a parent cannot escape income tax on savings income by putting his or her savings in the name of a child. This rule is subject to a £100 annual income limit.

To get around this rule parents have, in the past, set up a trust.

A trust for a minor child in which the child has an indefeasibly vested interest in the income and capital of the trust – known as a bare trust for tax purposes – ensured that any income arising to the trust, which was not distributed, was treated as the child's even if the funds in the trust came from the parent. It therefore generally escaped tax. So parents could set up a trust to escape tax on their savings and investments and, at the same time, provide for their children's futures.

However, as of the 1999 Budget these bare trusts are no longer so tax-efficient. Any income from trusts set up after then is treated and taxed as that of the parent (subject to the £100 limit) as is any income arising to funds added to exiting trusts after Budget day 1999. Just because the parent is now liable for tax on these trusts does not mean they are not useful for income tax and IHT planning. Grandparents can make use of them – particularly if they want to help with school fees for the grandchildren.

Pensions

A pension is one of the most tax-efficient ways to escape IHT. Tax relief is given at the individual's highest rate on contributions to the pension. A tax-free lump sum can be taken on retirement and if the individual lives a long life he or she can benefit from an income in retirement.

In addition, if the individual dies before retirement, the lump sum paid out by the pension fund (up to four times salary for those in occupational schemes) is not included in the estate for IHT purposes.

If the individual dies after retirement, the spouse (and possible other dependants) will receive a pension for life, which also escapes being included in the estate for IHT purposes (although the pension itself will be subject to income tax if, as a result, it pushes the individuals' annual income to a level above their personal tax allowances). Death benefits from personal and stakeholder pensions also escape IHT. The policyholder needs to ensure that the insurance is written in trust for their beneficiaries.

Making a will

Nearly two in three people in the UK do not have a will – although this drops to a third among the over-65s – leaving confusion over who should receive any inheritance.

Those who die intestate (without making a will) could find, as in the case of unmarried couples, that those closest to them receive nothing. Worse, if the state cannot trace anyone to inherit, the taxman gets the lot.

Writing a will is more than just a means of stating precisely the names of beneficiaries and what they will receive: it is also a means of minimizing tax bills.

Married couples should think twice before writing a will leaving their estate to the surviving partner. By doing so they are failing to make the most of each spouse's inheritance tax nil-rate band (or exemption) on the first death. As the nil-rate band is £285,000 for the 2006/7 tax year, this gives a potential tax loss of £114,000 (that is, 40 per cent tax on £285,000).

Tax Tips

- Married couples with substantial assets and those of more moderate means with property that is likely to exceed the IHT threshold should write their wills making the most of the nil-rate band giving away assets up to this threshold either outright or through trusts. Word the will referring to the 'nil-rate band available on the date of death' rather than specifying an amount. Leave the remainder to the surviving spouse.

- Even if a will does not take full advantage of the IHT nil-rate band, all is not lost. It is possible to change a will after a person dies so that the inheritance is given in a more tax-efficient manner. As long as all the beneficiaries who would lose out as a result of a change agree, a deed of variation can change the way the assets are distributed. The Inland Revenue publishes a free leaflet *IHT8 Alterations to an Inheritance Following Death*.

Who gets what if no will is made

The rules of intestacy depend on whether or not the deceased is married or not.

If someone is married:

- only the first £125,000 automatically goes to the spouse
- if the estate is worth more than this and there are children, the spouse receives the first £125,000, and a life interest in half the remainder as well as any personal effects. Their children (or their children's children if they are no longer alive) get the rest
- if there are no surviving children the deceased's parents will inherit half the balance in excess of £200,000 (with the spouse getting any personal effects)
- if there are no surviving children or parents, the brothers and sisters of the deceased share in half the balance in excess of £200,000 (with the spouse getting the personal effects). If the brothers and sisters are no longer alive, their children can inherit.

If the deceased was not married:

- any children inherit the entire estate, with it shared equally between them or their issue
- if there are no children the deceased's parents inherit with the estate shared equally between them
- if the parents are no longer alive, the brothers and sisters, or their issue, inherit
- if there are none of the above still alive, first grandparents, and if they are not alive, then aunts and uncles or their issue then inherit
- if there are no relatives everything goes to the Crown.

Further information

IFA Promotion has a free brochure called *Time to Think About Inheritance Tax*. For a copy, visit www.unbiased.co.uk or call (0800) 085 3250.

For a copy of the Inland Revenue's *IHT8 Alterations to an Inheritance Following Death*, visit www.hmrc.gov.uk or call (0845) 234 1000.

Index

Buy two titles at the offer price and get the cheapest book ½ price
All titles are in the Daily Telegraph series.

Title	RRP	Offer price	No. of copies	Total
Learning and Attention Disorders	£7.99	£6.98		
Alzheimer's Disease	£7.99	£6.98		
Chronic Pain	£7.99	£6.98		
Crohn's Disease & Ulcerative Colitis	£9.99	£8.98		
A Survival Guide to Late Life	£9.99	£8.98		
Epilepsy	£9.99	£8.98		
Parkinson's Disease	£9.99	£8.98		
Food Medicine	£9.99	£8.98		
Sleep Really Well	£9.99	£8.98		
Stroke	£9.99	£8.98		
Overcoming & Preventing Heart Problems	£9.99	£8.98		
Migraine	£7.99	£6.98		
Menopause	£9.99	£8.98		
Prostate Disorders	£7.99	£6.98		
Depression	£9.99	£8.98		
Hip Replacement	£9.99	£8.98		
P&P & Insurance				£3.00
Grand Total (please calculate your 50% discount on your second book)				£

Name ....

Address ....

.... Postcode ....

Daytime Tel. No./Email...

Three ways to pay:
1. **For express service telephone the TBS order line on 01206 255 800 and quote "BPHD". Order lines are open Monday–Friday 8.30a.m.–5.30p.m.**
2. I enclose a cheque made payable to TBS Ltd for £.........
3. Please charge my ☐Visa ☐Mastercard ☐Amex ☐Switch (switch issue no. ......) £.........

Card number ....

Expiry date................................... Signature ....

(your signature is essential when paying by credit card)

Please return forms (no stamp required) to, Constable & Robinson Ltd, FREEPOST NAT6619, 3 The Lanchesters, 162 Fulham Palace Road, London W6 9BR. All books subject to availability.
Enquiries to: readers@constablerobinson.com
www.constablerobinson.com

Constable & Robinson Ltd (directly or via its agents) may mail or phone you about promotions or products. Tick box if you do not want these from us ☐ or our subsidiaries ☐